VISIONS
Language ✦ Literature ✦ Content

Mary Lou McCloskey

Lydia Stack

THOMSON

HEINLE

Australia ✦ Canada ✦ Mexico ✦ Singapore ✦ United Kingdom ✦ United States

VISIONS STUDENT BOOK B
Mary Lou McCloskey and Lydia Stack

Publisher: *Phyllis Dobbins*
Director of Development: *Anita Raducanu*
Developmental Editor: *Tania Maundrell-Brown*
Associate Developmental Editor: *Yeny Kim*
Associate Developmental Editor: *Kasia Zagorski*
Editorial Assistant: *Audra Longert*
Production Supervisor: *Mike Burggren*
Marketing Manager: *Jim McDonough*
Manufacturing Manager: *Marcia Locke*
Director, ELL Training and Development: *Evelyn Nelson*
Photography Manager: *Sheri Blaney*
Development: *Proof Positive/Farrowlyne Associates, Inc.; Quest Language Systems*
Design and Production: *Proof Positive/Farrowlyne Associates, Inc.*
Cover Designer: *Studio Montage*
Printer: *R.R. Donnelley and Sons Company, Willard*

Cover Image: *© Grant Heilman Photography*

Printed in the United States of America.
1 2 3 4 5 6 7 8 9 10   08   07   06   05   04   03

For more information, contact Heinle, 25 Thomson Place, Boston, Massachusetts 02210 USA, or you can visit our Internet site at http://www.heinle.com

ISBN: 0-8384-5248-5

Reviewers and Consultants

We gratefully acknowledge the contribution of the following educators, consultants, and librarians who reviewed materials at various stages of development. Their input and insight provided us with valuable perspective and ensured the integrity of the entire program.

Program Advisor

Evelyn Nelson

Consultants

Deborah Barker
Nimitz High School
Houston, Texas

Sharon Bippus
Labay Middle School
Houston, Texas

Sheralee Connors
Portland, Oregon

Kathleen Fischer
Norwalk LaMirada Unified
    School District
Norwalk, California

Willa Jean Harner
Tiffin-Seneca Public Library
Tiffin, Ohio

Nancy King
Bleyl Middle School
Houston, Texas

Amy Hirasaki Moore
Houston, Texas

Julie Rines
The Thomas Crane Library
Quincy, MA

Lynn Silbernagel
The Catlin Gabel School
Portland, Oregon

Cherylyn Smith
Fresno Unified School District
Fresno, California

Jennifer Trujillo
Fort Lewis College
Teacher Education Department
Durango, Colorado

Teresa Walter
Chollas Elementary School
San Diego, California

Reviewers

Susan Alexandre
Trimble Technical High School
Fort Worth, Texas

Deborah Almonte
Franklin Middle School
Tampa, Florida

Donna Altes
Silverado Middle School
Napa, California

Ruben Alvarado
Webb Middle School
Austin, TX

Sheila Alvarez
Robinson Middle School
Plano, Texas

Cally Androtis-Williams
Newcomers High School
Long Island City, New York

Minerva Anzaldua
Martin Middle School
Corpus Christi, Texas

Alicia Arroyos
Eastwood Middle School
El Paso, Texas

Douglas Black
Montwood High School
El Paso, Texas

Jessica Briggeman
International Newcomer Academy
Fort Worth, Texas

Diane Buffett
East Side High School
Newark, New Jersey

Eva Chapman
San Jose Unified School
    District Office
San Jose, California

Elia Corona
Memorial Middle School
Pharr, Texas

Alicia Cron
Alamo Middle School
Alamo, Texas

Florence Decker
El Paso Independent School District
    (retired)
El Paso, Texas

Janeece Docal
Bell Multicultural Senior High School
Washington, DC

Addea Dontino
Miami-Dade County School District
Miami, FL

Kathy Dwyer
Tomlin Middle School
Plant City, Florida

Olga Figol
Barringer High School
Newark, New Jersey

James Harris
DeLeon Middle School
McAllen, Texas

Audrey Heining-Boynton
University of North Carolina-
    Chapel Hill
School of Education
Chapel Hill, North Carolina

Carolyn Ho
North Harris Community College
Houston, Texas

Donald Hoyt
Cooper Middle School
Fresno, California

Nancy A. Humbach
Miami University
Department of Teacher Education
Oxford, Ohio

Erik Johansen
Oxnard High School
Oxnard, California

Marguerite Joralemon
East Side High School
Newark, New Jersey

Karen Poling Kapeluck
Lacey Instructional Center
Annandale, Virginia

Lorraine Kleinschuster
Intermediate School 10 Q
Long Island City, New York

Fran Lacas
NYC Board of Education (retired)
New York, New York

Robert Lamont
Newcomer Center
Arlington, Texas

Mao-ju Catherine Lee
Alief Middle School
Houston, Texas

Gail Lulek
Safety Harbor Middle School
Safety Harbor, Florida

Natalie Mangini
Serrano International School
Lake Forest, California

Graciela Morales
Austin Independent School District
Austin, Texas

Karen Morante
School District of Philadelphia
Philadelphia, Pennsylvania

Lorraine Morgan
Hanshaw Middle School
Modesto, California

Dianne Mortensen
Pershing Intermediate School 220
Brooklyn, New York

Denis O'Leary
Rio del Valle Junior High School
Oxnard, California

Jeanette Page
School District of Philadelphia
   (retired)
Philadelphia, Pennsylvania

Claudia Peréz
Hosler Middle School
Lynwood, California

Yvonne Perez
Alief Middle School
Houston, Texas

Penny Phariss
Plano Independent School District
Plano, Texas

Bari Ramírez
L.V. Stockard Middle School
Dallas, Texas

Jacqueline Ray
Samuel High School
Dallas, Texas

Howard Riddles
Oak Grove Middle School
Clearwater, Florida

Randy Soderman
Community School District Six
New York, New York

Rita LaNell Stahl
Sinagua High School
Flagstaff, Arizona

Dean Stecker
School District of Palm Beach County
West Palm Beach, Florida

Mary Sterling-Cruz
Jackson Middle School
Friendswood, Texas

Rosemary Tejada
Carlsbad High School
Carlsbad, California

Camille Sloan Telthorster
Bleye Middle School
Houston, Texas

Vickie Thomas
Robinson Middle School
Plano, Texas

Claudio Toledo
Lynwood Middle School
Lynwood, CA

Christopher Tracy
Garnet-Patterson Middle School
Washington, DC

Stephanie Vreeland
T.A. Howard Middle School
Arlington, Texas

Jennifer Zelenitz
Long Island City High School
Long Island City, New York

We wish to thank the students at the following schools who helped us select high-interest readings at an appropriate language level. Their feedback was invaluable.

Student reviewers

Intermediate School 10 Q
Long Island City, New York

Jackson Middle School
Friendswood, Texas

L.V. Stockard Middle School
Dallas, Texas

Memorial Middle School
Pharr, Texas

Newcomer Center
Arlington, Texas

Nimitz High School
Houston, Texas

Oxnard High School
Oxnard, California

Pershing Intermediate School 220
Brooklyn, New York

Samuel High School
Dallas, Texas

Silverado Middle School
Napa, California

T.A. Howard Middle School
Arlington, Texas

Trimble Technical High School
Fort Worth, Texas

Contents

UNIT 4   Discoveries   222

To the Student

We hope you like *Visions*
We wrote it for you
To learn speaking, reading, writing,
And listening, too.

You'll read all kinds of things —
Stories, poems, and plays,
And texts that will help you understand
What your content teacher says.

Use this book to "grow" your English,
To talk about what you write and read.
Use it to learn lots of new words
And new reading strategies you'll need.

Good authors, good activities,
And especially your good teachers,
Can also help you learn grammar and writing,
And lots of other language features.

So please open this book
And learn everything you can.
Then write and show us how far you've come
Since you first began.

M.L.M. and L.S.

www.visions@heinle.com

Mary Lou McCloskey

Lydia Stack

UNIT 1

Challenges

Runners, Robert Delaunay, 1926.

View the Picture

1. What challenge are the people in the picture facing?
2. Compare your ideas with those of a partner.

In this unit, you will read a poem, a fable, stories, and a historical narrative. In these readings, people face challenges in their lives, such as staying alive or learning to feel comfortable in a new place. You will learn about the features of these writing forms and how to write them yourself.

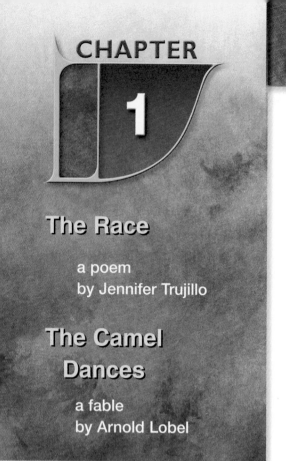

CHAPTER 1

The Race

a poem
by Jennifer Trujillo

The Camel Dances

a fable
by Arnold Lobel

Objectives

Reading Make inferences as you read a poem and a fable.

Listening and Speaking Describe something you like to do.

Grammar Study past tense verbs.

Writing Write a poem.

Content Science: Classify animals.

Use Prior Knowledge

Discuss Competition

Prior knowledge is something that you already know. Use your prior knowledge to help you understand what you do not know.

When you try to win against someone else, or against another team, this is called a competition.

1. With a partner, talk about competitions people take part in.
2. Copy the web on a piece of paper. Write your ideas in the web. Add more ovals if necessary.
3. Talk about an activity that you have each competed in. Use the following questions as a guide:

a. What was the activity?
b. Were you on a team or alone?
c. How did you feel before you competed? After?
d. Did you win?

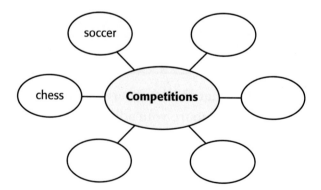

Build Background

Ballet

Background is information that can help you understand what you hear or read.

You will read about ballet in one of the readings. Ballet is a kind of dance. Ballet steps and body positions take a lot of practice. Dancers learn special ways to stand. These are called the five basic positions.

Content Connection

In a *pirouette,* dancers spin around on the toes or ball of one foot.

First Steps in Ballet

First Position
Second Position
Third Position
Fourth Position
Fifth Position

Build Vocabulary

Find Synonyms Using a Reference Aid

When you learn new words, you **build your vocabulary.**

A **synonym** is a word that has a similar meaning to another word.

happy = glad   mad = angry

A dictionary is a **reference** book that gives the meanings of words. Dictionaries often use synonyms for meanings.

1. The word *gallop* is used in "The Race." Look at this dictionary entry.

gal•lop /'gæləp/ *n.* the fastest run of four-legged animals, esp. horses: *The horse raced to the rescue at full gallop.* —*v.* (usu. of horses) to run at a gallop: *Race horses gallop around the race track.*

2. Notice that the word *run* is used in the definition of *gallop*. A synonym for *gallop* is *run*.
3. Copy this chart. Use a dictionary to look up the words. Find synonyms for them in the definitions. Write the words and their synonyms in your Personal Dictionary.

Word	Synonym
whoop	
shy	
chuckle	

Personal Dictionary

The Heinle Newbury House Dictionary

Activity Book p. 1

Student CD-ROM

Text Structure

Poem and Fable

The **text structure** of a reading is its main parts and how they fit together.

This chapter contains two reading selections, a poem and a fable.

1. "The Race" is a poem. Look for these things as you read or listen to it.

Poem	
Rhyming Words	words that sound the same at the end
Images	words that help you make pictures in your mind
Stanzas	groups of lines

2. "The Camel Dances" is a fable. Look for these things as you read or listen to it.

Fable	
Structure	short beginning, middle, and end
Characters	animals are often the main characters
A Moral	a lesson about life

3. As you read the poem and the fable, think about how they are the same and how they are different.

Student
CD-ROM

Reading Strategy

Make Inferences

A **reading strategy** is a way to understand what you read. You can become a better reader if you learn good reading strategies.

To **make an inference** is to make a guess. You use what you know when you make the guess. For example, if your brother comes home sweating and wearing his running shoes and shorts, you can make an inference that he went running. When you read, you use information from the reading selection and your own life to make inferences.

1. Read the first two lines of "The Race" on page 6. What do you learn about the girl? What inference can you make?

2. As you read or listen to "The Race" and "The Camel Dances," look for information about the characters. Use this information to make inferences.

The Girl	The Camel
lets her hair down when she rides	likes to dance

Student
CD-ROM

The Race

a poem
by Jennifer Trujillo

The Camel Dances

a fable
by Arnold Lobel

The Race

a poem by Jennifer Trujillo

Audio

1   She rode a horse named Fina
when women didn't ride.
They galloped around the mountain,
her legs on Fina's side.

Make Inferences

What is the rider like
when she is not on a
horse? What words
in the poem support
your answer?

2   She let her hair down from its **bun**
and felt it whip and fly.
She laughed and sang and whooped out loud.
Up there she wasn't shy!

3   One day great-grandma found her out
and planned to stop it all.
But down in town they'd heard some news . . .
they told her of a call.

4   A call for the caballeros
from all **the highs and lows**
to race their fancy **caballos**
to try and win the rose.

---

bun hair wrapped in a round shape

the highs and lows land up high (mountains) and
    low (valleys)

caballos horses

5 Abuela looked at Fina,
a **twinkle** in her eye.
Abuela said, "Let's enter!
This race deserves a try."

6 At **dawn** she was the only girl,
but didn't even care.
She came to meet the challenge, and
her horse was waiting there.

Make Inferences

Did the girl think she would win? What information supports your answer?

7 They swept across the finish line
much faster than the rest.
She **flung** her hat without surprise;
she'd always done her best.

8 Fina shook her **mane** and stomped.
Abuela flashed a smile.
She sniffed the rose and trotted off
in **caballera** style!

---

twinkle   a shine that goes on and off
dawn   sunrise
flung   threw or tossed

mane   the hair on a horse's neck
caballera   proud horse-riding style

About the Author — Jennifer Trujillo (born 1970)

Jennifer Trujillo was born in Denver, Colorado. Her family came from Caracas, Venezuela. She spent part of her childhood there and part of it in Colorado. Today Trujillo teaches at a Navajo Indian Reservation and at Fort Lewis College in Colorado. She says, "Writing is like swimming. Sometimes I dive in with a splash! Other times, I have to step in slowly—one toe at a time."

➤ What advice do you think Jennifer Trujillo would give a girl or a boy who wants to enter a competition?

The Camel Dances
a fable by Arnold Lobel

Audio

Make Inferences

What does the Camel's practicing tell you about her character?

1   The Camel had her heart set on becoming a ballet dancer. "To make every movement a thing of grace and beauty," said the Camel. "That is my one and only desire."

2   Again and again she practiced her pirouettes, her **relevés,** and her **arabesques.** She repeated the five basic positions a hundred times each day. She worked for long months under the hot desert sun. Her feet were **blistered,** and her body ached with fatigue, but not once did she think of stopping.

---

relevés ballet steps in which the dancer rises on tiptoe on one or both legs

arabesques movements in ballet in which the dancer stands on one leg with the other leg extended straight back

blistered covered with pockets of skin filled with fluid

3   At last the Camel said, "Now I am a dancer." She announced a **recital** and danced before an invited group of camel friends and **critics.** When her dance was over, she made a deep **bow.**

4   There was no **applause.**

5   "I must tell you **frankly,**" said a member of the audience, "as a critic and a **spokesman** for this group, that you are lumpy and humpy. You are baggy and bumpy. You are, like the rest of us, simply a camel. You are *not* and never will be a ballet dancer!"

6   Chuckling and laughing, the **audience** moved away across the sand.

7   "How very wrong they are!" said the Camel. "I have worked hard. There can be no doubt that I am a splendid dancer. I will dance and dance just for myself."

8   That is what she did. It gave her many years of pleasure.

9   *Satisfaction will come to those who please themselves.*

Make Inferences

Do you think the audience liked the recital? What information supports your answer?

---

recital   a show of dancing or music for people to watch
critics   people who give opinions about the arts
bow   bend at the waist
applause   clapping that shows approval

frankly   truthfully
spokesman   one who speaks for a larger group
audience   the people who come to watch an event

About the Author

Arnold Lobel (1933–1987)

Arnold Lobel grew up in Schenectady, New York. He studied art at the Pratt Institute in Brooklyn, New York. There he became interested in book illustration. Most of Lobel's books include characters who are animals. His most famous book, *Frog and Toad Are Friends,* contains humorous stories about friendship.

➤ Why do you think Arnold Lobel chose to tell this story using animals instead of people?

Beyond the Reading

Reading Comprehension

Question-Answer Relationships (QAR)

You can understand a reading better if you answer different kinds of questions.

"Right There" Questions

1. **Recall Facts** In "The Race," what does the main character like to do?
2. **Recall Facts** How does the race end?
3. **Recall Facts** In "The Camel Dances," what does the Camel like to do?

"Think and Search" Questions

4. **Understand Characters** How do Abuela and her granddaughter feel at the end of the race?
5. **Understand Characters** What steps does the Camel take to become a ballet dancer?
6. **Understand Main Ideas** What does the Camel's audience think of her dancing?

"Author and You" Questions

7. **Recognize Character Traits** How do you think the girl from "The Race" feels when she is riding horses?
8. **Make Inferences** In the beginning of "The Race," why do you think Abuela wants to stop her granddaughter from riding horses?
9. **Recognize Character Traits** How do you think the Camel feels when she is dancing?
10. **Explain Main Ideas** What is the moral, or lesson, of "The Camel Dances"?

"On Your Own" Question

11. **Compare** How do you feel when you are doing something that is special to you?

Activity Book
p. 2

Student
CD-ROM

Build Reading Fluency

Reading Key Phrases

When you build reading fluency, you learn to read faster and to understand better.

Reading key phrases will help you learn to read faster. Read these phrases aloud and raise your hand each time you read the key phrase: "rode a horse."

rode a horse	ride a horse	race horses
ride ponies	ride horses	rode a horse
raced a horse	rode a horse	raced horses
rode a horse	raced horses	rode horses

Listen, Speak, Interact

Describe Something You Like to Do

When people listen and talk to each other, they **interact.**

In both the poem and the fable, the characters like to do something.

1. Reread the poem and fable with a partner. Identify the activity each main character likes to do.

2. Tell your partner about an activity that you like to do. What do you like about it? How does it make you feel? Are you good at it?

3. How is your activity similar to or different from the activities the main characters like to do?

Elements of Literature

Distinguish Sounds of Rhyming Words

Literature is something that you read. Writers use many different ways to express themselves. These ways are the **elements of literature.**

Poetry often contains words that **rhyme.** Words that rhyme have the same ending sound. In stanza 1 of "The Race," *side* and *ride* are rhyming words. Often, the words that rhyme appear at the end of a line of poetry.

1. Read "The Race" with a partner. Take turns reading it out loud.

2. Be sure you make the correct sounds as you read. This will help you distinguish rhyming words. Ask your teacher to help you pronounce words you do not know.

3. Listen for the rhyming words as your partner reads. What similar sounds do the words have? How do the words sound different?

4. As you listen, think about the effects of the rhyming words. What mood, or feeling, do the rhyming words give the poem? Why do you think the author uses this style of writing?

5. List the rhyming words for each stanza in the poem in a chart.

Stanza (Group of Lines)	Rhyming Words
1	ride, side
2	fly, ___

Activity Book
p. 3

Student
CD-ROM

Word Study

Analyze the Suffix -*er*

Words can have several parts. In this section, you will learn what the different parts mean.

A **suffix** is a group of letters added to the end of a word. A suffix changes the meaning of a word.

The suffix -*er* often means that something or someone does something. For example, a teach**er** is someone who teaches.

Note that most base words ending in -*e* drop the final -*e* before adding the suffix -*er*. For example: *ride* ➞ *rider.*

1. Here are some action words. On a piece of paper, add -*er* to the words to make a word meaning someone who does the action.
   a. sing **b.** paint **c.** speak
2. Find a word with the suffix -*er* in "The Camel Dances." Write the word on a piece of paper.
3. Divide the word into the base word and the suffix -*er.*

Activity Book
p. 4

Student
CD-ROM

Grammar Focus

Study Past Tense Verbs

Grammar is the way that a language is put together. Grammar helps us understand each other.

To tell about actions in the past, use the past tense of verbs. Regular verbs form the past tense like this:

Simple Form	Ending	Past Tense
gallop	**-ed**	gallop**ed**

Most verbs are regular verbs. Irregular verbs form the past tense in different ways.

Simple Form	Past Tense
feel	**felt**
find	**found**
hear	**heard**
ride	**rode**
sweep	**swept**

Activity Book
pp. 4–5

Student
Handbook

Student
CD-ROM

From Reading to Writing

Write a Poem

In school, after you read some literature, you often have to write about it. This section shows you how to do this.

Write a short poem that tells about a challenge.

1. Choose an event that was a challenge for you or someone you know.
2. Give your poem a title.
3. Group your lines into sets of two lines. Use rhyme at the end of your lines. Look at the example.

> ### What Went Wrong
> She didn't want to be friends anymore.
> She said this as she went out the door.

4. Use past tense verbs.
5. Produce a visual such as a picture to go with your poem.
6. Present your poem to the class. Speak clearly and with expression.

Activity Book
p. 7

Across Content Areas

Classify Animals

Content areas are the subjects you study in school. Math, science, social studies, language arts, and other arts such as music and drawing are content areas.

Scientists who study animals **classify** them, or put them in groups. We can classify animals by what they eat.

Herbivores eat mostly plants.
Carnivores eat mostly other animals (meat).

1. Look at this list of animals.

Animals

camels	tigers	boa constrictors
wolves	cows	chimpanzees
elephants		

2. Work with a partner. Decide whether the animals in the list are herbivores or carnivores. If you do not know, use a reference resource such as an encyclopedia.
3. Copy this chart on a piece of paper. Write the name of each animal in the correct column.

Herbivores	Carnivores
horses	

Activity Book
p. 8

Student
CD-ROM

CHAPTER 2

Hatchet

an excerpt from a novel
by Gary Paulsen

Objectives

Reading Identify cause and effect as you read a realistic adventure story.

Listening and Speaking Act out events in a story.

Grammar Use the past tense of the verb *be.*

Writing Write a realistic adventure story.

Content Science: Learn about combustion.

Use Prior Knowledge

Share Knowledge About Forests

A forest is a large area with many trees. What do you already know about forests?

1. Read these statements. Decide if each one is true or false. Write your answers on a piece of paper.
   a. A forest has things in it that can be used to make a campfire.
   b. Dry leaves can catch fire—they are flammable.
   c. There is food that people can eat in a forest.
   d. Some forests have lakes and rivers.
   e. A dry, empty bird's nest is not flammable.
   f. A forest can have rocks in it.
2. Compare your answers with a partner's.
3. Check your answers with other students or your teacher.

Build Background

Fire

People who camp in forests often make a campfire. Campfires are used for cooking and staying warm.

It is easy to start a campfire with matches. If you do not have matches, you can start a fire with sparks (bits of light and heat). You make sparks by scraping two hard surfaces such as stone together.

Fire can be very dangerous. You should always have sand or water close by when you make a campfire.

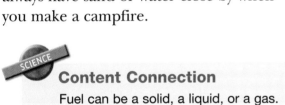

Content Connection

Fuel can be a solid, a liquid, or a gas.

Build Vocabulary

Use Context

Sometimes you can guess the meanings of new words by using the **context,** or nearby words and sentences.

1. In "Hatchet," the sparks made by the boy in the story "just *sputtered* and died." You can use the word *died* to guess what *sputtered* means.
2. Look at the underlined words in the following sentences. Use the context to help you understand the meaning of each word.

He tried small <u>twigs</u>, breaking them into little pieces, but that was worse than the grass.

Then he tried a <u>combination</u> of the two, grass and twigs.

3. Write the underlined words and your definitions in your Personal Dictionary. Then check your definitions in a dictionary.

Personal Dictionary

The Heinle Newbury House Dictionary

Activity Book
p. 9

Student CD-ROM

Text Structure

Realistic Adventure Fiction

Fiction is a **genre** (kind) of literature. In fiction, the writer makes up people and events. A novel is a kind of fiction. Novels are long. They are published as entire books.

You are going to read an excerpt (a short part) from a novel. This novel is **realistic adventure fiction.** The features of realistic adventure fiction are listed in the chart.

As you read, look for these features of realistic adventure fiction.

Realistic Adventure Fiction	
Setting	where the story takes place
Characters	people in the story
Events	things that could happen in real life
Problem	difficulty that the characters face

Student
CD-ROM

Reading Strategy

Identify Cause and Effect

A **cause** is an action or event that produces an effect or makes something happen. An **effect** is the result that happens. For example:

Cause: You study hard.

Effect: You get better grades.

Understanding the connection between a cause and an effect can help you better understand your reading.

1. As you read "Hatchet," ask yourself: What happens? What causes it to happen?
2. List your answers in a chart like the one on the right.

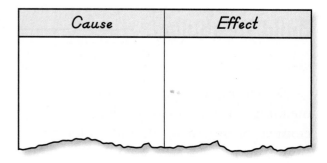

Student
CD-ROM

HATCHET

an excerpt from a novel
by Gary Paulsen

Prologue

In this story, the main character is a teenager named Brian Robeson. He is on a plane to visit his father in the oil fields in Canada. The only other person on the plane is the pilot. When the pilot has a heart attack, Brian must guide the plane to land. After he lands on a lake, he finds himself alone and scared. The only belongings he has are his clothing and a small ax called a hatchet. Brian must find a way to survive alone in the wilderness.

1   Brian found it was a long way from sparks to fire.

2   Clearly there had to be something for the sparks to ignite, some kind of tinder or kindling—but what? He brought some dried grass in, tapped sparks into it and watched them die. He tried small twigs, breaking them into little pieces, but that was worse than the grass. Then he tried a combination of the two, grass and twigs.

3   Nothing. He had no trouble getting **sparks,** but the tiny bits of hot stone or metal—he couldn't tell which they were—just sputtered and died.

4   He settled back **on his haunches** in **exasperation,** looking at the **pitiful** clump of grass and twigs.

5   He needed something finer, something soft and fine and fluffy to catch the bits of fire.

6   Shredded paper would be nice, but he had no paper.

7   "So close," he said aloud, "so close . . ."

Identify Cause and Effect

Why is Brian exasperated (frustrated)?

---

sparks   small bits of light caused by hard surfaces scraping together

on his haunches   sitting in a crouching position close to the ground

exasperation   extreme frustration

pitiful   sad, worth feeling sorry for

8 He put the hatchet back in his belt and went out of the shelter, limping on his sore leg. There had to be something, had to be. Man had made fire. There had been fire for thousands, millions of years. There had to be a way. He dug in his pockets and found the twenty-dollar bill in his wallet. Paper. Worthless paper out here. But if he could get a fire going . . .

Identify Cause and Effect

What happens when Brian tries to light his twenty-dollar bill? Why?

9 He ripped the twenty into tiny pieces, made a pile of pieces, and hit sparks into them. Nothing happened. They just wouldn't take the sparks. But there had to be a way— some way to do it.

10 Not twenty feet to his right, leaning out over the water were birches and he stood looking at them for a full half-minute before they **registered** on his mind. They were a beautiful white with bark like clean, slightly speckled paper.

11 Paper.

12 He moved to the trees. Where the bark was peeling from the trunks it lifted in tiny **tendrils,** almost fluffs. Brian plucked some of them loose, rolled them in his fingers. They seemed flammable, dry and nearly powdery. He pulled and twisted bits off the trees, packing them in one hand while he picked them with the other, picking and gathering until he had a **wad** close to the size of a baseball.

---

registered made an impression on, came to the attention of

tendrils thin pieces, like hairs

wad a ball made by pressing something soft together

13   Then he went back into the shelter and arranged the ball of birchbark peelings at the base of the black rock. As an afterthought he threw in the remains of the twenty-dollar bill. He struck and a stream of sparks fell into the bark and quickly died. But this time one spark fell on one small hair of dry bark—almost a thread of bark—and seemed to glow a bit brighter before it died.

14   The material had to be finer. There had to be a soft and incredibly fine nest for the sparks.

Identify Cause and Effect

What do you think will happen if Brian makes a home for the sparks? Why?

15   I must make a home for the sparks, he thought. A perfect home or they won't stay, they won't make fire.

16   He started ripping the bark, using his fingernails at first, and when that didn't work he used the sharp edge of the hatchet, cutting the bark in thin slivers, hairs so fine they were almost not there. It was **painstaking** work, slow work, and he stayed with it for over two hours. Twice he stopped for a handful of berries and once to go to the lake for a drink. Then back to work, the sun on his back, until at last he had a ball of fluff as big as a grapefruit—dry birchbark fluff.

---

painstaking   needing great care and effort

17   He **positioned** his spark nest—as he thought of it—at the base of the rock, used his thumb to make a small **depression** in the middle, and slammed the back of the hatchet down across the black rock. A cloud of sparks rained down, most of them missing the nest, but some, perhaps thirty or so, hit in the depression and of those six or seven found fuel and grew, smoldered and caused the bark to take on the red glow.

18   Then they went out.

19   Close—he was close. He repositioned the nest, made a new and smaller dent with his thumb, and struck again.

20   More sparks, a slight glow, then nothing.

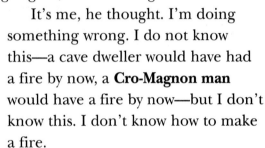

21   It's me, he thought. I'm doing something wrong. I do not know this—a cave dweller would have had a fire by now, a **Cro-Magnon man** would have a fire by now—but I don't know this. I don't know how to make a fire.

22   Maybe not enough sparks. He settled the nest in place once more and hit the rock with a series of blows, as fast as he could. The sparks poured like a golden waterfall. At first they seemed to take, there were several, many sparks that found life and took briefly, but they all died.

23   Starved.

24   He leaned back. They are like me. They are starving. It wasn't quantity, there were plenty of sparks, but they needed more.

---

positioned   put into the right place
depression   an area that is lower than what is nearby

Cro-Magnon man   a prehistoric human

25   I would kill, he thought suddenly, for a book of matches. Just one book. Just one match. I would kill.

26   What makes fire? He thought back to school. To all those science classes. Had he ever learned what made a fire? Did a teacher ever stand up there and say, "This is what makes a fire . . ."

27   He shook his head, tried to focus his thoughts. What did it take? You have to have fuel, he thought—and he had that. The bark was fuel. Oxygen—there had to be air.

28   He needed to add air. He had to fan on it, blow on it.

29   He made the nest ready again, held the hatchet backward, **tensed,** and struck four quick blows. Sparks came down and he leaned forward as fast as he could and blew.

30   Too hard. There was a bright, almost intense glow, then it was gone. He had blown it out.

> **Identify Cause and Effect**
>
> Why does Brian blow on his nest of shredded bark?

---

tensed held the muscles tightly just before using them

31 Another set of strikes, more sparks. He leaned and blew, but gently this time, holding back and aiming the stream of air from his mouth to hit the brightest spot. Five or six sparks had fallen in a tight mass of bark hair and Brian centered his efforts there.

32 The sparks grew with his gentle breath. The red glow moved from the sparks themselves into the bark, moved and grew and became worms, glowing red worms that crawled up the bark hairs and caught other threads of bark and grew until there was a pocket of red as big as a quarter, a glowing red coal of heat.

33 And when he ran out of breath and paused to **inhale,** the red ball suddenly burst into flame.

34 "Fire!" He yelled. "I've got fire! I've got it, I've got it, I've got it . . ."

---

inhale   breathe in to take in air

About the Author — Gary Paulsen (born 1939)

Gary Paulsen has written many novels for young readers. Several involve young characters facing challenges. Paulsen also faced some difficult problems as a child. His father was in the army, and Paulsen had to change schools often. Paulsen was a shy boy and changing schools was very hard for him. One day, a librarian gave him a library card and books, and he found a new world. Paulsen said, "I write because it's all I can do . . . [Because I want my] years on this ball of earth to mean something. Writing furnishes a way for that to happen."

➤ If you could ask Gary Paulsen a question about this story, what would it be?

Beyond the Reading

Reading Comprehension

Question-Answer Relationships (QAR)

"Right There" Questions

1. **Recall Facts** Who is Brian?
2. **Recall Facts** What problem does Brian have? Why does Brian have this problem?
3. **Recall Facts** What is the first thing Brian tries to burn?

"Think and Search" Questions

4. **Paraphrase Text** Tell someone what the story is about in your own words. What details do you recall when you paraphrase the story?
5. **Identify Cause and Effect** Why does Brian chop the peeled bark into smaller pieces?

"Author and You" Question

6. **Analyze Characters** What do you learn about Brian from his efforts to start the fire?

"On Your Own" Questions

7. **Analyze Characters** How does Brian feel at the end of the story? Why do you think he feels this way?
8. **Predict** What do you think Brian will do now that he has a fire going?
9. **Identify Author's Strategy** What would you ask the author about strategies he uses to make the story seem real? How do you think he would answer?

Activity Book
p. 10

Student
CD-ROM

Build Reading Fluency

Reading Chunks

Reading chunks, or groups, of words is better than reading word by word. With a partner, practice reading the underlined chunks of words aloud two times.

Clearly there had to be something for the sparks to ignite, some kind of tinder or kindling—but what? He brought some dried grass in, tapped sparks into it and watched them die.

He tried small twigs, breaking them into little pieces, but that was worse than the grass. Then he tried a combination of the two, grass and twigs. Nothing. He had no trouble getting sparks, but the tiny bits of hot stone or metal—he couldn't tell which they were—just sputtered and died.

Listen, Speak, Interact

Act Out Events in a Story

Brian is lost in the woods with only a hatchet for a tool. He faces difficult challenges, but does not give up. He keeps trying.

1. With a partner, reread the story. List the challenges that Brian faces.
2. Find and discuss the different things Brian does to meet these challenges.
3. Find clues that show how Brian feels about his situation. When does he show frustration or excitement?

4. Choose one of the challenges in the story to act out for the class.
5. When you present the event, speak slowly and clearly. Show how Brian feels through his words and his actions.

Elements of Literature

Use Figurative Language

To make their stories more interesting, writers often describe one thing by comparing it to another thing. This is called **figurative language. Similes** are one kind of figurative language. Similes use the words *like* or *as* to show comparison: *Brian ran like the wind.*

1. Read paragraphs 10, 16, 22, and 32 aloud with a small group. Find the simile in each paragraph.
2. Make a section called "Similes" in your Reading Log. Copy the sentences from the selection with similes.

3. Record other similes that you find as you read other pieces of literature.

The chair is like a throne.

She is as tall as the sky.

Reading Log   Activity Book   Student
                 p. 11   CD-ROM

Word Study

Understand Compound Words

Some words are made up of two other words. These are called **compound words.** You can usually guess the meaning of a compound word if you look at each part separately. Look at this example from "Hatchet."

Then he went back into the shelter and arranged the ball of <u>birchbark</u> peelings at the base of the black rock.

birch	a kind of tree
bark	the rough outside part of a tree

↓

birchbark	the bark of a birch tree

1. Copy the following sentences on a piece of paper. Find the compound words and underline them.
   a. As an afterthought, he threw in the remains of the paper.
   b. He started ripping the bark, using his fingernails at first . . .
   c. The sparks poured like a golden waterfall.
2. Divide each compound word into two words.
3. Write these compound words and their meanings in your Personal Dictionary. If you need help with the meanings, look them up in a dictionary or ask your teacher.

Personal Dictionary   The Heinle Newbury House Dictionary   Activity Book p. 12   Student CD-ROM

Grammar Focus

Use the Past Tense of the Verb *Be*

The verb **be** is an irregular verb. The past tense of **be** has two forms, **was** and **were.**

1. Find examples of the past tense of *be* in paragraphs 1, 2, and 10.
2. Write a sentence using each subject in the chart. Include a past tense of *be* in each sentence.

Subjects	Past Tense of *Be*
I He/She/It/Brian	**was** in the forest.
You We They/The students	**were** in the forest.

Activity Book pp. 13–14   Student Handbook   Student CD-ROM

From Reading to Writing

Write a Realistic Adventure Story

You have analyzed "Hatchet" and looked at its text structure. Use the selection as a model for writing your own adventure story.

1. Organize your story using the chart. Decide where the story takes place. Who are the characters? What is the problem?
2. Use the past tense of *be* correctly.
3. Include similes to help readers picture the people, places, and things you are describing.
4. Be sure your story has a beginning, a middle, and an end.
5. Indent each paragraph.

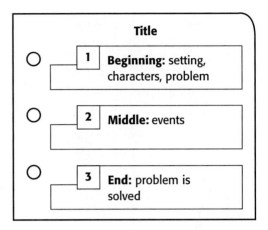

Title

1 **Beginning:** setting, characters, problem

2 **Middle:** events

3 **End:** problem is solved

6. Be sure to capitalize the title of your story, the names of the characters, and other proper nouns.

Activity Book
p. 15

Across Content Areas SCIENCE

Learn About Combustion

When scientists talk about fire, they use the word **combustion.** Combustion requires three things:

fuel	something that will burn, such as paper or wood
oxygen	a colorless, odorless gas in the air (you must breathe oxygen in order to live)
heat	to start, or **ignite,** the combustion

Which of these does Brian use in each of the following situations?

1. Brian blew on the fire.
2. He gathered birchbark.
3. He made sparks with his hatchet and a rock.
   a. fuel **b.** oxygen **c.** heat

Remember: Always observe fire safety rules. Always have something that can **extinguish** (put out) the fire. In the science lab, always follow instructions.

Activity Book
p. 16

CHAPTER 3

Into the Reading

Antarctic Adventure

an excerpt from
a historical narrative
by Meredith Hooper

Objectives

Reading Predict events as you read a historical narrative.

Listening and Speaking Retell order of events.

Grammar Use *and* to join words and sentences.

Writing Write a historical narrative.

Content Social Studies: Learn about bodies of land and water.

Use Prior Knowledge

Discuss Directions

What do you know about directions?

1. Look at the map and answer these questions.
   a. Which state is to the north of Texas?
   b. Which state is to the west?
   c. What country is to the south?
   d. Which direction is Louisiana from Texas?
2. Choose a city, state, or country where you have lived. Draw a map and label the directions. Tell your partner what is to the north, south, east, and west of it.

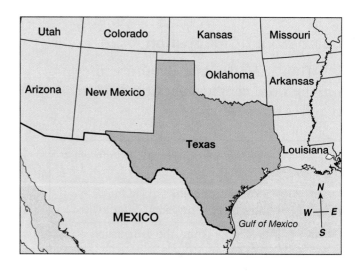

Build Background

Antarctica

Antarctica is a continent located at the South Pole, the most southern point on Earth. The temperature in Antarctica is rarely above 32°F (0°C). Antarctica is almost completely covered by ice. Today, scientists live in and study Antarctica from underground buildings. No other people live in this very cold place.

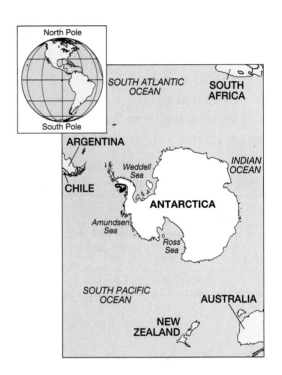

Content Connection

Explorers began trying to reach the South Pole in the early 1900s.

Build Vocabulary

Identify Words About Ships

You are going to read a story about a ship that sinks. To understand the action, learn some words about ships.

Write these sentences in your Personal Dictionary. Complete the sentences with words from the picture.

1. The front of a ship is the —— .
2. The back of the ship is the —— .
3. The man is standing on the —— .
4. The —— makes the ship move in a specific direction.
5. The wind blows into the —— and makes the ship move.

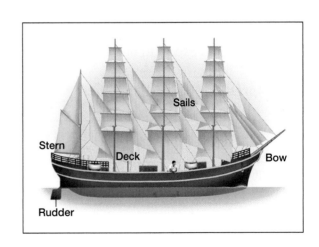

Personal Dictionary

Activity Book
p. 17

Student CD-ROM

Text Structure

Historical Narrative

"Antarctic Adventure" is a **historical narrative.** It tells a story about the experiences of real people from history. As you read, look for these features of a historical narrative:

Historical Narrative	
Events	what happened
Dates	when events happened in history
Characters	real people
Setting	descriptions of real places

As you read "Antarctic Adventure," identify the real people in the narrative. Think about what their experiences were like.

Student
CD-ROM

Reading Strategy

Predict

As you read "Antarctic Adventure," try to **predict,** or guess, what you think will happen next in the narrative. When you predict as you read, you are a more active reader.

To predict what will happen:

Use clues.	Clues are hints from what you read.
Change predictions.	New clues may change what you think.

1. Read paragraphs 3 and 4 on page 32. What do you think will happen next? Why?
2. Now read paragraph 5. Was your prediction correct?
3. Did you use clues from the story (the cracking sound) and your prior knowledge (boats with holes can sink) to make your prediction?
4. Continue predicting as you read the selection.

Student
CD-ROM

Antarctic Adventure

an excerpt from a historical narrative

by Meredith Hooper

Prologue

Ernest Shackleton was an explorer who wanted to cross Antarctica on foot. He formed a crew and was the leader of a brave expedition that set sail for this continent in 1914. The name of his ship was *Endurance*. After six weeks of pushing through ice, the ship became locked in ice.

The *Endurance* Sinks

1   The beginning of the end came on Sunday, October 24, 1915, just after dinner. The *Endurance* lost the fight.

2   For 278 days the wooden ship had been stuck fast in the dangerous **pack ice** of the Weddell Sea.

3   Now three huge ice **floes** were pressing **relentlessly** around the ship. The *Endurance* groaned and quivered. Suddenly, there was a terrible crash! Twisted and **fatally** bent, the *Endurance* began to let in water.

4   The men pumped water out until they were exhausted. But still the ice floes pressed in, twisting and grinding with a dreadful roaring noise. The ship's **timbers** cracked and splintered under the pressure.

> **Predict**
>
> What do you think will happen to the *Endurance*?

Audio

The *Endurance*.

---

pack ice   a large area of sea ice with a mixture of floating ice pieces packed together
floes   sheets of floating ice

relentlessly   without stopping
fatally   in a way that causes death
timbers   large pieces of wood

**Photographer Frank Hurley
and Ernest Shackleton.**

5   The end came on Wednesday. The *Endurance* was being crushed. It was **sickening** to feel the decks breaking up and the ship's great wooden beams bending, then snapping with a noise like gunfire.

6   The ship's stern lifted 20 feet into the air, the rudder tore off, and water rushed forward and froze, weighing down the bow. The icy black sea poured in.

Predict

Will Shackleton tell his men to leave the ship?

7   Ernest Shackleton looked down into the engine room and saw the engines dropping sideways. He gave the order: **abandon** ship!

8   The men tumbled out onto the ice, shocked and exhausted. They were standing on a shaking ice floe, just 2 feet thick, floating on the surface of the deep, dark ocean.

9   That night they camped on the ice. All around them the ice floes groaned and crashed. Three times the ice started splitting and smashing underneath them, and they had to move their tents.

---

sickening making you feel sick

abandon leave without planning to return

10　　Shackleton decided that they had to walk across the pack ice to reach land. But the land he was aiming for was 312 miles away.

11　　They set out on Saturday, dragging food, equipment, and the lifeboats from the *Endurance* over the ice. But in three days, they traveled less than 2 miles.

12　　Shackleton decided they had to stop and camp on the ice. The ice would drift north, taking them nearer to land and safety.

Predict

Do you think the men will reach the land 312 miles away?

13　　In a way, the ice was friendly. It was solid underfoot. It gave them water to drink. Seals and penguins used the ice, so there would be food to catch.

14　　They chose a large, thick floe for "Ocean Camp." They could still see the *Endurance* in the distance. Parties of men **salvaged** what they could from the crushed wreck.

15　　One evening, Shackleton saw the *Endurance* begin to sink. "She's going, boys!" he shouted sadly. The men ran to watch. Their ship **upended,** bow first, and sank slowly under the ice.

16　　The *Endurance* had been their home for so long. She was their last link with the outside world. They felt very lonely now.

---

salvaged　rescued objects sure to be lost in the ship

upended　turned so that one end points upward and the other downward

17   Five months later they were still camping. They had drifted slowly north, and now the floes were starting to break up. Their floe heaved and suddenly split. The men crammed into their three lifeboats.

18   After seven days they managed to reach **uninhabited** Elephant Island and set up camp on the coast. There, Shackleton left 22 of his men in a small hut.

19   With five men, he planned to make a dangerous and daring journey. The island of South Georgia lay 800 miles away, across the wild ocean. They would sail there and get help at one of the whaling stations.

20   In the little *James Caird,* they made one of the greatest sea journeys ever. After 17 days, they stumbled **exhausted** onto the shore of South Georgia. But they were on the wrong side of the island.

21   No one had ever crossed the glaciers and mountains of South Georgia on foot, but Shackleton and two of his men did it to reach help.

22   It took three months before Shackleton was able to rescue the men on Elephant Island. But everyone who had sailed on the *Endurance* had been saved.

---

uninhabited   without any people living there
James Caird   the name of a ship

exhausted   very tired

About the Author

Meredith Hooper (born 1939)

Meredith Hooper has written more than 20 nonfiction books for young readers. She researches each book carefully to make sure that it contains correct information. She explains this challenge, "I bring . . . research skills to bear on each subject, believing that each audience deserves the best." Many of Hooper's books are about science or history.

➤Why do you think that Meredith Hooper wrote about Shackleton's trip to Antarctica? To inform the reader? To entertain the reader? To influence the reader?

Beyond the Reading

Reading Comprehension

Question-Answer Relationships (QAR)

"Right There" Questions

1. **Recall Facts** When do the events in this narrative happen?
2. **Recall Facts** What is Ernest Shackleton's role?
3. **Recall Facts** What problems do Shackleton and his men face?
4. **Recall Facts** What is the first thing that goes wrong for the *Endurance*?

"Think and Search" Questions

5. **Find Cause and Effect** Why does the *Endurance* begin to sink after 278 days stuck in the ice?
6. **Identify the Main Idea** Why does Ernest Shackleton give the order to abandon ship?
7. **Analyze Characters** Why does Shackleton decide to stop crossing the ice and camp out instead?

"Author and You" Questions

8. **Understand Character Traits** What words would you use to describe Ernest Shackleton as a leader?
9. **Understand Plot** What do you think it was like to be stranded on the ice of Antarctica?
10. **Use Visual Elements** How did looking at the photographs on the pages of the selection help you to understand the narrative?

"On Your Own" Question

11. **Express Your Opinion** Would you like to take a challenging trip like the one in this story? Why or why not?

Activity Book
p. 18

Student
CD-ROM

Build Reading Fluency

Rapid Word Recognition

Rapidly recognizing words helps increase your reading speed.

1. With a partner, review the words in the box.
2. Next, read the words aloud for one minute. Your teacher or partner can time you. How many words did you read in one minute?

fight	deck	ice	pack	ice	fight
stuck	pack	deck	ice	pack	stuck
pack	huge	stuck	fight	huge	pack
ice	ice	each	stuck	fight	ice
huge	stuck	deck	huge	deck	deck

Listen, Speak, Interact

Retell Order of Events

The events in "Antarctic Adventure" cover nearly two years. The writer tells the events in the order they happened. Time words help you keep track of events.

Examples of Time Words
Dates (June 15, 2003)
Days of the week (Monday, Tuesday . . .)
Months of the year (January, February . . .)

1. Read the selection aloud as a partner listens. Stop each time you come to a time word. On a piece of paper, list the words and the events in time order.
2. Then make a timeline that shows the events you recorded.
3. Using the timeline as a guide, retell the events to your partner.
4. Tell your partner about an adventure you had. Keep all events in the correct time order. Use time words to make the order of events clear.

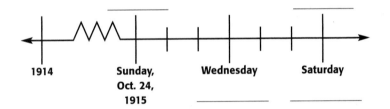

1914   Sunday, Oct. 24, 1915   Wednesday   Saturday

Elements of Literature

Identify Personification

Writers use **personification** to make nonfiction writing more interesting. Personification gives human thoughts, feelings, and actions to an object or animal.

In "Antarctic Adventure," the author describes the ship as if it were a person. For example: "The *Endurance* groaned."

Groaned is a word usually used for people and animals. The use of the word makes the ship seem alive.

Look through the rest of the selection and find other examples of personification. Record them in your Reading Log.

Reading Log   Activity Book
                        p. 19

Student
CD-ROM

Word Study

Use Adverbs

Adverbs can describe verbs. Many adverbs end in *-ly*.

The ship sailed slow**ly.**

Writers use adverbs to make their writing more precise or vivid.

1. In "Antarctic Adventure," find examples of adverbs that end in *-ly*. Look in paragraphs 3 and 15.

2. Write the adverbs in your Personal Dictionary. Underline the *-ly.*

3. Write an example sentence of your own using one of the adverbs.

Personal Dictionary

Activity Book
p. 20

Student CD-ROM

Grammar Focus

Use *And* to Join Words and Sentences

The word *and* means "also." *And* can join words and sentences.

And joining nouns:	They set out on Saturday, dragging food, equipment, **and** the lifeboats.
And joining verbs:	The ice floes groaned **and** crashed.
And joining adjectives:	The men tumbled out onto the ice, shocked **and** exhausted.
And joining adverbs:	Slowly **and** sadly, the people left the ship.
And joining sentences:	The ice started splitting, **and** they had to move their tents.

1. Find the uses of *and* in paragraphs 4, 6, and 7 of "Antarctic Adventure." What words or groups of words are joined?

2. Combine these two sentences into one. Use *and.*

The ship made a terrible noise. It sank.

Activity Book
pp. 21–22

Student Handbook

Student CD-ROM

From Reading to Writing

Write a Historical Narrative

Write a historical narrative about someone who faced danger. You may write about a person you know or someone you have learned about.

1. Use time words to tell when the events took place.
2. Make sure that your narrative has a beginning, a middle, and an end.
3. Use personification to bring things to life.
4. Use *and* to join words and sentences.
5. Be sure to indent each paragraph.
6. Add a timeline that shows the order in which important events occur.
7. Be sure to capitalize days of the week and months of the year.

Activity Book
p. 23

Across Content Areas

Learn About Bodies of Land and Water

The surface of Earth is made up of land and water. The main bodies of land are called **continents.** The main bodies of water are called **oceans.**

Continents	Oceans
Asia	The Atlantic Ocean
Africa	The Pacific Ocean
North America	The Indian Ocean
South America	The Arctic Ocean
Australia	
Europe	
Antarctica	

Smaller bodies of salt water are called **seas.** Some examples are the Mediterranean Sea (between Europe, Asia, and Africa) and the Caribbean Sea (along the coasts of Venezuela, Colombia, and Central America). Seas are often parts of oceans.

Islands are smaller bodies of land completely surrounded by water. Puerto Rico is an island in the Caribbean Sea.

1. Look at a map of the world and find the continents and oceans.
2. Look at the map of Antarctica on page 29. List the oceans, seas, continents, and islands that you see on the map.

Activity Book
p. 24

CHAPTER 4

Yang the Youngest

an excerpt from a novel
by Lensey Namioka

Objectives

Reading Compare a reading with your experiences as you read a first-person narrative.

Listening and Speaking Identify and use colloquial speech.

Grammar Study complex sentences with dependent clauses.

Writing Write a first-person narrative.

Content Social Studies: Learn the meanings of *culture*.

Use Prior Knowledge

Discuss the First Day of School

The main character in "Yang the Youngest" is attending a new school. In most cultures, the first day of school is a big day. You introduce yourself, meet new people, and learn school rules.

1. Copy the web on a piece of paper.
2. With a partner, brainstorm things that might happen on the first day of school. Write your ideas on the web.
3. Share your information with the class.

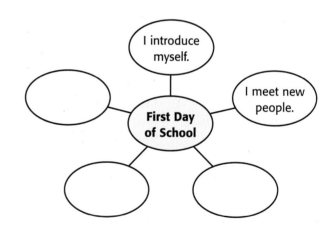

- I introduce myself.
- I meet new people.
- **First Day of School**

Build Background

China

China is a very large country in eastern Asia. It has a long history and has had a great influence on other countries. Paper and silk were first developed there. Family life, politeness, and respect for authority are very important in China.

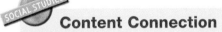

Content Connection

More than three billion people live in Asia. Over one billion live in China.

Build Vocabulary

Identify Homonyms

Homonyms are words that are pronounced and usually spelled the same but have different meanings.

Read these sentences. Choose the definitions that make sense.

1. "It was really hot, so I went to the <u>pool</u> to swim." In this sentence, *pool* means:
   a. a small body of water
   b. a game played on a special table

2. "When the teacher called my name, I <u>rose</u>." In this sentence, *rose* means:
   a. got up from my seat
   b. a flower with a beautiful smell

3. "May I borrow your <u>pen</u>?" In this sentence, *pen* means:
   a. a place to put animals in
   b. something to write with

Write these homonyms in your Personal Dictionary.

Personal Dictionary

Activity Book p. 25

Student CD-ROM

Text Structure

First-Person Narrative

"Yang the Youngest" is an excerpt from a novel. The story is told by Yang himself. In this type of writing, **first-person narrative,** the speaker tells you about his or her life.

As you read, look for these features of first-person narrative.

First-Person Narrative	
Story	beginning, middle, end
Personal Pronouns	I, me, we, us
Problem	The speaker faces a problem.
Problem Resolution	The speaker tells how he or she resolves the problem.

Student
CD-ROM

Reading Strategy

Compare a Reading with Your Experiences

As you read, think about how the experiences of the main character, Yang, might be like yours. Yang feels he does not know enough English to make friends. He also surprises his parents with his "American" behavior.

1. Read paragraph 1 on page 44. Compare your experiences with what happens in the paragraph by answering questions such as these:
   a. Have I ever had trouble because I did not know anyone?
   b. Have my parents ever been surprised by changes in my behavior?

2. As you read the selection, continue making comparisons between your experiences and the story. For example, have you ever felt afraid to meet new people?

Student
CD-ROM

YANG THE YOUNGEST

an excerpt from a novel
by Lensey Namioka

Audio

Compare a Reading with Your Experiences

Have you ever been afraid to join a new situation? What made you feel afraid?

1   Our family arrived in America in the winter, and the school year was almost half over. So when I started school, the other students in my class already knew each other. To make things worse, I didn't even know enough English to try to make friends.

2   But language was only one of my problems. American kids scared me at first. They yelled terribly loud and ran fast in the hallways.

3   For the first few weeks, I found myself hugging the walls. It was like the time in China when I learned to swim. I was afraid to let go of the side of the pool because in the middle were other swimmers splashing around like sharks.

4   Once when I was walking in the hallway at school, I turned a corner and bumped into a boy. He was running so fast that he knocked me off my feet.

5   He pulled me **upright** and shook me a little. Maybe he wanted to see if any parts were **rattling** loose. When he saw that I wasn't hurt, he **winked** at me, laughed, and said, "Hey, no sweat!"

---

upright   standing up
rattling   making short, sharp noises by banging around

winked   closed only one eye in order to make a friendly face

6   He looked so cheerful that I laughed, too. "No sweat" sounded like a good phrase, and I told Third Sister about it. She added it to her list.

7   In a few weeks I learned to walk just as fast and shove my way just as hard as the other kids.

8   My parents even complained about it. "You're becoming too rough, Yingtao. Why do you have to **stomp** your feet so hard?"

9   Before I got used to the American school, the other kids laughed at some of the things I did. Each morning, as soon as the teacher came into the room, I jumped to my feet and stood **stiffly** at attention. That was how we showed our **respect** to the teacher in China.

10   The first time I did it here, the teacher asked me whether I needed something. I looked around and saw that nobody else was standing up. Feeling foolish, I shook my head and sat down.

11   When I did it again the next day, a couple of kids behind me started to **snigger**. After that, I remembered not to jump up, but I half rose a few times. One boy used to watch me, and if he saw my bottom leave my seat, he would whisper, "Down, **Fido!**"

12   Third Sister was a great help during those early days. While the other kids were busy talking or playing games at **recess,** she and I stood in a corner and kept each other company.

Compare a Reading with Your Experiences

Have you ever been embarrassed by behaving differently from others?

---

stomp   walk heavily or loudly
stiffly   in a formal manner, not bending the body
respect   honor, admiration

snigger   snicker, laugh meanly
Fido   a traditional name for a dog
recess   a break from work or school to relax

13   Every day we walked together to our **elementary school,** which was not far from our house. Eldest Brother and Second Sister took a big yellow bus to a school that was farther away.

14   If Eldest Brother had trouble making friends, it didn't seem to bother him. Music was the only thing he really cared about.

15   I think Second Sister felt the loneliest. In China, people always said she would turn out to be a real beauty. She had been popular at school there, always surrounded by friends. But in America not many people told her she was beautiful. These days she was often **cranky** and sad. Mother told the rest of us that we just had to be patient with Second Sister.

16   Third Sister had no trouble at all making friends. Even before she could speak much English, she began **chatting** with other kids. She could always fill in the gaps with laughter.

---

elementary school   a school for grades 1–6 and students about the ages of 6–12

cranky   acting annoyed, in a bad mood

chatting   talking in a friendly and informal way

17   During lunch she and I sat at a table with mostly **Asian-Americans.** At first we didn't understand what Asian-Americans were. When we were filling out **registration forms** at school, we put down "Chinese" in the space marked "race."

18   The secretary at the school told us to change it to "Asian-American." With a big smile, she said, "We have a number of Asian-Americans at this school, so you'll be able to make friends easily."

19   My teacher must have felt the same because on my first day in class, she seated me next to a girl who was also Asian-American.

20   I greeted her in Chinese, but she just shook her head. "I'm afraid I don't understand Japanese," she said in English.

21   "I wasn't speaking Japanese," I told her. "I was speaking Chinese."

22   "Sorry. I don't understand that, either. My family is from Korea."

23   I didn't know much about Korea, except that my country had once **invaded** her country. I hoped she didn't hold it against me.

24   "You speak good English," I said. "When did you arrive?"

25   "I was born in America," she said. "So were my parents."

26   **In spite of** this bad start, she tried to be helpful to me. But we never became close friends.

27   So I was lonely. After Third Sister made friends in her class, she began to spend less and less time with me.

Asian-Americans Americans whose parents or ancestors came from Asia

registration forms papers showing lists of students who are signed up for school

invaded sent armies to take over and control

in spite of *in spite of* introduces an idea that may seem surprising

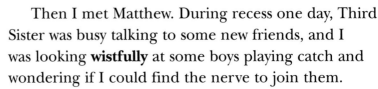

28　Then I met Matthew. During recess one day, Third Sister was busy talking to some new friends, and I was looking **wistfully** at some boys playing catch and wondering if I could find the nerve to join them.

29　Suddenly I felt someone **pluck** my pen from my pocket. This was a ballpoint pen I had brought with me from China, with a picture of a panda on the side of it. Whenever I thought about China and missed the friends I had left behind, I would take out the pen and look at the picture.

Compare a Reading with Your Experiences

Has anyone ever teased you? How did you feel?

30　The boy who had taken the pen was running away, laughing. I ran after him, shouting. The teacher came up and asked me what the trouble was.

31　"He took my . . . my . . ." I stopped, because I didn't know the English word for pen. In Chinese we have the same word, *bi,* for pen, pencil, and brush. "He took my writing stick," I finished **lamely.**

32　The boy **who'd** taken the pen stood there and grinned, while the teacher looked **puzzled.**

33　"Jake took his ballpoint pen," said a tall, **freckled** boy with curly brown hair. "I saw the whole thing."

34　The teacher turned and frowned at Jake. "Is this true?"

35　"Aw, I was just teasing him a little," said Jake, quickly handing the pen back to me. "He's always playing with it, so I got curious."

36　I thanked the boy with the curly hair. "Don't mind Jake," he said. "He didn't mean anything."

---

wistfully　in a manner that is sadly wishful
pluck　pull or grab
lamely　in a manner that is weak or not convincing

who'd　who had
puzzled　confused
freckled　having small spots of darker skin on the skin

37   "My name is Yang Yingtao," I introduced myself. Then I remembered that in America people said their **family name** last and their **given name** first.

38   "Yingtao is my last name," I told him. "Except that in America my last name is really my first name and my first name is my last name. So I'm Yang Yingtao in China and Yingtao Yang in America."

39   The boy looked confused. Just then the bell rang. "I'm Matthew Conner," he said quickly. "See you around."

40   I began to feel a little less lonely.

> **Compare a Reading with Your Experiences**
>
> Have you ever confused anyone? What happened? How did you feel?

---

family name the name you share with your parents and brothers or sisters

given name the name given to you by your parents when you were born

About the Author   Lensey Namioka (born 1929)

Like her character Yang, Lensey Namioka was born in China and later came to the United States. Her father worked for the Chinese government, and the family moved around a lot. Because of this, Namioka understands some of the problems young people face when they come to a new place or feel that they do not fit into the group. She says that she writes books "because it's fun. There's nothing else I enjoy more."

➤ Why do you think Lensey Namioka wrote "Yang the Youngest"? To entertain? To inform? To persuade?

Beyond the Reading

Reading Comprehension

Question-Answer Relationships (QAR)

"Right There" Questions

1. **Recall Facts** What is the setting of the story?
2. **Recall Facts** Who walks to school with Yang?

"Think and Search" Questions

3. **Analyze Setting** How would you describe the place where the story happens?
4. **Recognize Character Traits** Why does Yang have trouble sharing his thoughts and feelings at school?
5. **Understand Characters** What is the main problem Yang faces?
6. **Analyze Characters** How does Yang change as he gets used to his new school?
7. **Draw a Conclusion** What happens to change Yang's feelings?

"Author and You" Questions

8. **Analyze Characters** Why do you think Second Sister is crankier in the United States than she had been in China?
9. **Compare and Contrast** What did you learn about Chinese culture from the selection? What things are similar to your culture? What things are different?

"On Your Own" Questions

10. **Predict** What do you think will happen between Yang and Matthew?
11. **Express Your Opinion** What do you think Yang should do to be more comfortable in his new school?

Activity Book
p. 26

Student
CD-ROM

Build Reading Fluency

Adjusting Reading Rate

You read many quotations in "Yang the Youngest." Reading quotations aloud helps you learn to adjust your reading rate. Pause and read as if you are speaking to a person.

1. With a partner, practice rereading paragraphs 18–25 on page 47.
2. Read the quotations with expression.
3. Pause after each quotation.
4. Choose the quotation you like the best and read it aloud in front of the class.

Listen, Speak, Interact

Identify and Use Colloquial Speech

When the boy runs into Yang in the hallway, he says, "Hey, no sweat." This kind of language is called **colloquial speech.** Colloquial speech is the way you speak with friends in everyday conversation. Using colloquial speech helps authors create characters that sound like real people.

1. Read aloud or listen to paragraphs 1–7 with a partner.

a. Act out the scene when Yang bumps into another student.
b. Discuss what you think the phrase "Hey, no sweat" means.
2. Together, find three other examples of colloquial speech in paragraphs 11, 35, and 39. What do they mean?
3. Colloquial speech can reflect a region or culture. What examples of colloquial speech do you know? How do they reflect a region or culture?

Elements of Literature

Analyze Characters

Characters are the people in a story. Writers tell about characters in two ways:

Direct Characterization	The author tells you how the character feels. Example: "The character is happy."
Indirect Characterization	The author *suggests* how a character feels or what a character is like. Example: "The character is laughing."

1. Copy the character web in your Reading Log.
2. Complete the web with details about Yang. Next to each detail write *D* if it shows *direct characterization* and *I* if it shows *indirect characterization*.

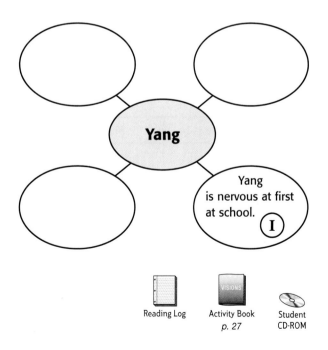

Yang

Yang is nervous at first at school. Ⓘ

Reading Log   Activity Book p. 27   Student CD-ROM

Word Study

Define Words with a Latin Root

Many English words and spellings come from other languages and cultures. For example, the word *respect* has the word part *spect*. *Spect* comes from the Latin word *spectare* that means "to look." (People who lived in Rome long ago spoke Latin.) The word *respect* means "to look at with honor."

Word	Meaning
re**spect**	to look at with honor
in**spect**	to look at closely
spectator	someone who watches something

Personal Dictionary   Activity Book p. 28   Student CD-ROM

1. Copy the words and definitions in the chart in your Personal Dictionary.
2. Work with a partner to write three sentences. Include one *spect* word in each sentence.

Grammar Focus

Study Complex Sentences with Dependent Clauses

A **clause** is a part of a sentence. It has a subject (S) and a verb (V).

Dependent Clause	Main Clause
When I study hard, ↑ ↑ ↑ S V comma	I get good grades.

Main clauses can be sentences by themselves. **Dependent clauses** must be used with main clauses. They cannot stand alone.

Dependent clauses can start with time words like *when, after, before, as soon as,* and *while.*

<u>Before</u> I got used to the American school, the other kids laughed at some of the things I did.

When the dependent clause comes first, a comma is used.

As soon as I finish**,** I will call you.

I will call you as soon as I finish.

1. Find other examples of sentences from the reading with clauses. Look in paragraphs 1, 4, 9, 11, 12.
2. Write three sentences with dependent clauses and main clauses. Use correct punctuation.

Activity Book pp. 29–30   Student Handbook   Student CD-ROM

From Reading to Writing

Write a First-Person Narrative

Write a first-person narrative about a challenge you are facing. A challenge usually involves a problem. Tell how you will resolve the problem.

1. Use the first-person pronouns *I, me, we,* and *us.*
2. Use direct and indirect characterization.
3. Write sentences with dependent and independent clauses. Use correct punctuation.
4. Be sure your narrative has a beginning, a middle, and an end.

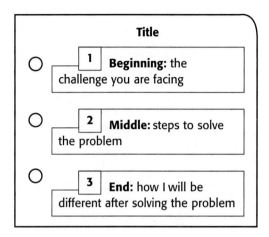

Title

○ **1 Beginning:** the challenge you are facing

○ **2 Middle:** steps to solve the problem

○ **3 End:** how I will be different after solving the problem

Activity Book
p. 31

Across Content Areas

SOCIAL STUDIES

Learn the Meanings of *Culture*

The word **culture** has two main meanings when it applies to people. Read this dictionary entry:

> **cul•ture** /ˈkʌl+ʃər/ *n.* **1** the ideas, activities (art, foods, businesses), and ways of behaving that are special to a country, people, or region: *In North American culture, men do not kiss men when meeting each other. They shake hands.* **2** the achievements of a people or nation in art, music, literature, etc.: *The Chinese have had a high culture for thousands of years.‖She is a person of culture and refinement.*

Read these sentences. Decide which definition—**1** or **2**—matches each sentence.

1. My sister goes to museums a lot because she loves art.
2. In many East Asian countries, most people eat with chopsticks.
3. Jazz music originated in the United States.
4. In Mexico, taking a siesta (a short nap) after lunch used to be common.

Activity Book
p. 32

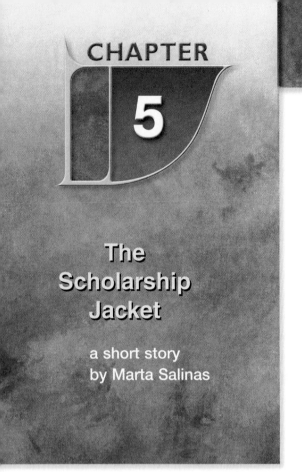

CHAPTER 5

The Scholarship Jacket

a short story
by Marta Salinas

Into the Reading

Objectives

Reading Find the main idea and details as you read a short story.

Listening and Speaking Debate issues.

Grammar Use *could* and *couldn't* for past ability.

Writing Write a short story.

Content Science: Learn about nutrition.

Use Prior Knowledge

Discuss Awards

An award is a prize or a special honor. The main character in this selection believes that she will win an award. Have you ever worked hard to win a prize or special honor?

1. Work in a small group.
2. On a piece of paper, list as many awards as you can.
3. Identify what a person needs to do in order to win the award. For example, in a footrace, a person needs to cross the finish line first.
4. Copy the chart. Complete it with information about how the awards are won.

Event	Prize	How You Win It
Essay Contest	1st place ribbon	Write the best essay
Soccer	1st place trophy	
Spelling Contest	1st place trophy	

5. Many people all over the world work hard to win awards. Discuss with a partner why this is a common theme in many cultures.

Build Background

School Traditions

Schools around the world have special traditions or customs. Some schools give awards to the best student. Others put pictures of the best athletes up on a wall. One tradition in schools in the United States is to give a jacket that has the initial, or first letter, of the school's name on it. For example, if your school is called Martinez School, the initial would be *M*.

Discuss school traditions with a partner. Describe traditions you know about from your school or schools in other cultures.

Content Connection

The valedictorian is the student in the graduating class who has the best grades. The valedictorian sometimes gives a speech on graduation day.

Build Vocabulary

Learn Words About Emotions

In "The Scholarship Jacket," the characters show their emotions. With a partner, read these sentences and choose the best explanation for the underlined words in each one. Check your answers in a dictionary.

1. I fidgeted with the papers on my desk because I didn't know what to say.
   a. I was happy.
   b. I was nervous.
2. I despaired every time I thought about the race. I knew I couldn't win.
   a. I had no hope.
   b. I felt excited.
3. When I won the contest, I was in shock.
   a. I was very surprised.
   b. I was very tired.

Write the words *fidget, despair,* and *in shock* in your Personal Dictionary, along with their meanings.

Personal Dictionary

The Heinle Newbury House Dictionary

Activity Book *p. 33*

Student CD-ROM

Text Structure

Short Story

"The Scholarship Jacket" is a **short story.** Short stories develop the characters and action very quickly. Look at the chart. It shows some features of a short story.

Short Story	
Characters	a few are presented in the story
Main Problem	comes at the beginning of the story
Narration	the author's words that describe the action and the characters
Dialogue	the words that the characters speak; the words are in quotation marks (" . . . ")

1. As you read "The Scholarship Jacket," notice how the writer carefully develops the characters and the story.

2. Stop at the end of each page and ask yourself, "What do I know about Martha? What is happening now?"

Student
CD-ROM

Reading Strategy

Find the Main Idea and Details

The **main idea** of a paragraph is the most important idea in the paragraph. The **details** include all the information that helps you understand the main idea.

Sometimes the author does not directly state the main idea. When this happens, you have to find it by paying attention to the details. Ask yourself, "What topic do the details share?"

1. Read paragraph 2 of "The Scholarship Jacket," on page 58. What is the paragraph's main idea? What are the details that you find?

2. Think about what the details tell you. How do they support the main idea?

Student
CD-ROM

THE SCHOLARSHIP JACKET

a short story by Marta Salinas

Audio

1 The small Texas school that I attended carried out a tradition every year during the eighth grade graduation; a beautiful gold and green jacket, the school colors, was awarded to the class valedictorian, the student who had maintained the highest grades for eight years. The **scholarship** jacket had a big gold S on the left front side and the winner's name was written in gold letters on the pocket.

2 My oldest sister Rosie had won the jacket a few years back and I fully expected to win also. I was fourteen and in the eighth grade. I had been a straight A student since the first grade, and the last year I had looked forward to owning that jacket. My father was a farm laborer who couldn't earn enough money to feed eight children, so when I was six I was given to my grandparents to raise. We couldn't participate in sports at school because there were registration fees, uniform costs, and trips out of town; so even though we were quite **agile** and athletic, there would never be a sports school jacket for us. This one, the scholarship jacket, was our only chance.

3 In May, close to graduation, **spring fever** struck, and no one paid any attention in class; instead we stared out the windows and at each other, wanting to speed up the last few weeks of school.

Find the Main Idea and Details

What is the main idea of this paragraph?

---

scholarship study, schoolwork
agile quick, able to move well

spring fever a feeling of great energy due to the warm weather of spring

I despaired every time I looked in the mirror. Pencil thin, not a curve anywhere, I was called "Beanpole" and "String Bean" and I knew that's what I looked like. A flat chest, no hips, and a brain, that's what I had. That really isn't much for a fourteen-year-old to work with, I thought, as I **absentmindedly** wandered from my history class to the gym. Another hour of sweating in basketball and displaying my toothpick legs was coming up. Then I remembered my P.E. shorts were still in a bag under my desk where I'd forgotten them. I had to walk all the way back and get them. Coach Thompson was a real bear if anyone wasn't dressed for **P.E.** She had said I was a good forward and once she even tried to talk Grandma into letting me join the team. Grandma, of course, said no.

4   I was almost back at my classroom's door when I heard angry voices and arguing. I stopped. I didn't mean to **eavesdrop;** I just hesitated, not knowing what to do. I needed those shorts and I was going to be late, but I didn't want to interrupt an argument between my teachers. I recognized the voices: Mr. Schmidt, my history teacher, and Mr. Boone, my math teacher. They seemed to be arguing about me. I couldn't believe it. I still remember the shock that rooted me flat against the wall as if I were trying to blend in with the graffiti written there.

> **Find the Main Idea and Details**
>
> How does the style (look and feeling) of the illustration help express the main idea of this paragraph?

---

absentmindedly   without one's mind on the task, thinking about other things

P.E.   physical education or gym class
eavesdrop   listen in on another person's conversation

Find the Main Idea and Details

How are the details about Joann's father important to the main idea of Mr. Boone's message? What is the main idea or meaning of his words to Mr. Schmidt?

5   "I refuse to do it! I don't care who her father is, her grades don't even begin to compare to Martha's. I won't lie or **falsify** records. Martha has a straight A plus average and you know it." That was Mr. Schmidt and he sounded very angry. Mr. Boone's voice sounded calm and quiet.

6   "Look, Joann's father is not only on the Board, he owns the only store in town; we could say it was a close tie and—"

7   The pounding in my ears drowned out the rest of the words, only a word here and there filtered through. ". . . Martha is Mexican. . . . **resign**. . . . won't do it. . . ." Mr. Schmidt came rushing out, and luckily for me went down the opposite way toward the **auditorium,** so he didn't see me. Shaking, I waited a few minutes and then went in and grabbed my bag and fled from the room. Mr. Boone looked up when I came in but didn't say anything. To this day I don't remember if I got in trouble in P.E. for being late or how I made it through the rest of the afternoon. I went home very sad and cried into my pillow that night so grandmother wouldn't hear me. It seemed a cruel **coincidence** that I had overheard that conversation.

---

falsify   make false, change to say something untrue
resign   choose to leave one's job
auditorium   a large room with seats as in a theater

coincidence   a combination of events that happens by chance but seems arranged or planned

Find the Main Idea and Details

The speaker tells us that the principal fidgeted with his papers. How does this detail help you identify the main idea in this paragraph?

8   The next day when the principal called me into his office, I knew what it would be about. He looked uncomfortable and unhappy. I decided I wasn't going to make it any easier for him so I looked him straight in the eye. He looked away and fidgeted with the papers on his desk.

9   "Martha," he said, "there's been a change in policy this year regarding the scholarship jacket. As you know, it has always been free." He cleared his throat and continued. "This year the Board decided to charge fifteen dollars— which still won't cover the complete cost of the jacket."

10   I stared at him in shock and a small sound of **dismay** escaped my throat. I hadn't expected this. He still avoided looking in my eyes.

11   "So if you are unable to pay the fifteen dollars for the jacket, it will be given to the next one in line."

---

dismay   unhappiness, shock

12　　Standing with all the **dignity** I could **muster,** I said, "I'll speak to my grandfather about it, sir, and let you know tomorrow." I cried on the walk home from the bus stop. The dirt road was a quarter of a mile from the highway, so by the time I got home, my eyes were red and puffy.

13　　"Where's Grandpa?" I asked Grandma, looking down at the floor so she wouldn't ask me why I'd been crying. She was sewing on a quilt and didn't look up.

14　　"I think he's out back working in the bean field."

15　　I went outside and looked out at the fields. There he was. I could see him walking between the rows, his body bent over the little plants, hoe in hand. I walked slowly out to him, trying to think how I could best ask him for the money. There was a cool breeze blowing and a sweet smell of mesquite in the air, but I didn't **appreciate** it. I kicked at a dirt clod. I wanted that jacket so much. It was more than just being a valedictorian and giving a little thank you speech for the jacket on graduation night. It represented eight years of hard work and **expectation.** I knew I had to be honest with Grandpa; it was my only chance. He saw me and looked up.

> **Find the Main Idea and Details**
>
> Why is the jacket so important to Martha? How do the details "eight years of hard work and expectation" help you understand the main idea?

---

dignity　pride
muster　collect, find

appreciate　enjoy
expectation　hope, desire

Find the Main Idea and Details

Do you think Grandpa will give her the money for the jacket? What details make you think this?

16   He waited for me to speak. I cleared my throat nervously and clasped my hands behind my back so he wouldn't see them shaking. "Grandpa, I have a big favor to ask you," I said in Spanish, the only language he knew. He still waited silently. I tried again. "Grandpa, this year the principal said the scholarship jacket is not going to be free. It's going to cost fifteen dollars and I have to take the money in tomorrow, otherwise it'll be given to someone else." The last words came out in an **eager** rush. Grandpa straightened up tiredly and leaned his chin on the hoe handle. He looked out over the field that was filled with the tiny green bean plants. I waited, desperately hoping he'd say I could have the money.

17   He turned to me and asked quietly, "What does a scholarship jacket mean?"

18   I answered quickly; maybe there was a chance. "It means you've earned it by having the highest grades for eight years and that's why they're giving it to you." Too late I realized the **significance** of my words. Grandpa knew that I understood it was not a matter of money. It wasn't that.

He went back to hoeing the weeds that sprang up between the **delicate** little bean plants. It was a **time consuming** job; sometimes the small shoots were right next to each other. Finally he spoke again.

19   "Then if you pay for it, Marta, it's not a scholarship jacket, is it? Tell your principal I will not pay the fifteen dollars."

---

eager   hurried, fast, excited
significance   importance

delicate   fragile, easily broken
time consuming   taking a lot of time

20   I walked back to the house and locked myself in the bathroom for a long time. I was angry with grandfather even though I knew he was right, and I was angry with the Board, whoever they were. Why did they have to change the rules just when it was my turn to win the jacket?

Find the Main Idea and Details

What words help you understand how Martha is feeling in this paragraph?

21   It was a very sad and **withdrawn** girl who dragged into the principal's office the next day. This time he did look me in the eyes.

22   "What did your grandfather say?"

23   I sat very straight in my chair.

24   "He said to tell you he won't pay the fifteen dollars."

25   The principal **muttered** something I couldn't understand under his breath, and walked over to the window. He stood looking out at something outside. He looked bigger than usual when he stood up; he was a tall **gaunt** man with gray hair, and I watched the back of his head while I waited for him to speak.

---

withdrawn   silent, not wanting to talk to anyone, unhappy

muttered   complained, spoken unclearly or quietly

gaunt   very thin

26   "Why?" he finally asked. "Your grandfather has the money. Doesn't he own a small bean farm?"

27   I looked at him, forcing my eyes to stay dry. "He said if I had to pay for it, then it wouldn't be a scholarship jacket," I said and stood up to leave. "I guess you'll just have to give it to Joann." I hadn't meant to say that; it had just slipped out. I was almost to the door when he stopped me.

28   "Martha—wait."

29   I turned and looked at him, waiting. What did he want now? I could feel my heart pounding. Something bitter and **vile** tasting was coming up in my mouth; I was afraid I was going to be sick. I didn't need any sympathy speeches. He sighed loudly and went back to his big desk. He looked at me, biting his lip, as if thinking.

30   "Okay. We'll make an exception in your case. I'll tell the Board, you'll get your jacket."

Find the Main Idea and Details

What is the main emotion of this paragraph? How do Martha and the principal feel? Use details from the paragraph to support your ideas.

vile terrible

31 I could hardly believe it. I spoke in a trembling rush. "Oh, thank you sir!" Suddenly I felt great. I didn't know about **adrenaline** in those days, but I knew something was pumping through me, making me feel as tall as the sky. I wanted to yell, jump, run the mile, do something. I ran out so I could cry in the hall where there was no one to see me. At the end of the day, Mr. Schmidt winked at me and said, "I hear you're getting a scholarship jacket this year."

32 His face looked as happy and innocent as a baby's, but I knew better. Without answering I gave him a quick hug and ran to the bus. I cried on the walk home again, but this time because I was so happy. I couldn't wait to tell Grandpa and ran straight to the field. I joined him in the row where he was working and without saying anything I crouched down and started pulling up the weeds with my hands. Grandpa worked alongside me for a few minutes, but he didn't ask what had happened. After I had a little pile of weeds between the rows, I stood up and faced him.

---

adrenaline   a chemical that the body makes when a person is very excited; it gives a boost of energy

33　　"The principal said he's making an exception for me, Grandpa, and I'm getting the jacket after all. That's after I told him what you said."

34　　Grandpa didn't say anything, he just gave me a pat on the shoulder and a smile. He pulled out the crumpled red handkerchief that he always carried in his back pocket and wiped the sweat off his forehead.

35　　"Better go see if your grandmother needs any help with supper."

36　　I gave him a big grin. He didn't fool me. I skipped and ran back to the house whistling some silly tune.

Find the Main Idea and Details

How would you describe Martha and Grandpa at this point in the story? What details or words tell you how they feel about each other at the end?

About the Author

Marta Salinas (born 1949)

Marta Salinas was born in California. She studied writing and received her degree from the University of California at Irvine. Her short story "The Scholarship Jacket" was first published in *Nosotras: Latina Literature Today,* a collection of works by Hispanic women writers.

➤ Based on this story, how do you think Marta Salinas feels about fighting for fairness?

Beyond the Reading

Reading Comprehension

Question-Answer Relationships (QAR)

"Right There" Questions

1. **Recall Facts** Who is the story's main character?
2. **Explain the Main Idea** What does Martha hope to win?
3. **Recall Facts** What happens when Martha returns to her classroom to get her P.E. clothes?
4. **Recall Facts** To whom does Mr. Boone want to give the scholarship jacket? Why?

"Think and Search" Questions

5. **Summarize** Why does the principal tell Martha that she must pay fifteen dollars for the scholarship jacket?
6. **Analyze Characters** What do you learn about Grandpa when he refuses to pay the fifteen dollars?

7. **Analyze Characters** In paragraph 29, the principal uses nonverbal language: "he sighed loudly . . . biting his lip . . ." What does this nonverbal language tell you about what he is thinking and feeling?

"Author and You" Question

8. **Make an Inference** Why is Martha angry at her grandfather, even though she knows he is right?

"On Your Own" Questions

9. **Draw a Conclusion** What do you think about the people who want to give the jacket to Joann?
10. **Put Yourself in a Character's Place** What would you do in Martha's position?
11. **Express Your Opinion** Did Grandpa make the right choice?

Activity Book
p. 34

Student
CD-ROM

Build Reading Fluency

Reading Chunks of Words Silently

Reading silently is good practice. It helps you learn to read faster.

1. Listen to paragraph 1 of "The Scholarship Jacket" on the Audio CD.

2. Listen to the chunks of words.
3. Reread paragraph 1 silently two times.
4. Your teacher will time your second reading.

Listen, Speak, Interact

Debate Issues

Should Martha and her grandfather have paid the money for the jacket? Debate this issue with your classmates.

In a debate, some people support one side of an issue. Other people support the other side. Good debaters make the best arguments possible, even if they disagree with the side that they are arguing.

Position	Argument	Facts and Opinions to Support the Position
1	Martha and her grandfather should pay for the jacket.	
2	Martha and her grandfather should not pay for the jacket.	

1. Fill out a chart like this. Be prepared to argue both sides.
2. Present one position in the debate. Be sure to support your position with facts and opinions.

3. Listen to your classmates' arguments. What evidence do your classmates use to support their opinions?
4. How do their opinions compare to yours? Do their arguments cause you to change your opinions? Why or why not?

Elements of Literature

Analyze Character Motivation

Motivation is the reason why a character acts in a certain way. To understand a character's motivation, ask: Why does the character say or do this? For example:

Why does Martha want the scholarship jacket?

She wants to be like her sister.
She wants to make her family proud.

1. Analyze the motivations of the following characters. Write your answers in your Reading Log.
   a. Mr. Boone: Why does he want to give the jacket to Joann?
   b. Grandpa: Why doesn't he want to pay for the jacket?
2. Work with a partner to explain other character motivations in the story. Be sure to look for nonverbal messages such as gestures, facial expressions, and body language (how the person moves his or her body).

Reading Log   Activity Book p. 35   Student CD-ROM

Word Study

Identify Root Words

Root words are the words from which other words are made. You can see the root word inside the larger words.

Root Word	Words Using the Root Word
except	exception, exceptional, unexceptional

Recognizing root words can help you understand and spell the larger words that include them.

1. Look at the underlined words in the following sentences. What root word do you see in them? Write the root words and the larger words in your Personal Dictionary.

   a. The jacket stood for eight years of hard work and <u>expectation</u>.
   b. My father was a farm <u>laborer</u>.
   c. I won't lie or <u>falsify</u> records.
   d. He looked <u>uncomfortable</u> and <u>unhappy</u>.

2. Each time you find a root word inside a larger word, write both words in your Personal Dictionary. This will increase your vocabulary.

Personal Dictionary   Activity Book p. 36   Student CD-ROM

Grammar Focus

Use *Could* and *Couldn't* for Past Ability

Use **could** to describe past abilities. If you were able to do something yesterday, then you *could* do it. If you were not able to do something yesterday, then you *could not* do it.

Sometimes writers combine *could* and *not* into the contraction **couldn't.** For example, "We *couldn't* participate in sports at school."

1. Find other examples of *could* and *couldn't* in the story. See paragraphs 2, 4, 15, and 29.

2. Write one sentence using *could* to describe something you were able to do sometime in the past. Write another sentence using *couldn't* to describe something you were not able to do in the past.

Activity Book pp. 37–38   Student Handbook   Student CD-ROM

From Reading to Writing

Write a Short Story

Write a short story about working for something that you want. Use the model to plan the important parts of your story.

1. Be sure your story has a beginning, a middle, and an end.
2. Introduce the characters right away.
3. Introduce the goal quickly.
4. Include only a few events.

Title

○ | **1** **Beginning**
Who are the characters? What are they like?
Remember: You are the main character.

○ | **2** **Middle**
What is your goal? What is your motivation? What events take place?

○ | **3** **End**
How do you meet your goal? How does the story end?

Activity Book
p. 39

Across Content Areas

Learn About Nutrition

Nutrition is the study of how the body needs and uses food. Look at these words related to nutrition.

nutritionist	someone who gives advice about nutrition
nutrient	something in food that feeds the body
nutritious	good for the health of your body

1. Copy these sentences on a piece of paper.
2. Complete each one with the correct word: *nutritionist, nutrient,* or *nutritious.*
   a. Are beans good for you? Many _____ say "Yes!"
   b. Beans are _____ because they contain protein, a _____ that builds muscles and other body tissues.

Listening and Speaking Workshop

Make a Speech: News Report

> **Topic**
>
> Choose one of the chapter stories you read and present it as a news report. Focus on the challenge or problem the characters faced.

Step 1: Use a graphic feature such as a Sunshine Organizer to organize your news report.

Step 2: Be specific.

Answer the following questions:

1. *Who* faces the challenge or problem?
2. *What* is the challenge or problem? Describe it in detail.
3. *When* do the main events take place? In the present or in the past?
4. *Where* do the main events take place (the setting)?
5. *Why* do the characters face the problem? (Describe how the problem came up.)

Step 3: Use an attention-grabbing opening.

Use one of these hints for openings:

1. Ask a question.
2. Say something funny.
3. Make a dramatic statement.
4. Refer to an authority and use quotes.

Step 4: Stay on the topic and use visuals.

1. The topic is about "A challenge." Don't wander.
2. Notecards will help you stay on track.
3. Use visuals with your speech to make it more interesting.
   a. Use pictures from a magazine or the Internet, or use a drawing.
   b. Consider using a video or a technology presentation.

Step 5: Practice your speech.

After you have at least one idea for an opening:

1. Put each group of ideas on a notecard.
2. Practice with a partner.
3. Answer the questions on the Checklists.
4. Revise your report based on feedback.
5. Practice with visuals.

Viewing Workshop

Compare and Contrast Electronic Media with Written Stories

Analyze Information

In Unit 1, you read about Ernest Shackleton and the ship the *Endurance*.

1. Get a video from the school or public library about Ernest Shackleton.
2. Compare and contrast the video to the reading selection "Antarctic Adventure." What new information do you learn from the video? What information is the same? What information do you learn only in the reading selection?

Further Viewing

Watch the *Visions* CNN video for Unit 1. Do the Video Worksheet.

CNN Video

Writer's Workshop

Write to Narrate: Tell How Someone Faced a Challenge

Writing Prompt

Choose someone you admire who has faced a challenge. Write his or her story. It could be someone in your family or community, a friend, or someone you know about from history or the news. You are writing because you think that the story is inspiring and you want to share it with other people.

Step 1: Make lists.

1. List important events, background information, and other details that are important to the challenge.
2. List other people who are important to the challenge.
3. Make a list of events. Put them in correct time order.

Step 2: Write your first draft.

1. Begin with a strong opening that makes the reader want to know what is coming next.
2. Write a sentence to introduce the topic.
3. Use details to describe the characters and their actions.
4. Use *and* to connect words.
5. Follow correct time order. Use time words like dates and *first, then, next* in dependent clauses.
6. In your ending, show that the story is over. Use a word like *finally*.

Story Chart

Title of Your Story

I. Beginning

  A. Strong opening

  B. State the topic

  C. Identify the characters and the setting

II. Middle

  A. Sequence of events

  B. Details

  C. Dialogue in quotation marks

III. End

  A. Connect the details of the story

  B. Tell why you admire the person and why

Step 3: Revise.

Collaborate with a partner to revise and organize your work. Listen as your partner reads your story aloud to you. Check for these things:

1. Did you use correct pronouns when talking about each character *(he, she, him, her)*?
2. Did you pay attention to the audience and your purpose for writing?
3. Did you use details to make the story interesting and exciting?
4. Did you describe actions?
5. Did you use correct time order?
6. Did you rearrange the text to give your story a clear beginning, middle, and end?

Step 4: Edit and proofread.

Read your story carefully and check for these things. If you have written your story on a computer, use the checks for spelling, punctuation, and grammar.

1. Did you write clearly by combining important parts of text? Did you delete parts that were not important to your story?
2. Did you use different sentence types to keep your writing interesting?
3. Did you use a dictionary or glossary to make sure your spelling is correct?
4. Did you use punctuation correctly to clarify and enhance your ideas?
5. Did you indent paragraphs?
6. Use the Editor's Checklist in your Student Handbook.

Step 5: Publish.

Prepare your story for presentation to your audience:

1. If you wrote your story on a computer, choose a font (style of type) that is easy to read. If you wrote it by hand, use your best handwriting.
2. Write a title page with the title of your story and "by (your name)."
3. Create a class collection of the stories. Make a Table of Contents to organize everyone's work.
4. As you read the stories, review them for their strengths and weaknesses.
5. Set your goals as a writer based on your writing and the writing of your classmates.
6. Meet with a small group to talk about each other's stories. Talk about challenges you and your classmates faced in writing the stories. Then talk about strategies you used to express your ideas.

The Heinle
Newbury House
Dictionary

Student
Handbook

Projects

Project 1: Create a Poster About Meeting Challenges

Do you know people who have successfully met challenges? In your opinion, what qualities do these people share?

1. Take a poll of ten people of different ages and/or cultures. Ask, "What are the three most important qualities to help people meet challenges?"
2. List each person's name and response in a chart.

My Mother
1. intelligence
2. courage
3. keeps trying

3. Look at your list. Are the qualities mentioned the same or different for all ages? For all cultures?
4. Find the three qualities named most often. Make a poster with illustrations that show these qualities.
5. Present your poster to the class and to your family.

Project 2: Write a Magazine Article or a Web Article

Research a place where it is difficult to live. It can be a place from the unit or a place that you have read or know about.

1. Make a list of five questions you want to answer about the challenge of living in the place. Include any questions you formed as you read the unit selections.
2. Use reference books and the Internet to answer your questions.
3. Your questions may change as you research. Revise your questions if you need to. Then continue to research answers.
4. Complete a chart with your questions and answers. Use these to write your article.

What I Want to Know	What I Learned
How does cold weather affect life there?	It is dangerous to go out without the right clothing and equipment.

5. Find photographs or make illustrations that show your place. Write short captions that tell about each image.
6. Compare and contrast your magazine or Web article with a reading selection that mentions a difficult place to live. How is your information similar? How is it different?

Further Reading

Here is some information about books that tell how people have faced challenges. Choose one or more of them. Record the ones you read in your Reading Log. Write your thoughts and feelings about what you read. Take notes about your answers to these questions:

1. What challenge did this book describe?
2. How did the people meet their challenges?

Hatchet
by Gary Paulsen, Pocket Books, 1996. After a plane crash, Brian must learn how to survive alone in the Canadian wilderness. With only a hatchet that his mother gave him, Brian must make it on his own.

Yang the Youngest and His Terrible Ear
by Lensey Namioka, Yearling Books, 1994. Yingtao recently moved with his family of musicians from China to Seattle, Washington. He is tone-deaf and is afraid of ruining the family recital.

That Was Then, This Is Now
by S. E. Hinton, Puffin, 1998. This book by the award-winning author of *The Outsiders* is about two 16-year-old friends, Byron and Mark, who have been close friends since childhood. However, their friendship suddenly changes when Byron discovers that Mark has committed a crime. Byron turns Mark over to the police. Now he must learn to face the guilt of betrayal and the loss of his best friend.

Quilted Landscape: Conversations with Young Immigrants
by Yale Strom, Simon & Schuster Children's, 1996. This book tells the stories of 26 immigrant children ages 11 through 17. They describe how they feel about living in the United States and discuss the challenges of adjusting to a new country.

The Cay
by Theodore Taylor, Yearling Books, 2002. In this award-winning book, a boy named Phillip travels on a freight boat that is torpedoed during World War II. Blinded by a blow to the head, he finds himself on a deserted Caribbean island.

Raptor
by Paul Zindel, Hyperion Press, 1999. Zack and his American Indian friend, Ute, are trapped in a cave with a living dinosaur, the deadly Utah raptor. In this thriller, the two boys struggle to outwit the dinosaur and escape from the cave.

Selkirk's Island: The True and Strange Adventures of the Real Robinson Crusoe
by Diana Souhami, Harvest Books, 2002. This book tells the true story of Alexander Selkirk, who spent four years on a deserted island in the eighteenth century.

Reading Log   Heinle
                     Reading Library

UNIT 2

Changes

Day and Night, M. C. Escher, woodcut, 1938.

View the Picture

1. Describe the changes that take place in the picture.
2. With a partner, discuss a change in your life.

In this unit, you will read a science article, a diary, a play, a story, a journal, and a poem about changes. You will learn some of the reasons for change, and some of the challenges that changes bring. You will learn about the features of these writing forms and how to write them yourself.

CHAPTER 1

Why Do Leaves Change Color in the Fall?

an excerpt from a science article from the World Wide Web

Into the Reading

Objectives

Reading Make inferences about a scientific informational text.

Listening and Speaking Role-play a scientific interview.

Grammar Identify and use the simple present tense.

Writing Write a scientific informational text.

Content Science: Learn about trees.

Use Prior Knowledge

Discuss the Change of Seasons

A season is several months that have a certain kind of weather. The northern part of North America has four seasons—summer, autumn (fall), winter, and spring. In some parts of the world, there are only two seasons—the dry season and the rainy season.

1. On a piece of paper, make a chart like the one here.
2. Choose a place where you have lived. On the chart, fill in the name of the place and the seasons.
3. Fill in the chart with information about each of the seasons.
4. Share your information with a partner.

Change of Seasons in _____				
Season				
Temperature is (hot, warm, cool, cold)				
Weather (rainy, sunny, snowy, windy)				
Clothes People Wear				
Things People Do				

80   **Unit 2** Changes

Build Background

North America and Climate

Climate is the kind of weather that an area has. The United States has many different climates. The southwestern United States has a desert climate—it is hot and dry. The Northeast and Midwest have a temperate climate—it is not extremely hot, and it is not extremely cold.

Content Connection

A **climate map** shows the different weather patterns in an area.

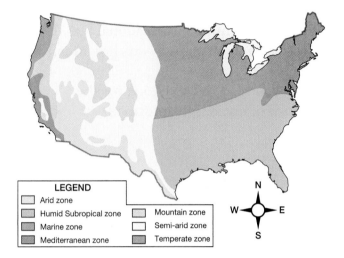

LEGEND
- Arid zone
- Humid Subropical zone
- Marine zone
- Mediterranean zone
- Mountain zone
- Semi-arid zone
- Temperate zone

N W—E S

Build Vocabulary

Use a Word Wheel

Making a **Word Wheel** will help you remember new words.

1. In your Personal Dictionary, draw a large circle. Divide it into four parts.
2. Write *photosynthesis* in one part of the circle.
3. Look up the word *photosynthesis* in the dictionary. What is the meaning of this word?
4. Write three words that are related to *photosynthesis*. Write the words in the other three parts of the circle.

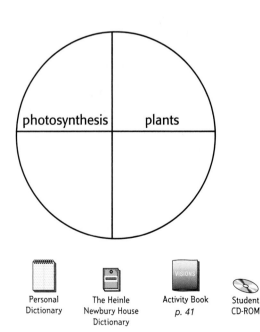

photosynthesis | plants

Personal Dictionary   The Heinle Newbury House Dictionary   Activity Book *p. 41*   Student CD-ROM

Text Structure

Scientific Informational Text

"Why Do Leaves Change Color in the Fall?" is a **scientific informational text.** It describes how changes in weather affect the color of leaves.

As you read the text, look for these features of a scientific informational text.

Scientific Informational Text	
Event	description of a natural event
Explanation	scientific explanation of how and why the event takes place
Cause and Effect	statements that describe a scientific process

Student
CD-ROM

Reading Strategy

Make Inferences

When you use what you already know to understand a reading, you **make inferences.** As you read "Why Do Leaves Change Color in the Fall?" make inferences about the text. This will help you understand the new ideas and information.

1. Read the selection title on page 83, and look at the pictures. Make inferences about the topic of the selection. Write your inferences on a piece of paper.

2. Read paragraphs 1 and 2. Were your inferences correct? Write down some facts from the selection that support your inferences.

3. As you read the rest of the selection, continue to make inferences.

Student
CD-ROM

Why Do Leaves Change Color in the Fall?

an excerpt from a science
article from the World Wide Web
from *Science Made Simple*

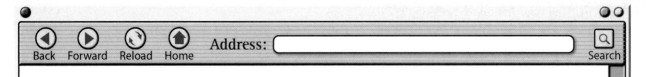

Audio

1   We all enjoy the beautiful show of colors as leaves change each autumn. Did you ever wonder how and why this happens? To answer that question, we first have to understand what leaves are and what they do.

2   Leaves are nature's food **factories.** Plants take water from the ground through their roots. They take a gas called carbon dioxide from the air. Plants use sunlight to turn water and carbon dioxide into glucose. Glucose is a kind of sugar. Plants use glucose as food for energy and as a building block for growing. The way plants turn water and carbon dioxide into sugar is called photosynthesis. That means "putting together with light." A chemical called chlorophyll helps make photosynthesis happen. Chlorophyll is what gives plants their green color.

3   As summer ends and autumn comes, the days get shorter and shorter. This is how the trees "know" to begin getting ready for winter.

Make Inferences

Why do trees have to "get ready" for winter?

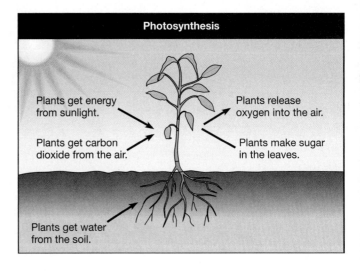

Photosynthesis

Plants get energy from sunlight.

Plants get carbon dioxide from the air.

Plants release oxygen into the air.

Plants make sugar in the leaves.

Plants get water from the soil.

---

factories   places where things are manufactured, or made

4　　During winter, there is not enough light or water for photosynthesis. The trees will rest, and live off the food they stored during the summer. They begin to shut down their food-making factories. The green chlorophyll disappears from the leaves. As the bright green fades away, we begin to see yellow and orange colors. Small amounts of these colors have been in the leaves all along. We just can't see them in the summer, because they are covered up by the green chlorophyll.

5　　The bright reds and purples we see in leaves are made mostly in the fall. In some trees, like maples, glucose is trapped in leaves after photosynthesis stops. Sunlight and the cool nights of autumn turn this glucose into a red color. The brown color of trees like oaks is made from wastes left in the leaves.

Make Inferences

Do oak trees have glucose trapped in their leaves after photosynthesis stops?

An oak tree in autumn.

6　　It is the combination of all these things that make the beautiful colors we enjoy in the fall.

7　　During summer days, leaves make more glucose than the plant needs for energy and growth. The **excess** is turned into **starch** and stored until needed. As the daylight gets shorter in the autumn, plants begin to shut down their food production.

---

excess　extra, more than is needed　　　　**starch**　food for the plant

8   Many changes occur in the leaves of **deciduous trees** before they finally fall from the branch. The leaf has actually been preparing for autumn since it started to grow in the spring. At the base of each leaf is a special layer of cells called the "abscission" or separation layer. All summer, small tubes which pass through this layer carry water into the leaf, and food back to the tree. In the fall, the cells of the abscission layer begin to swell and form a cork-like material, reducing and finally cutting off flow between leaf and tree.

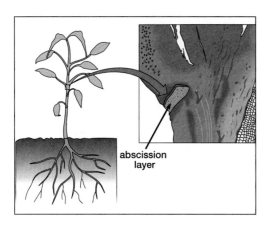

abscission layer

Glucose and waste products are trapped in the leaf. Without fresh water to **renew** it, chlorophyll begins to disappear.

Make Inferences

What do you think will happen to the leaf when chlorophyll begins to disappear?

9   Other colors, which have been there all along then become visible. The orange colors come from carotene ('kar-uh-teen) and the yellows from xanthophyll ('zan-thuh-fil). They are common pigments, also found in flowers, and foods like carrots, bananas and egg yolks. We do not know their exact role in leaves, but scientists think they may be involved somehow in photosynthesis.

10   The bright red and purple colors come from anthocyanin (an-thuh-'si-uh-nuhn) **pigments.**

---

deciduous trees   trees that lose their leaves
renew   make new or better

pigments   colors in plants

These are also common in plants; for example, beets, red apples, and purple grapes, and flowers like violets and hyacinths. In the leaves, these pigments are formed in the autumn from trapped glucose. Brown colors come from tannin, a bitter waste product. Different combinations of these pigments give us a wide range of colors each fall.

As the bottom cells in the separation layer form a seal between leaf and tree, the cells in the top of the separation layer begin to **disintegrate.** They form a tear-line, and eventually the leaf is blown away or simply falls from the tree.

Make Inferences

Are pigments present in leaves?

---

disintegrate   dissolve or break into pieces

Beyond the Reading

Reading Comprehension

Question-Answer Relationships (QAR)

"Right There" Questions

1. **Recall Facts** How do plants take water from the ground?
2. **Recall Facts** What is glucose? Why is glucose important for plants?

"Think and Search" Questions

3. **Recall Steps in a Process** How do plants turn water and carbon dioxide into sugar?
4. **Recall Steps in a Process** What are the steps that make maple leaves red?
5. **Compare and Contrast** How are trees different in the winter and the summer?

"Author and You" Questions

6. **Determine Causes and Effects** What eventually happens to the leaves?
7. **Make Inferences** What do you think happens to the trees in the spring?

"On Your Own" Questions

8. **Make Inferences** Some kinds of trees do not change color in the autumn. Do you think that these trees also use photosynthesis to make food?
9. **Think About Language** English has two words for one of the seasons—*autumn* and *fall*. Why do you think the word *fall* is used for this season?
10. **Interpret Visual Images** Why do you think illustrations are used instead of photos on pages 84 and 86? How do different parts of the illustrations help you understand the text?

Activity Book
p. 42

Student
CD-ROM

Build Reading Fluency

Repeated Reading

Rereading one paragraph at a time can help increase your reading rate and build confidence.

1. With a partner read aloud paragraph 1 in "Why Do Leaves Change Color in the Fall?" three times.
2. Did your reading rate increase each time?
3. Next, read paragraph 2 three times.
4. Continue rereading each paragraph.
5. Stop after ten minutes.

Listen, Speak, Interact

Role-Play a Scientific Interview

Scientists who understand processes such as photosynthesis must be able to answer questions about the subject.

1. With a partner, reread the selection.
2. Ask each other questions about the text. Be sure you both understand the steps of photosynthesis.
3. Role-play an interview. One of you will be a scientist and one of you will be an interviewer. Write five questions about photosynthesis that the interviewer will ask the scientist.
   a. Use several different question words, such as *why, where, how, when,* and *what.*
   b. Use a question mark at the end of each question.
4. Prepare answers to all five questions.

Interviewer: Dr. Perez, what does the word *photosynthesis* mean?

Scientist: It means "made with light." It is also the way that plants make sugar.

---

5. Perform your interview for the class.

Elements of Literature

Identify Processes

Scientific writing describes **processes,** or the order in which things happen. One kind of process is a cycle. A cycle is a process that begins and ends with the same thing. For example, the life cycle of a chicken is from an egg to a baby chick to an adult chicken. The adult chicken then lays eggs.

1. Find the paragraph in the reading that gives the cycle of a plant making food.
2. Find the paragraph that gives the cycle of what happens to leaves in the autumn.

Activity Book
p. 43

Student
CD-ROM

Word Study

Use Pronunciation in Context: *ph*

Some English words and spellings come from the Greek language. Some Greek words use the letters *ph* together. They are pronounced like an *f*.

<u>photo</u>synthesis	<u>tele</u>phone
<u>graph</u>	<u>alpha</u>bet
<u>physical</u>	<u>sym</u>phony

1. The box lists six words that have the letters *ph*.

2. Say the words aloud. Pronounce the *ph* like an *f* as in *fact*. Say the word *fact* so you can feel and hear the correct sound. Use the pronunciation in the dictionary to help you say the word.

3. Find the meaning of the Greek roots underlined in each word. Use a dictionary or glossary.

4. Write original sentences using the words in the box.

The Heinle Newbury House Dictionary

Activity Book p. 44

Student CD-ROM

Grammar Focus

Identify and Use the Simple Present Tense

The **simple present tense** is used to describe things that happen regularly or are generally true.

The green chlorophyll **disappears.**

The simple present tense is the **simple form** of the verb or the simple form plus -*s* or, sometimes, -*es*. The simple form of a verb is the verb with no endings or other changes.

1. Find the uses of the simple present tense in paragraph 2.

2. Write three sentences about things you do every day. Use the simple present tense.

Simple Present Tense	
Subject	**Verb**
I You We They The leaves	disappear.
He She It The color	disappear**s.**

Activity Book pp. 45–46

Student Handbook

Student CD-ROM

From Reading to Writing

Write a Scientific Informational Text

Write an informational text that explains a scientific process—the water cycle. Use the terms *evaporation, condensation,* and *precipitation.* Look at the Water Cycle diagram to plan your informational text.

1. Use the simple present tense.
2. Be sure to add *-s* to a verb if its subject is *he, she, it,* or a singular noun.
3. List events in order.
4. Collaborate with a partner to revise your writing. Add or delete text to make your writing clearer.

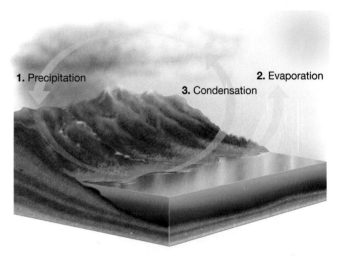

1. Precipitation   2. Evaporation   3. Condensation

Activity Book
p. 47

Across Content Areas

Learn About Trees

You read about **deciduous trees**—trees whose leaves change color and drop off in the fall. Not all trees are deciduous. Some stay green all year. These trees have **needles** instead of leaves. They also have **cones** (rounded, woody structures). They are called **coniferous** trees. The needles of coniferous trees do die and drop off, but they do this at different times. Therefore, the tree is always green.

Complete the diagram to show the similarities and differences between deciduous and coniferous trees.

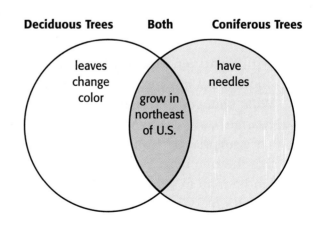

Deciduous Trees   Both   Coniferous Trees

leaves change color

grow in northeast of U.S.

have needles

Activity Book
p. 48

Into the Reading

Elizabeth's Diary

an excerpt from a
historical fiction diary
by Patricia Hermes

Objectives

Reading Summarize a historical fiction
diary.

Listening and Speaking Talk about the
sequence of events.

Grammar Use the future tense with *will*.

Writing Write a diary entry.

Content Language Arts: Understand
genres of literature.

Use Prior Knowledge

Discuss Moving to a New Place

Have you, or has someone you know,
ever moved to a new place? What was it
like to move?

1. With a partner, discuss what you
   know about moving to a new place.
   What changes were hard? What
   changes were easy? What changes
   were surprising? Complete a chart
   like the one here.
2. Find a map in your classroom or in
   a textbook. With your finger, mark
   the path of the move—from country
   to country or city to city.

Hard Changes	Easy Changes	Surprising Changes

Build Background

Jamestown

In 1607, a group of English people traveled by ship to make new homes on the east coast of North America. They settled in what is now Virginia, in a place called Jamestown. It was the first permanent English colony in North America.

You are going to read about a girl and her family who moved to this new land.

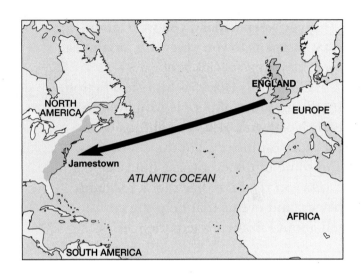

Content Connection

A **colony** is a new place where a group of people have moved but are still governed by their home country.

Build Vocabulary

Use Varied Word Choices

Writers often find different ways to say similar things. This makes their writing more vivid and precise. Sometimes you can understand a word or a phrase by finding another one nearby with a similar meaning. Here is an example from "Elizabeth's Diary":

Five of our ships were gone. One missing ship is the *Sea Venture*.

In these sentences, *gone* and *missing* mean almost the same thing.

Work with a partner. Read these sentences and look at the **bold** words or phrases. Then find a word in the right-hand column that has a similar meaning.

1. I **could not hold back my tears.**

2. I **swatted** three mosquitoes.

3. The sky was **blacker than night.**

a. hit
b. cried
c. dark

The Heinle Newbury House Dictionary

Activity Book *p. 49*

Student CD-ROM

Text Structure

Historical Fiction Diary

If you keep a **diary,** you write about what happens to you every day, or almost every day, in a special book.

"Elizabeth's Diary" is historical fiction. It tells the story of people who lived in early North America. The author bases the story on history, but the characters and some of the events are not real.

As you read the diary, look for dates, places, and events that help the author tell about Elizabeth's experiences.

Historical Fiction	
Dates	The months, days, and years are real dates.
Setting	The cities and countries are real places.
Events	Some events really happened. Other events are made up.
Characters	Some characters are real. Some are made up.

Student
CD-ROM

Reading Strategy

Summarize

When you **summarize** a reading you say or write down the most important information or events.

As you read "Elizabeth's Diary," summarize the information in each paragraph. Summarizing will help you understand and remember what you read.

1. Read the first and the last sentence in each paragraph. The most important information is often found there.

2. Read the entire paragraph quickly. The other sentences provide details.

3. Ask yourself, "What is the most important idea in the paragraph?"

Student
CD-ROM

Elizabeth's Diary

an excerpt from a
historical fiction diary
by Patricia Hermes

Still, we are safely in Jamestown. I am here with my papa. Soon, our new baby will be born. But it will be a home n...

Audio

1
2
3

Summarize

What happened during the trip?

August 11, 1609

Today, we came to land at last! It seems there are no bones in my legs. I hugged my friend Jessie. We held each other up. Still, the land seemed to bob around beneath us. Seventy-one days. That is how long we were on the ocean.

Nine ships sailed from Plymouth, England. But at sea, a hurricane struck. Oh, how it struck! It became blacker than night. The waves brought us up into the dark sky, and then **slammed** us down. Men were washed off deck and into the sea. Some men tied themselves to the **mast.** But then—the mast broke off. Our ship rolled and rats came out. I tried to hold back tears, but could not. Jessie cried, too. Mama said we should not show fear or **dismay.** But soon, she cried, too. Prayers flew up to heaven like little

birds. After the storm, when it became quiet, we looked about. Then, even Papa had tears in his eyes. For five of our ships were gone. One missing ship is the *Sea Venture*. It held our food! Were the ships blown off course? Or are they at the bottom of the ocean? We do not know.

Still, we are safely in Jamestown. I am here with my mama and papa. Soon, our new baby will be born. But it will be a home without Caleb, my **twin.** He stayed behind with Mama's cousin because his lungs are weak. He will join us come spring. I pray that spring comes soon, because without Caleb it will be a sad home.

---

slammed   struck or hit with great force
mast   a very tall pole on a ship that holds up the sails
dismay   upset or worry

twin   one of two children born to the same mother at the same time

till we are safely in Jamestown. I am here with my pa. Soon, our new baby will be born. But it will be a home wit

August 11, later

Summarize

What problem does Elizabeth have?

4   It is *hot* inside this fort where we shall live for a while. Nothing stirs but nasty **mosquitoes.** They bite and sting. They get in my ears. Jessie and I **compete** for who can swat the most. I have killed twenty-seven. Jessie is winning, for she has **slain** thirty. Mama rubs **fennel** into the bites. Already, though, my neck is as fat as a **melon.**

5   Papa says that tomorrow we shall begin to build our house. He says there will be no bugs inside our house. Captain Gabriel Archer was one of those in charge of our **expedition.** He has lived here before. He says, "You wait and see. There are always bugs."

6   Gabriel Archer is a **dreadful,** unpleasant man.

---

mosquitoes   small insects that bite and suck blood
compete   work hard to beat others at a contest or race
slain   killed
fennel   a tall herb or plant used as a medicine or to flavor food

melon   a kind of juicy, large fruit
expedition   a long journey with a goal such as exploring a new land
dreadful   awful, terrible

About the Author — Patricia Hermes (born 1936)

Patricia Hermes was born in Brooklyn, New York. She writes fiction and nonfiction. One of her novels, *Fly Away Home* (1996), was made into a movie. She enjoys writing because it allows her to be any character that she wants to be. Hermes says, "It gives me the opportunity to live other lives . . . I can write about things that scare me. . . . I can be silly. I can be brave. I can make everything work out." *Our Strange New Land: Elizabeth's Diary* is the first part of two books. The second book is *The Starving Time: Elizabeth's Diary.*

➤ Describe how Patricia Hermes' point of view affects "Elizabeth's Diary." Do you think she enjoyed writing the book?

Beyond the Reading

Reading Comprehension

Question-Answer Relationships (QAR)

"Right There" Questions

1. **Determine Chronological Order** What is the date of the first diary entry?
2. **Identify** Who is Jessie?
3. **Recall Facts** Where did Elizabeth's ship sail from?

"Think and Search" Questions

4. **Identify** Where did Elizabeth and her family travel to?
5. **Identify** Who is Caleb?
6. **Explain** What happened when the hurricane struck?

"Author and You" Questions

7. **Draw Conclusions** What members of Elizabeth's family traveled with her? Who stayed behind?

8. **Analyze Setting** Where is Elizabeth living? Why?
9. **Understand Characterization** Is Elizabeth happy to be in North America? How do you know?
10. **Visualize** What is the fort like? Do you think it is a safe place to live? Why or why not?

"On Your Own" Question

11. **Compare with Your Experiences** How would you feel if you were in Elizabeth's situation?

Activity Book
p. 50

Student
CD-ROM

Build Reading Fluency

Rapid Word Recognition

Rapidly recognizing words helps increase your reading speed.

1. With a partner, review the words in the box.
2. Next, read the words aloud for one minute. Your teacher or partner will time you.
3. How many words did you read in one minute? Was it more than on page 36?

there	tied	struck	each	night
each	night	there	sea	tied
struck	each	sea	night	stuck
night	sea	each	there	sea
sea	there	tied	tied	each

Listen, Speak, Interact

Talk About the Sequence of Events

"Elizabeth's Diary" tells Elizabeth's thoughts. She writes about her present, past, and future.

1. With a partner, reread the story. Find one event that happens in the past, one event that happens in the present, and one event that will happen in the future. How do you think Elizabeth feels about each of these events?
2. Tell your partner about three events:
   a. an important event in your past
   b. an important event in your present
   c. an important event that you want for your future

3. Draw a timeline that shows the sequence of these events. Include small pictures in your timeline.
4. Present a short speech about your life using the illustrated timeline.
5. When your classmates present their speeches, listen to be sure you understand. If you do not, ask your classmate to repeat or to use different words.

Elements of Literature

Identify Flashbacks

Writers use **flashbacks** to tell about something that happened to a character before the time that the story is set. A character remembers something that happened in the past. In "Elizabeth's Diary," there is a flashback.

1. Copy the following sentences in your Reading Log. The sentences are listed in the order that they appear in the diary.
   a. Today, we came to land at last!
   b. But at sea, a hurricane struck.

   c. Still, we are safely in Jamestown.
   d. It is *hot* inside this fort.
   e. Papa says that tomorrow we shall begin to build our house.
2. Now rewrite the sentences in the order they really happened.

Reading Log   Activity Book   Student
            p. 51   CD-ROM

Word Study

Understand the Suffix -ty

A **suffix** is a word part added to the end of a word. A suffix changes the word's meaning. The suffix -ty added to a number word means *tens* or *times ten*.

six + -ty = six**ty**

Note that the spelling of the numbers two through five changes when the suffix -ty is added.

1. Copy the chart in your Personal Dictionary.
2. Complete the chart. Follow the example.
3. Find three number words ending with the suffix -ty in paragraphs 1 and 4.

Suffix + ty (times ten)		
2	two + ty ⇒ twenty	20
3	three + ty ⇒ thirty	30
4	four + ty ⇒ forty	40
5	five + ty ⇒ fifty	50
6	*six + ty ⇒ sixty*	60
7		70
8		80
9		90

Personal Dictionary

The Heinle Newbury House Dictionary

Activity Book
p. 52

Student CD-ROM

Grammar Focus

Use the Future Tense with *Will*

"Elizabeth's Diary" tells about some events that take place in the future. One way to form the **future tense** is:

will + base form of verb

Look at this example:

Without Caleb it <u>will be</u> a sad home.

Find other examples of the future tense with *will* in paragraphs 3 and 5 of "Elizabeth's Diary." Write them on a piece of paper.

Activity Book
pp. 53–54

Student Handbook

Student CD-ROM

From Reading to Writing

Write a Diary Entry

Write a diary entry about your past and your future.

1. Brainstorm ideas for a diary entry. Use a chart to organize your ideas.

Past	Future
I lived in ___.	I will live in ___.

2. In your chart, write answers to these questions.
   a. What important things happened to you last year? How did you feel?
   b. Think about your future. How will your life change?

3. Write a diary entry using the information in your chart. Be sure to use the appropriate diary form shown in the reading.
4. Check your work for the following:
   a. Did you indent each paragraph?
   b. Did you write the date?
   c. Did you use *I* or *we*?
   d. Did you use a question mark (?) when you asked a question?
   e. Did you use an exclamation point (!) when you wanted to show excitement?

Activity Book
p. 55

Across Content Areas

Understand Genres of Literature

In literature, people write about their experiences in several **genres**, or forms, of literature.

A **diary** is a book with blank pages in which you record your experiences every day. Diaries are usually very private.

A **journal** is like a diary, but it is often a record of special events. Journals are often written for other people to read.

A **memoir** is a record of the writer's experiences in the distant past.

In this book, there are selections from two diaries, one journal, and one memoir. Find these selections in the table of contents at the beginning of this book.

Activity Book
p. 56

And Now Miguel

a play based on a novel
by Joseph Krumgold

Objectives

Reading Determine the sequence of events in a play.

Listening and Speaking Perform a scene.

Grammar Identify and use the future conditional.

Writing Write dialogue for a scene in a play.

Content Social Studies: Understand state flags.

Use Prior Knowledge

Talk About Farming

In the selection you are going to read, Miguel and his family make their living by farming. What do you know about farming?

1. Make a chart like the one here.
2. With a partner, brainstorm a list of daily tasks (jobs) on a farm.
3. Guess the time it would take to do each job.
4. Add up the time for all the jobs.
5. Share your chart with the rest of the class. Discuss how many people it might take to run a farm.

Daily Tasks on a Farm	Time
care for animals	3–4 hrs. a day
fix equipment	2 hrs. a day

Build Background

The Sangre de Cristo Mountains

Miguel, the main character of the selection, hopes to go to the Sangre de Cristo Mountains. The Sangre de Cristo Mountain chain is one of the longest on Earth. It stretches from Poncha Pass, Colorado, to Glorieta Pass, New Mexico.

Content Connection

There are ten peaks in the Sangre de Cristo Mountain chain that are higher than 14,000 feet (4,268 meters).

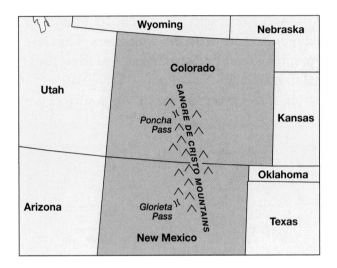

Build Vocabulary

Use the LINK Strategy

The LINK strategy is one way for you to build your vocabulary. LINK stands for **L**ist, **I**nquire, **N**ote, and **K**now.

Use the word *goal* as an example. A *goal* is something that you want to achieve. Complete a LINK chart for your goals in your Personal Dictionary.

L	**L**ist words related to a topic.
I	**I**nquire, or ask about the meanings of words.
N	**N**ote ideas using the words from your list.
K	**K**now more about a topic.

1. **List:** List all the words you can think of that relate to your goals in life.
2. **Inquire:** Share your list of words with a partner. If your partner wrote any words you do not know, ask what they mean.
3. **Note:** Write sentences about your goals. Use as many words as you can from your lists.
4. **Know:** Think about what you know about goals.

Personal Dictionary

Activity Book
p. 57

Student CD-ROM

Text Structure

Play

"And Now Miguel" is a **play.** In a play, actors pretend to be the characters. They memorize and perform a script of what the characters say.

In a play, you will find these features.

Play	
Scenes	parts of the story in the play
Narrator	the person who describes the scene and gives background information
Characters	their names appear before each line of dialogue to tell who is speaking
Dialogue	conversations between different characters

Student CD-ROM

Reading Strategy

Determine the Sequence of Events

The **plot,** or main events, of a play follows a certain order. This is called the **sequence of events.**

1. Below you will find a group of sentences from the play. They are not in the right order. On a piece of paper write the sentences in the order in which they happen in the play. To help you decide the sequence of events, look for words that serve as clues such as *before, after,* and *next.*

a. The next morning, more than a dozen sheep are gone.
b. One night, there is a storm.
c. "It's all right Miguel. We'll find them. This is not a job for you."
d. Miguel says, "I can find them! I can help!"

2. As you read the play, check to see if you put the events in the correct sequence.

Student CD-ROM

And Now Miguel

a play based on a novel
by Joseph Krumgold

Scene 1

1 **Miguel:** *I am Miguel Chavez. To my family, I am just a boy. But I want to be a man. The men in my family raise sheep in the mountains of New Mexico. It has been our work for hundreds of years. I, too, will be a shepherd someday. I hope and I wait. But "someday" never comes.*

2 **Narrator:** Miguel and his brother Gabriel are driving out to the new **pasture.** Miguel is quiet.

3 **Gabriel:** What's up, Miguel?

4 **Miguel:** I've been thinking how easy it is for you—to be Gabriel.

5 **Gabriel** *(laughing):* I guess so, little brother. After all, that's who I am!

6 **Miguel:** But it's not easy for me—to be Miguel.

7 **Gabriel:** Maybe not. It takes a little time. Wait a year or two, and it'll be easier.

8 **Miguel:** Isn't there something I can do *now*? Like practice?

9 **Gabriel** *(shaking his head):* Being Miguel—it's not like playing basketball. As I say, it takes time.

> **Determine the Sequence of Events**
>
> Who was born first, Miguel or Gabriel?

---

pasture   land with grass where animals can eat

Scene 2

10 **Miguel:** *I had a wish, to take the sheep into the Sangre de Cristo Mountains along with the other men.*

If they know you are ready, you will go. But if they don't, you must wait again for another year.

I must try to make them see that I am ready.

Determine the Sequence of Events

What is Miguel doing when his grandfather speaks to him?

11 **Narrator:** The first **lamb** of the year is born. Before long, there are many new lambs. Miguel gets the job of painting numbers on the sheep. That way, it is easy to tell which lamb belongs to which mother in case they get separated. During a break in the work, Miguel's grandfather speaks to him.

12 **Grandfather:** That's the real work of a *pastor*, of a shepherd. To see that no sheep **strays** away from the **flock.** All must stay together.

13 **Miguel:** Why do they go off by themselves? Why are sheep so dumb?

14 **Grandfather** *(laughing):* That's a good question! Sheep are like people.

15 **Miguel** *(confused):* What do you mean?

16 **Grandfather:** When people don't stick together, they get lost. Now let's get back to work!

---

lamb a baby sheep
strays leaves a group, gets lost

flock a group of animals

Scene 3

17 **Miguel:** *Some boys dream of becoming policemen or airplane pilots. But for me, there is only one kind of work. At night, I look at the mountains and I dream of becoming a shepherd.*

18 **Narrator:** One night, there is a storm. The next morning, more than a **dozen** sheep are gone. At breakfast, Miguel and his father talk.

19 **Miguel** *(excited):* I can find them! I can help!

20 **Father:** It's time for school, isn't it?

21 **Miguel:** All I want to say—

22 **Father** *(shaking his head):* It's all right, Miguel. We'll find them. This is not a job for you.

23 **Narrator:** Miguel runs out of the house. At school, a boy tells Miguel he saw the sheep.

24 **Miguel:** Where did you see them? Where?

25 **Juby:** What's the matter, Miguel? Is something wrong?

26 **Miguel** *(impatiently):* Just tell me, where are the sheep?

27 **Juby:** Give me a chance, OK?

28 **Narrator:** The bell rings as Juby explains where he saw the sheep. It's in the opposite direction from where the others plan to look.

29 **Miguel:** *I stood there thinking. But not for long. I knew if I came home with the missing sheep, they would have to say I'm ready.*

I didn't look back as I ran down the hill, away from the school.

30 **Narrator:** Miguel **searches** for hours, but he can't find the sheep. He is tired, and his feet hurt. He is about to give up when he spots the sheep coming up the hill toward him.

Determine the Sequence of Events

Put these events in order:
Miguel went to school.
There was a storm.
Juby said he saw the sheep.

---

dozen twelve   **searches** looks for someone or something

Scene 4

Determine the Sequence of Events

What happens after the men shout "Bravo!"?

31 **Narrator:** A little while later, Miguel arrives home with the sheep. *"Bravo!"* the men shout. But Miguel's father has something to say.

32 **Father:** I am glad that the sheep are back. Sheep are important. But school is even more important. If you stayed away from school every time something had to be done, you'd grow up to be a ***burro.***

33 **Miguel:** I understand, Papá.

34 **Father** *(smiling):* I want to thank you for what you did, though.

35 **Narrator:** Later, Miguel tries to ask his father about going up to the mountains when school is over.

36 **Miguel:** I can go to the mountains? Yes?

37 **Father** *(firmly):* No! It cannot be arranged. Not this year. *(He nods toward Gabriel.)* Gabriel will go. That is part of his work. It's not yet time for you to go.

38 **Miguel** *(disappointed):* Yes, Papá.

39 **Narrator:** That night, Miguel prays to San Ysidro.

40 **Miguel** *(praying):* If you think it is a good idea, please arrange it so I may go up into the Sangre de Cristo Mountains.

---

burro Spanish word for "donkey," a person who is not very smart

Scene 5

41 **Narrator:** It's June. After the sheep are **sheared,** the flock will leave for the mountains. During the shearing, Miguel sweeps the floor.

42 **Miguel:** *It's a big job, to be the one with the broom. When the fleeces come off the sheep, they fall on the floor. And if they get dirty, the buyer is disappointed. So the floor has to be swept in the best and most careful way.*

My father trusts me to do a good job. Maybe he believes I'm becoming a man.

43 **Narrator:** Miguel is a hard worker. The men praise him because he sweeps up so much dust. Miguel feels proud. But suddenly one day, Miguel slips. He falls into the bottom of a big sack of fleeces.

44 **Eli:** Did anyone see Miguel?

45 **Gabriel** *(looking down in the sack):* Here! He's in the sack!

46 **Narrator:** All the men yell and laugh, except for Miguel's father.

47 **Father** *(snapping):* Is this any time to start playing games, like you were a little boy? Now come on! Up!

48 **Miguel:** *I was ashamed. I no longer felt like a man. If I could have stayed at the bottom of the sack, I would have stayed there.*

Determine the Sequence of Events

What events made Father unhappy with Miguel's behavior?

---

sheared cut (the wool of the sheep)   **snapping** speaking in an annoyed or angry voice

Scene 6

49 **Narrator:** Two days later, Miguel's father has news for Miguel.

50 **Father** *(seriously):* You will go with us to the mountains, Miguel.

51 **Miguel** *(puzzled):* Me? Go to the Sangre de Cristo Mountains for the whole summer?

52 **Father:** Yes.

53 **Miguel:** I'm glad, Papá.

54 **Father:** I'm glad, too.

55 **Miguel:** How did this happen?

56 **Father:** Gabriel can't go. He has to go into the army to train to be a soldier. There was a letter this morning.

57 **Miguel:** *I stood there quietly. I did not know what to think. There was too much good mixed up with the bad.*

> **Determine the Sequence of Events**
>
> What happened earlier that Miguel did not know about?

---

puzzled not understanding

Scene 7

Determine the Sequence of Events

Put these events in order: Miguel prayed to St. Ysidro. Gabriel has to go away.

58 **Narrator:** Miguel feels terrible. He thinks it's because of his prayers that Gabriel has to go away. Finally, he and Gabriel talk together.

59 **Gabriel:** It's dangerous to wish so hard, Miguel. Sometimes wishes come true in ways that surprise you.

60 **Miguel:** I'm sorry.

61 **Gabriel:** I made a wish, too. For a long time, I have wished to see other places—like an ocean. Now I have my wish.

62 **Miguel:** I think I understand.

63 **Gabriel:** While I'm gone, Miguel, you learn everything about sheep. When I come back, you and I will be the best two *pastores* in all New Mexico.

64 **Miguel** *(smiling):* I promise.

---

pastores Spanish word for "shepherds"

Scene 8

65   **Miguel:** *The next morning, I left with the men for the mountains. And Gabriel left for the army.*

Five days later, we reached our camp, high up in the Sangre de Cristo Mountains. Many men named Chavez had come to this place. And now, watching the country below I, Miguel, stood there at last.

Determine the Sequence of Events

What two events happened at the same time?

About the Author   Joseph Krumgold (1908–1980)

Joseph Krumgold was born in New Jersey. He wrote novels, children's books, and screenplays for movies. Krumgold's books tell stories about growing up and how we learn to accept and respect one another. In 1966, his book *About Miguel Chavez* was made into a movie called *And Now Miguel*.

➤Krumgold wrote this story as a narrative. It was adapted into a play. How are the two genres the same? How are they different? Which one do you like better? Why?

Beyond the Reading

Reading Comprehension

Question-Answer Relationships (QAR)

"Right There" Questions

1. **Recall Facts** What job do the men in Miguel's family do for a living?
2. **Understand Chronological Order** What happens after the storm?

"Think and Search" Questions

3. **Identify** What two jobs does Miguel get to do?
4. **Analyze** How important are these two jobs?
5. **Explain** What does Miguel think will happen if he comes home with the missing sheep?

"Author and You" Questions

6. **Draw Conclusions** Why do you think Miguel tells his brother that "it is not easy to be Miguel"?

7. **Analyze Characters** Why do you think Father tells Miguel he will be a *burro* if he does not go to school?
8. **Analyze Characters** In paragraph 57, what does Miguel mean when he says, "There was too much good mixed up with the bad"?
9. **Make Inferences** How do you think Miguel will spend the rest of his life?

"On Your Own" Question

10. **Relate the Story to Your Life** What is something that you would like to do, but your parents think you are too young to do?

Activity Book
p. 58

Build Reading Fluency

Adjust Your Reading Rate

When you read a play you must adjust your reading rate to read with expression.

1. Listen to the Audio CD for "And Now Miguel."
2. Read along with the Audio CD.
3. Read with expression.

Listen, Speak, Interact

Perform a Scene

Good actors read their lines as if they are feeling the characters' emotions. Choose one scene from "And Now Miguel" and perform it with a small group.

1. Decide how the events in the story would affect the characters' emotions.

2. Perform the scene for the class, acting out the emotions you discussed. Use your own experiences to help you in your presentation.

3. If possible, record the presentation on video.

4. Listen to the other groups in the class. What emotions do you hear and see in their presentations?

Elements of Literature

Understand Scenes in a Play

Playwrights (people who write plays) usually divide a play into different parts, or **scenes.** In "And Now Miguel," each scene happens in a different place, or setting. Sometimes the narrator describes the setting. Other times you have to guess where the scene takes place by getting clues from the dialogue.

1. Choose one scene in "And Now Miguel" and describe how to show the setting in a theater. What is the scenery behind the actors? List props (things on the stage such as chairs and tables), and costumes (what the actors are wearing), lighting, and sounds you would use.

2. Copy this chart in your Reading Log. Complete it with your ideas.

3. Draw your scene.

Scene	Setting	Props	Costumes	Lighting
1	in a truck	wheel	work clothes	bright

Reading Log

Activity Book
p. 59

Student
CD-ROM

Word Study

Contrast *Its* and *It's*

The words **its** and **it's** look alike but have different meanings.

Its is used to show possession. *It's* is a **contraction** (short form) of *it* and *is*. The apostrophe (') shows that a letter has been left out.

Possessive Form: *Its*
The sheep's ears are soft.
Its ears are soft.
Contraction Form: *It's*
It is rainy on the mountains.
It's rainy on the mountains.

1. Skim the reading to find examples of *its* and *it's*. Write the sentences with these words in your Personal Dictionary.
2. Rewrite the sentences to include the nouns and verbs.
3. Note that most possessive forms include apostrophes. For example, *Anna's book* means "the book that belongs to Anna."

Personal Dictionary

Activity Book p. 60

Student CD-ROM

Grammar Focus

Identify and Use the Future Conditional

The **future conditional** is used to describe what might happen in the future. The condition is what must happen first. It begins with the word *if*. The result happens later. It has a verb referring to the future, often with *will*.

If Joe needs help, he <u>will</u> ask the teacher.

Write three sentences like these using the future conditional:

If Miguel finds the sheep, he will be happy.

If I save some money, I might buy some CDs.

Activity Book pp. 61–62

Student Handbook

Student CD-ROM

From Reading to Writing

Write Dialogue for a Scene in a Play

Write dialogue for a scene in a play with two characters. One character wants to do something, but the other character does not.

1. Write your characters' names.
2. Decide the reason for the conflict.
   a. Write the first character's reasons for wanting to do the activity.
   b. Write the second character's reasons for why the first character cannot do the activity.
   c. Use the future conditional.
   d. Be sure to use apostrophes correctly when writing contractions and possessives.
3. Write the dialogue between the two characters.
4. Perform a dramatic interpretation of the scene. Speak with expression. Use gestures and body language.

Activity Book
p. 63

Across Content Areas

Understand State Flags

Each state in the United States has its own flag. The colors and symbols on a state flag usually tell something about the state's people and history.

For example, the New Mexico flag shows a Native American symbol for the sun. The red and yellow colors come from the Spanish flag because Spanish explorers came to New Mexico in the 1500s.

1. Draw the flag for your state or another state.
2. Research what the design and colors stand for. Use the library or the Internet.
3. Explain the colors and symbols in your flag.

Activity Book
p. 64

CHAPTER 4

Tuck Triumphant

an excerpt from a novel
by Theodore Taylor

Objectives

Reading Draw conclusions as you read realistic fiction.

Listening and Speaking Interview a newcomer.

Grammar Use adjectives before nouns.

Writing Write a realistic story.

Content Social Studies: Learn about families.

Use Prior Knowledge

Discuss Surprises

Think about a time when you heard surprising news.

1. Copy the Sunshine Organizer on a piece of paper.
2. Name the surprise in the center of the circle.
3. Write answers to these questions around the circle.
   a. Who told you the surprising news?
   b. What was the surprise?
   c. When did you learn about the surprise?
   d. Where did the surprise happen?
   e. Why was it a surprise?
   f. How did you react to the surprise?

4. Share your outline information with a partner.

Build Background

Korea

Korea is a part of Asia south of China. Approximately 70 million people live there. A few years after World War II, Korea was divided into North Korea and South Korea.

SOCIAL STUDIES

Content Connection

Korea is a **peninsula**. A peninsula is a body of land that has water on three sides.

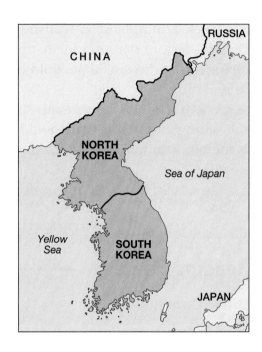

Build Vocabulary

Identify Related Words

"Tuck Triumphant" takes place in an airport in Los Angeles, California. There are several words about travel in the story.

1. On a piece of paper, draw a web like the one here.
2. Read the sentences below and find five words that relate to travel. Write these words in the web.
  a. Passengers began to come and go out of Customs and Immigration.
  b. We saw a pretty Korean stewardess.
  c. Handing over his Korean passport, she said, "I admire your courage."

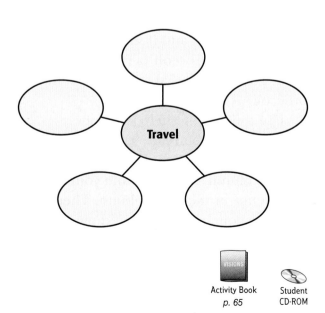

Activity Book
p. 65

Student
CD-ROM

Text Structure

Realistic Fiction

"Tuck Triumphant" is **realistic fiction**—a story that uses made-up characters and events that could happen in real life.

As you read, look for details such as the setting and events that could be real. Write two examples of each in your Reading Log.

Realistic Fiction	
Setting	a real place
Plot	events that could happen in real life
Characters	people who take part in the events; they talk and act like real people

Reading Log

Student CD-ROM

Reading Strategy

Draw Conclusions

You **draw a conclusion** when you decide that something is true, or not true, after thinking carefully about all of the facts. For example, if you see that your friend never chooses broccoli in the cafeteria (a fact), and if she makes a face when she sees broccoli (a fact), you can draw a conclusion that she does not like broccoli.

Use the chart to help you draw conclusions as you read "Tuck Triumphant." List facts from the reading in one column. List facts from your experience in the next column. Then write the conclusion you can draw.

Facts from Reading	Facts from Experience	Conclusions
Helen calls the other person "Mother."	Children call only their mothers "Mother."	The other person is Helen's mother.

Student CD-ROM

TUCK
Triumphant

an excerpt from a novel
by Theodore Taylor

1 "Will that **adoption** lady be here?" I asked again, wishing I were somewhere else. At the very best, I'd gone along with this whole thing **halfheartedly,** hiding my true feelings, since learning we weren't getting a baby.

2 *Here* was the old, **tottering** Los Angeles airport of my childhood, mostly wood and **corrugated** iron. A new one was being built.

3 Mother shook her head. "She called yesterday. She had to go to Salt Lake City. We're on our own, Helen."

4 We'd survive, I thought. As usual.

5 There was a family poem that we all recited on appropriate occasions. Birthdays and such.

> *We are the Ogdens*
> *Tougher than leather*
> *We are the Ogdens*
> *We stick together*

Draw Conclusions

Who do you think Stan is?

6 Stan had written it when he was about ten and now thought it was silly. He was **embarrassed** by it.

7 After a while passengers from Pan Am Flight 12, a three-tailed, four-motored **Constellation,** began to come out of **Customs and Immigration,** relatives running to meet them, hugging and kissing, **jabbering,** laughing. Most of the passengers were carrying packages wrapped in straw. The greeters had bouquets of flowers.

---

adoption the act of choosing to take legal responsibility for a child

halfheartedly without interest or energy

tottering moving unsteadily, almost falling down

corrugated having a wavy surface

embarrassed feeling ashamed

Constellation a type of airplane

Customs and Immigration the part of government that keeps track of the goods and people entering a country

jabbering talking quickly without making much sense

Draw Conclusions

Who is the family waiting for?

8   I'd left Tuck and Daisy* at home, telling them this was the day their new brother was arriving.

9   The rest of us Ogdens—father, mother, Luke and myself—stood silently watching for *our* passenger. Finally, we saw a pretty Korean stewardess holding the hand of a little boy who looked even younger than six. On his chest was a big sign: Chok-Do Choi. In his right hand was a small straw bag. In her free hand the stewardess held a little gray stuffed **koala.**

10   Chok-Do was a war **orphan** and war orphans usually had few possessions. The fighting between North Korea and South Korea hadn't been over too long.

11   *He's beautiful,* I thought, flat admitted it. I melted at the sight of him, unlike the new me.

* Tuck and Daisy are the Ogden family's dogs.

---

koala   a small, furry animal from Australia that lives in trees

orphan   a child whose parents have died

12   He was wearing a white shirt and his dark shorts were held up by **suspenders.** Beneath sturdy legs, shiny black shoes were on his small feet. His black-black hair was **crew-cut** and his face was as round as a lemon pie and about the same color. Truly beautiful.

Draw Conclusions

Did each member of the family have a similar reaction when they saw Chok-Do?

13   I glanced at my mother and saw tears. I saw that my father was **dabbing** at his eyes. Luke was swallowing. Why were we all so sad? Then I suddenly realized my own eyes were wet. I couldn't believe myself.

14   We moved to meet him.

15   Smiling widely, the stewardess said, "You are Chok-Do's new family?"

16   My father said, "Yes, I'm Tony Ogden."

CHOK

---

suspenders   straps worn over the shoulders to hold up a pair of pants, used instead of a belt

crew-cut   a haircut with the hair cut very short

dabbing   touching quickly

17   Mother was already kneeling down, hugging her new son, kissing him, saying "*An-nyŏng-ha-shim-ni-kka.*"

18   "How are you?"

19   We'd all learned a little Korean.

20   Then she stood up, wiping her eyes, introducing the family. "This is your father and this is Helen, your sister, and this is Luke, your brother."

21   **Bewildered,** he looked at us as if we were Martians, saying nothing. His eyes were huge and brown and I was wishing they were mine.

22   "Do you have identification?" asked the stewardess.

23   My father quickly displayed the adoption papers and his driver's license.

24   She glanced at them and then seemed to be sizing up Chok-Do's new family, going to each of our faces, an **inquisitive** look on hers.

---

bewildered   very confused

inquisitive   curious, asking a lot of questions

25   Finally handing over his Korean passport and a visa, she said, in almost **flawless** English, "Well, I have delivered him as I promised. I must say I admire your courage to adopt a little deaf boy."

26   She glanced down at Chok-Do and smiled.

27   I heard my mother gasp and then my father said, in a squeezed voice, "What? What did you say?"

28   "Deaf boy?" Mother said. "There's some mistake." On her face was shock, **disbelief.**

29   "Weren't you told?" asked the stewardess. "He does not hear, does not speak."

30   Staring at her and then at Chok-Do, my parents answered together a **breathless:** "No!"

31   "I'm sorry," said the stewardess. "I wish you good luck."

32   Then she knelt down by the boy, kissed his cheek, smiled briefly, handed him the koala and disappeared back into Customs and Immigration.

Draw Conclusions

Did the Ogdens know that Chok-Do was deaf? How can you tell?

---

flawless perfect

disbelief unable or unwilling to believe

breathless out of breath

33   Daddy called after her, "Wait a minute!"

34   Mother said she had to sit down and went over to a low **concrete-block** wall, taking Chok-Do by the hand. My father went over and sat down beside her. They were in a state of **shock.** So were Luke and myself. So much for the tough Ogdens.

> **Draw Conclusions**
>
> How do the Ogdens feel about the news that Chok-Do is deaf?

---

concrete-block   large bricks made of concrete

shock   upsetting surprise

About the Author

Theodore Taylor (born 1921)

Theodore Taylor grew up during the Great Depression, a time when many people in the United States didn't have jobs or money. Taylor helped his family by delivering newspapers and selling candy. His parents worked very hard, and Taylor learned to take care of himself. He started writing when he was 13 years old. He wrote about sports for a local newspaper. In his books, Taylor's characters face problems alone, the same way he did as a child. He said, "I like that kind of kid. I think kids like that kind too, and if it helps them aim for self-reliance, then I've done a good job."

➤ Based on what you know about Taylor's writing, how do you think the Ogden family will react to this change in their lives?

Beyond the Reading

Reading Comprehension

Question-Answer Relationships (QAR)

"Right There" Questions

1. **Recall Facts** Who is Helen?
2. **Recall Facts** Why is Helen at the airport with her parents?
3. **Recall Facts** What surprise do the Ogdens learn about Chok-Do?

"Think and Search" Questions

4. **Make Inferences** Why do you think Stan is embarrassed by the Ogden family poem?
5. **Make Inferences** How did Chok-Do become an orphan?
6. **Compare and Contrast** How do the family's feelings change after they learn that Chok-Do is deaf?

"Author and You" Question

7. **Draw Conclusions** How do you think Chok-Do feels about traveling to another country and having a new family?

"On Your Own" Questions

8. **Predict** What do you think will happen between the Ogdens and Chok-Do? Explain.
9. **Relate the Reading to Your Personal Experiences** Have you ever had to stay with strangers? How did you feel, or how do you think you would feel?

Activity Book
p. 66

Student
CD-ROM

Build Reading Fluency

Choral Read Aloud

A choral read aloud means the teacher reads aloud together with the class. This helps you connect spoken language with the text.

1. Read "Tuck Triumphant" aloud with your teacher.

2. Try to keep up with the class.
3. You may point to the text as you read.

Listen, Speak, Interact

Interview a Newcomer

One of your cousins is coming to your city for a visit. However, you have never met this cousin. You are meeting at the airport. You want to find out about your cousin, and your cousin wants to find out about you.

1. With a partner, decide who lives in the city and who is the visitor. What would you like to learn about each other? Use the list of questions in the box. Add your own questions.

2. Practice your interview. Be sure to use intonation to show you are asking a question.

3. Record your interview or present it to the class.

Questions
1. How old are you?
2. What do you like to do?
3. What classes do you like at school?
4. What sports do you like?
5. What is your favorite (food, movie, band, television program)?

Elements of Literature

Recognize Style in a First-Person Narrative

In a **first-person narrative,** a character in the story tells the story. This character is the **narrator.**

In "Tuck Triumphant," Helen Ogden is the narrator.

We'd survive, I thought. As usual.

The first sentence is a complete sentence. The second sentence is an incomplete sentence. It does not have a subject or a verb.

Sometimes writers use incomplete sentences as part of their **style.** Style is the way that writers use language to express themselves.

In "Tuck Triumphant," the author uses incomplete sentences as part of his style. Helen's incomplete sentences make her thinking seem real to us, because we often use incomplete sentences when we think.

1. Find two examples of incomplete sentences in Helen's thoughts. Look in paragraphs 5 and 12.

2. Listen to the Audio CD for these paragraphs. How does this language make the reader feel?

Activity Book
p. 67

Student
CD-ROM

Word Study

Use the Suffix -less

A **suffix** is a group of letters added to the end of a word. It changes the word's meaning. The words *flawless* and *breathless* have the suffix *-less*.

> flaw + -less ⟶ flawless
>
> breath + -less ⟶ breathless

The suffix *-less* means "without." When *-less* is added to the end of the nouns *flaw* and *breath*, the meanings of the words change.

She spoke in almost <u>flaw**less**</u> English.

My parents answered together, a <u>breath**less**</u>: "No!"

1. Look up the definitions of *flaw* and *breath* in a dictionary.

2. Use your knowledge of these words and the suffix *-less* to guess the meanings of *flawless* and *breathless*. Look these words up in a dictionary to check your answers.

3. Copy the sentences below in your Personal Dictionary. Complete each sentence with a word that ends in the suffix *-less*.

   a. The long road ahead seemed without end. The road seemed _____ .

   b. During the storm, the family lost its home. The family was _____ .

Personal Dictionary The Heinle Newbury House Dictionary Activity Book p. 68 Student CD-ROM

Grammar Focus

Use Adjectives Before Nouns

An **adjective** describes a **noun** (a person, place, or thing). Adjectives go before the nouns they describe.

a <u>big</u> sign: The adjective *big* tells you about the noun *sign*.

a <u>little</u> boy: The adjective *little* tells you about the noun *boy*.

1. Find three examples of adjectives in paragraph 12.
2. Name the nouns that the adjectives describe.
3. Write a sentence containing an adjective on a piece of paper. Identify the adjective and the noun.

Activity Book pp. 69–70 Student Handbook Student CD-ROM

From Reading to Writing

Write a Realistic Story

Write a story about meeting someone new. You can write about someone you really met, or you can make up a realistic character.

Use the chart below to plan the main parts of your story. List what you knew about the person before the meeting. Then list what you learned from the meeting.

What I Knew Before We Met	What I Learned When We Met

1. Write in the first-person voice, using the pronouns *I, me, we,* and *us*.
2. Use incomplete sentences to express some of your thoughts.
3. Use adjectives before some of your nouns to make your writing more interesting and precise.
4. Include realistic details about the characters, events, and setting so that readers can picture the story.
5. Produce a visual such as a drawing that shows something about the setting and characters of your story.

Activity Book
p. 71

Across Content Areas

Learn About Families

In "Tuck Triumphant," we meet the mother, the father, and the two children of the Ogden family. This is called a **nuclear family.**

However, the Ogden family is more than just four people. There are probably grandparents, aunts, uncles, and cousins. This larger family is called an **extended family.**

In some parts of the world, it is traditional for many members of an extended family to live together. In the United States, members of a nuclear family usually live together, but sometimes other family members live with them, too.

How are families in your culture the same as the Ogden family? How are they different?

What do you think are the advantages and disadvantages of each kind of family?

Activity Book
p. 72

Student
CD-ROM

CHAPTER 5

The Journal of Jesse Smoke

an excerpt from a historical fiction journal by Joesph Bruchac

Ancient Ways

a poem by Elvania Toledo

Into the Reading

Objectives

Reading Understand the sequence of events as you read a historical fiction journal.

Listening and Speaking Identify how language reflects culture and regions.

Grammar Use the present continuous tense.

Writing Write a poem.

Content Math: Use rank order.

Use Prior Knowledge

Plan for a Trip

How do you get ready for a trip?

1. On a piece of paper, draw a chart like the one here.
2. Decide where you are going. Write the name of your destination (the place where you are going) on the chart.
3. Complete the chart. Under each heading, list the things that you will take on a trip. Add more headings if you wish.
4. Using your chart, share your ideas with the class. Ask for suggestions to add to your list.

Destination: _____		
Clothes	Food	Other Needs
jacket		
hiking boots		

Build Background

The Trail of Tears

"The Journal of Jesse Smoke" describes a time when Cherokee Native Americans were forced to leave their homes. Other people wanted their land. In 1838, General Winfield Scott forced thousands of Cherokee to march to a new home in what is now the state of Oklahoma. They called the route they took "The Trail of Tears" because many of them died.

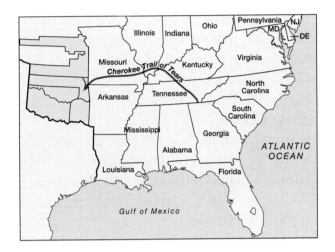

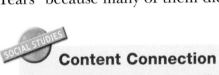

Content Connection

Other Native American tribes include the Cheyenne, Seminole, Apache, Comanche, Sioux, and Navajo.

Build Vocabulary

Find Root Words

You can sometimes understand the meaning of a word by looking at the word's **root,** or base.

1. Copy the chart in your Personal Dictionary.
2. Find the root of each word. Write it in the chart.
3. Write the meaning of the root word. Use a dictionary if you need to.
4. What is the meaning of the original word? If you are still uncertain, look it up in the dictionary.

Word	Root	Meaning of Root
possession	possess	own
approaching		
traditional		
existence		
plantation		

Personal Dictionary

The Heinle Newbury House Dictionary

Activity Book
p. 73

Student CD-ROM

Text Structure

Historical Fiction Journal

A journal is similar to a diary. They are both books in which you record your daily experiences. A journal is usually public. It is written for others to read. A diary is usually private. It is written only for the author to read.

In this chapter, you will read an excerpt from "The Journal of Jesse Smoke," a **historical fiction** journal. It tells the story of a Native American youth whose people are forced to move.

As you read "The Journal of Jesse Smoke," look for these features:

Historical Fiction	
Dates	chronological sequence of events
Characters	people in the story; they can be real or made-up
Dialogue	speech between characters; what real people might have said

Student
CD-ROM

Reading Strategy

Understand the Sequence of Events

The **sequence of events** in a story is the order in which events happen.

Remembering the most important events in a story can help you recall details that go with the events.

1. Draw a timeline like this on a piece of paper.

2. Read paragraphs 1–5 of "The Journal of Jesse Smoke."

3. Write the important events and dates on your timeline.

4. Continue reading the journal, writing the important events on your timeline.

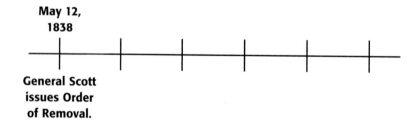

May 12, 1838

General Scott issues Order of Removal.

Student
CD-ROM

The Journal of Jesse Smoke

an excerpt from a historical fiction journal

by Joseph Bruchac

Ancient Ways

a poem by Elvania Toledo

Audio

The Journal of Jesse Smoke
an excerpt from a historical fiction journal by Joseph Bruchac

May 12, 1838

1   The worst has happened. Scott has issued an order for our immediate Removal*. All must hasten to prepare for **emigration** and come forward so that we may be transported. His **address,** dated May 10, has been posted widely throughout the Cherokee Nation.

May 15, 1838

Understand the Sequence of Events

What important event happens in this paragraph? Which details should you remember?

2   A few of our people are following the orders of General Scott. Carrying what possessions they can, they are making their way to one of the three collection points. They are along the rivers at Gunter's Landing, Ross's Landing, and Cherokee Agency. Although the waters are low in the Tennessee, they plan to take us west on flatboats.

3   Many of my people, like my mother, have made no preparations for leaving.

4   "We shall trust in Kooweeskoowee*," my mother says. "John Ross has a plan."

5   Our second chief, George Lowrey, has remained here in our Cherokee Nation while John Ross fights for us in Washington. Whenever he speaks, he echoes my mother's words. He also reminded us of the words spoken in council by the old warrior Woman Killer, who died not long after speaking these words that many of us know by heart.

*Removal was the government's policy of ordering American Indians to leave their land and go to reservations.

*Kooweeskoowee, or John Ross, was a leader of the Cherokee Nation.

---

emigration   leaving one's country to live in another   **address**   a speech

6   "My companions," Woman Killer said, "men of renown, in council, who now sleep in the dust, spoke the same language and I now stand on the verge of the grave to bear witness to their love of country. My sun of existence is fast approaching to its setting, and my aged bones will soon be laid in the bosom of this earth we have received from our fathers, who had it from the Great Being above. When I sleep in forgetfulness, I hope my bones will not be deserted by you."

7   Chief Lowrey has assured us that John Ross is still **negotiating** and having some success. The secretary of war himself has promised that there will be no forcible roundup of our people before the fall, when it is more practical to travel.

8   The great majority of our people speak no English, have no great **plantations,** and live closer to our old ways. They have little or no knowledge of all that is happening. All they have is their deep love for this land and their trust that our leaders, especially Tsan Usdi, will abide by the will of our people.

Understand the Sequence of Events

What important event is reported in this paragraph? Which details should you remember?

---

negotiating   talking in order to reach an agreement   **plantations**   large farms

9   I observed this today when I spoke to a friend of mine. His name is Standing Turkey. His family numbers ten and they farm land along the Hiwassee River. He and three others in the family are readers of Cherokee. He and his brother are mechanics, and the four women in their family are weavers. Though their place is small, it has fine soil, good water, a small herd of cattle. It is much **coveted** by the white men who have been surveying it with hungry eyes.

10   Standing Turkey was on his way to the blacksmith to have a tool mended. He greeted me as we passed on the road. I turned and followed him. Neither of us spoke for half a mile or so as we walked together.

11   "You are still filling your book with words?" he said to me at last, motioning with his chin at the journal under my arm.

Understand the Sequence of Events

What important event happens in this paragraph? Which details should you remember?

---

coveted   wanted with great desire and envy

12   I nodded. It seems that everyone knows of my journal now. I have been teased about it often. Such gentle teasing, though, means that people approve of what I am doing.

> **Understand the Sequence of Events**
>
> What important event is reported in this paragraph? Which details should you remember?

13   The sound of galloping hooves approaching came from around the bend. We stepped to the side, climbing over a rail fence just in time to avoid being run over by a **company** of white soldiers on horseback. Their faces were grim, and the sun glinted off their guns and bayonets. They seemed to take no notice of us and they soon disappeared, leaving nothing behind but the choking clouds of swirling dust.

14   Standing Turkey and I returned to the road, clouds of red dust rising from us as well as we brush ourselves off.

15   "They seem determined," Standing Turkey said. "But Kooweeskoowee will defeat them."

---

company   a military unit of soldiers

About the Author   Joseph Bruchac (born 1942)

Joseph Bruchac is of Abenaki Indian descent. He says: "I think I always knew I would be a writer someday, but it wasn't until I was grown and had children of my own that I turned to telling Native American stories. My Indian grandfather never told those stories to me. Instead, I began to seek them out from other Native elders as soon as I left home for college. I wanted to share those stories with my sons."

Bruchac still lives in the house he grew up in, near the foothills of the Adirondack Mountains in New York.

➤When authors write, they often have a perspective (opinions and attitudes) about what they describe. What do you think Joseph Bruchac's perspective is on the removal of the Cherokee people?

Audio

Ancient Ways
a poem by Elvania Toledo

1   They're traditional.

2   They **used to** live in a **hogan**
      but now they live in a trailer.

3   They used to live in a village
      but now they live in a neighborhood.

4   They used to herd sheep
      but now they go to the grocery store.

5   They used to exercise
      but now they drive vehicles.

6   The father tells his daughter
      "Things are changing."

---

used to *used to* means that something happened in the past, but it does not happen in the present

hogan a traditional American Indian house

Elvania Toledo

Elvania Toledo is a Native American and a resident of a Navajo community in New Mexico. Toledo wrote "Ancient Ways" when she was a student at Atza Biyaazh Community School in Shiprock, New Mexico.

➤ What do you think Elvania Toledo's perspective is on the changes that she describes in this poem? Compare and contrast changes in your culture to those in the Navajo community.

When you listen to the poem, how does the use of "but now they . . ." make you feel?

Beyond the Reading

Reading Comprehension

Question-Answer Relationships (QAR)

"Right There" Questions

1. **Recall Facts** On what day does Jesse Smoke begin his journal?
2. **Recall Facts** Who gave the orders to the people to make their way to the collection points?
3. **Recall Facts** Will Jesse Smoke's mother make preparations to leave her land?
4. **Recall Facts** List three things that changed for the people in "Ancient Ways."

"Think and Search" Questions

5. **Evaluate Evidence** Do you think the people of the Cherokee Nation want to move away from their land? Why or why not?
6. **Summarize** What is happening to the Cherokee people?

"Author and You" Questions

7. **Analyze Characters** Why do you think Jesse is keeping a journal about what is happening?

8. **Draw Conclusions** Why do you think the Cherokee people believe that Kooweeskoowee will save them from the Removal?

"On Your Own" Questions

9. **Analyze Characters** Do you think Standing Turkey and Jesse Smoke were afraid when the white soldiers with guns and bayonets came behind them on the road? Why or why not?
10. **Relate to Your Experience** Have you or any people you know had a similar experience to the Cherokee's? Describe it.
11. **Relate to Your Experience** In "Ancient Ways," people's lives changed. How has your life changed over the years? Have the changes been good, bad, or both?

Activity Book
p. 74

Student
CD-ROM

Build Reading Fluency

Read to Memorize

You must adjust your reading rate to read slowly when you memorize.

1. Use the Audio CD to listen to "Ancient Ways."
2. Read each line slowly.
3. Practice memorizing the poem.
4. In small groups, present the poem without looking at the words.

Listen, Speak, Interact

Identify How Language Reflects Culture and Regions

Speakers' choices of words can tell listeners about their culture and their country or region.

1. With a partner, listen to the audio recording of page 137 as you read. Find words that tell you about Cherokee culture and the region where they live. What do these words tell you?

2. With a partner, find a sentence in paragraph 6 that means "When I die, I hope that you will not forget me." Discuss how the two ways of expressing this idea are different. What does the speaker's choice of expression tell you about his role in Cherokee culture and society?

3. Think of a story that was passed down to you in your family. Tell your partner the story. Use words that say something about your culture or region.

4. Tell your story to the class. Listen to your partner's story. What do the words he or she uses tell you about the culture or region? Talk about your ideas with your partner.

Elements of Literature

Understand Metaphors

A **metaphor** is a way of describing something by comparing it to something else. For example, if you say that someone has "a heart of stone," you do not really mean that the person's heart is made of stone. You are using a metaphor to compare this person's heart to a stone. Both are cold and hard.

1. Look at these metaphors. Explain what they mean to a partner.

a. My sun of existence is fast approaching to its setting.

b. When I sleep in forgetfulness, I hope my bones will not be deserted by you.

2. On a piece of paper, write two or three metaphors to describe someone or something you know.

Activity Book
p. 75

Student
CD-ROM

Word Study

Use the Suffix *-ness*

When the suffix *-ness* is added to some adjectives, it forms a noun. This noun describes the condition that the adjective describes. Look at this example:

> When I sleep in <u>forgetfulness</u>, I hope my bones will not be <u>deserted</u> by you.

The adjective *forgetful* is the base, or root, of the noun *forgetfulness*.

> I am a very <u>forgetful</u> person.

> My <u>forgetfulness</u> sometimes gets me into trouble.

1. Copy this chart in your Personal Dictionary.

The Suffix *-ness*	
Adjective	**Noun**
forgetful	forgetfulness
kind	kindness
happy	happiness
loud	loudness

2. The last letters of some adjectives change when you add the suffix *-ness*. Find an example in the chart.

Personal Dictionary

Activity Book
p. 76

Student CD-ROM

Grammar Focus

Use the Present Continuous Tense

The **present continuous tense** describes an action that is happening *right now*. Look at this example:

> John Ross <u>is</u> still <u>negotiating</u>.

Look at the chart to see how this tense is formed.

1. Find three examples of the present continuous tense. Look in paragraphs 2 and 6.

2. Write two sentences of your own that use the present continuous.

The Present Continuous Tense		
Subject	**am/are/is**	**Verb + *ing***
I	am	working.
You We They	are	working.
He She It	is	working.

Activity Book
pp. 77–78

Student Handbook

Student CD-ROM

From Reading to Writing

Write a Poem

Write a poem with six to ten lines that describes how you have changed since you were younger. Brainstorm a list of ways you have changed. Use the list to help you plan your poem.

1. Use the structure of "Ancient Ways":

> I used to eat mangoes
>   but now I eat apples.

2. Make sure your poem has a pattern or rhythm.
3. Separate your lines into stanzas.
4. Read your poem to the class. Read it dramatically. Use gestures and body language to show meaning.

Activity Book
p. 79

Across Content Areas

Use Rank Order

Rank order places things according to quantity or importance.

1. On a piece of paper, write a list of the numbers 1–10.
2. Put the states in the chart in rank order of Native American population.
3. The first state should have the largest population. The last state should have the smallest population.
4. Include the population numbers in your list.

State	Native American Population
Arizona	265,367
California	345,011
Florida	49,190
Michigan	59,945
New Mexico	173,773
New York	76,046
North Carolina	98,235
Oklahoma	273,348
Texas	127,950
Washington	95,808

Activity Book
p. 80

Student
CD-ROM

Listening and Speaking Workshop

Interview and Report

Topic

In small groups, prepare an interview about changes that should take place in your school.

Before you begin, assign roles:
The interviewer: asks questions to gain information
The interviewees: answer the questions
The reporter: reports the interview results to the class

Step 1: Write interview questions.

Use your own experience to list issues and concerns about your school. Then form questions for your interview.

Issues / Concerns	Questions
The school day starts too early.	What time do you think school should start?

Step 2: Ask and answer the questions.

1. The interviewer should show respect when asking questions.
   a. Ask if the interviewee wants to be interviewed.

"Excuse me. Could I ask you a few questions about our school?"

b. The interviewer should pay attention to the interviewee. Look the interviewee in the eyes when he or she is speaking. Accept the answers. Do not argue.

"I see. My next question is, . . ."

"That is an interesting answer."

c. At the end of the interview, thank the interviewee.

"Thank you for your time."

2. The reporter should take notes.

Step 3: Summarize and report the responses to the class.

1. All group members should go over the reporter's notes and choose the most interesting answers.

Wei-Mon:
school should start at 9:00
has to help her mother in the morning

Rosa:
wants school to start at 7:00
works in the afternoon

2. Organize the answers that you chose into a report.
3. The reporter reports to the class.

Step 4: Ask classmates to evaluate your report.

Ask your classmates to evaluate the report by using the Active Listening Checklist. Then have a discussion in your group about how you could improve your performance.

> **Active Listening Checklist**
> 1. I liked _____ because _____.
> 2. I didn't like _____ because _____.
> 3. I want to know more about _____.
> 4. I don't understand _____.

Viewing Workshop

Analyze Film or Video

Tell How a Scene Is Effective

In this unit, you read a selection about the Cherokee Native Americans in the 1830s and a selection about the English colonists in Virginia. Select one of these two topics. Then compare and contrast the written account with a video story.

1. Rent a video about the Native Americans or the colonists, or borrow a video from your school library.
2. Watch the video. What is the purpose of the video? To inform, entertain, persuade? How does the video show this purpose?
3. Identify a scene that was powerful for you. Maybe it made you think, or maybe it gave you strong emotional reactions.
4. Think about how the video created this effect. Consider the following elements: the acting, the dialogue, the music, the images themselves.
5. Compare and contrast the video to the selections. How are they similar? How are they different?
6. Take notes on your thoughts. How does the maker of the video use these things to show important ideas? What are the strengths and weaknesses of these elements? Describe the scene to your class and explain how it was effective.

Further Viewing

Watch the *Visions* CNN Video for Unit 2. Do the Video Worksheet.

CNN Video

Writer's Workshop

Write to Persuade: Write a Letter to the Editor

Writing Prompt

Suppose you know someone who is no longer interested in school and wants to quit and get a job. Write a persuasive letter to the editor of a newspaper. You want to persuade readers that it is better to stay in school than to drop out.

Step 1: Research.

1. Make a list of all the reasons why people should stay in school. Fill out a Comparison Chart like this one.

Advantages of Staying in School	Disadvantages of Dropping Out
gain knowledge and skills	low pay

2. Use your own experience and the library or the Internet to find facts and statistics about why people should stay in school. Look for information in the following subject areas or search topics: employment, level of education, U.S. Department of Labor, and jobs.
3. Use tables of contents and headings in books to find these topics. Use key words to find them on the Internet.
4. Organize and summarize the facts you find. Write them in the chart to help you create your persuasive letter.

Step 2: Write your first draft.

1. Write the letter opening.
2. In the first paragraph, write an introduction. Explain why you are writing, and give an idea of what your letter will be about.
3. Write a paragraph that summarizes your ideas. Use full sentences. A good way to write persuasive letters is to ask and answer questions. For example:

    "Do students who work always earn more than those who stay in school? The evidence says no."

4. Write a conclusion sentence to summarize your ideas and finish your letter.
5. End your letter with the closing.

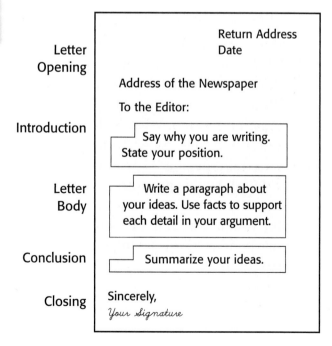

Step 3: Revise.

1. Reread your draft and ask yourself these questions:
   a. Is my introduction clear?
   b. Did I present my ideas in a logical order?
   c. Did I use persuasive language?
   d. Did I support my opinions with facts and details?

   Revise your work using the points above. Combine and rearrange text to make your ideas clear.

2. Be sure you have all the facts and details you need to write your letter. Use the Internet or school library if you need to find more information. Use the information to revise your letter.

3. Collaborate with a partner. Ask each other the following questions to help revise and organize your work:
   a. Would the letter persuade me to stay in school?
   b. If not, how could the letter be more persuasive?
   c. How can I add or delete text to make it more persuasive?

4. Use your partner's responses to the questions above to make any final changes to your letter.

Step 4: Edit and proofread.

1. Proofread your work. Check your spelling. Use a dictionary to check the spelling of difficult words. Make sure you have ended all sentences with a punctuation mark.

2. Be sure you used apostrophes correctly when writing possessives and contractions.

3. Use the Editor's Checklist in your Student Handbook.

Step 5: Publish.

Write the final version of your letter. Follow these steps:

1. If possible, use a computer to make your final version. If not, copy the letter onto writing paper. Use your best handwriting so that others can read your work.

2. Put the letter in an envelope. Address the envelope to "Editor." Add the name and address of the newspaper. Ask your teacher to help you send the letter to a local newspaper.

3. Read a copy of your letter to the class. Ask your classmates for feedback.

4. Listen to your classmates read their letters. Would their letters persuade someone to stay in school? What facts and details helped you to believe your classmates' opinions?

The Heinle Newbury House Dictionary

Student Handbook

Projects

In this unit, you learned about changes. In these projects, consider what changes are taking place.

Project 1: Research Life in the United States Since the Colonial Period

Present a compare and contrast poster between life in the United States now and in the colonial period (1607 to 1776). Use the library or the Internet to gather information and images to present to classmates. Examples include:

Population: Were there more people or fewer people living in the United States than there are today?

City Life Versus Country Life: Did more people or fewer people live in cities than they do now?

Transportation and Travel: How has the way people move from place to place changed?

Employment: What jobs from today were more common in the colonial period than today? What jobs did not exist in the colonial period?

Entertainment: How has the way people spend their free time changed?

Project 2: Write a Magazine Article About a Historical Site

In the United States, there are several places where buildings have been returned to their original condition. In some of these places, people dress as the early settlers did. They also show you how the original people lived and worked.

Choose one of the sites below or another site that you know about. Research using the Internet or the library, and write an article for a travel magazine about it. Answer these questions:

Where is the site?
Who lived in this area originally?
When did they live there?
How did they live?
What can you see and do there?
Why do people like to go there to visit?

1. As you research, form new questions you want to find answers to.
2. List your sources with your article. (Sources are places where you gathered information.)

Some Historical Restorations in the United States:

Colonial Williamsburg, in Williamsburg, Virginia (Search: Colonial Williamsburg)

Plimoth Plantation, in Plymouth, Massachusetts (Search: Plimoth Plantation)

Old City Park, in Dallas, Texas (Search: Old City Park)

Calico Ghost Town in Barstow, California (Search: Calico Ghost Town)

St. Augustine Lighthouse, in St. Augustine, Florida (Search: St. Augustine Lighthouse)

Further Reading

These books tell how people have dealt with changes in their lives. Choose one or more of them to read. Write your thoughts and feelings about what you read in your Reading Log. Take notes about your answers to these questions:

1. Did any of the changes you read about remind you of an experience that you have had?
2. In the books you read, how did the characters adjust to the changes?

Our Strange New Land: Elizabeth's Jamestown Colony Diary
by Patricia Hermes, Scholastic, Inc., 2002. Elizabeth is a member of the first English colony in Jamestown, Virginia. She keeps a diary of her experiences.

And Now Miguel
by Joseph Krumgold, HarperTrophy, 1984. Miguel Chavez spends the entire year trying to convince the Chavez men that he is ready to help herd the sheep to the mountains.

Tuck Triumphant
by Theodore Taylor, Camelot, 1996. Helen tries to convince her family to keep the deaf Korean boy they adopted. Helen's blind Labrador, Friar Tuck, helps her accomplish her goal.

Eagle Song
by Joseph Bruchac, Puffin, 1999. Danny's family moves from a Mohawk reservation to Brooklyn, New York. Danny must learn how to deal with not fitting in and being teased at school. He learns the value of courage and how to adjust to his new home.

Dream Soul
by Laurence Yep, HarperTrophy, 2002. Joanie's parents are immigrants from China. Joanie faces the conflict of living in two cultures, American and Chinese, when she moves to West Virginia.

Taking Sides
by Gary Soto, Harcourt, 1992. Fourteen-year-old Lincoln Mendoza moves from a Hispanic inner-city neighborhood to a suburb. An aspiring basketball player, Lincoln must learn how to handle a difficult new coach and his new team.

The Giver
by Lois Lowry, Laurel Leaf, 1994. This Newbery Award–winning book is set in a future society governed by a Committee of Elders. At the annual Ceremony of Twelve, the elders assign each 12-year-old person a life assignment. They select Jonas to be a "receiver of memories." In his new assignment, Jonas begins to uncover the truth about his society.

Reading Log

Heinle
Reading Library

UNIT 3

Courage

The Glacier de Tacconay, from *Scenes from the Snowfields,* Vincent Brooks, engraving, 1859.

View the Picture

1. How do you think this picture shows courage?
2. With a partner, discuss times when you needed courage.

In this unit, you will read a poem, a biography, a diary, a speech, and a memoir about courage. You will learn about situations in which people needed courage to survive or to face a challenge in their lives. You will also learn about the features of these writing forms and how to write them yourself.

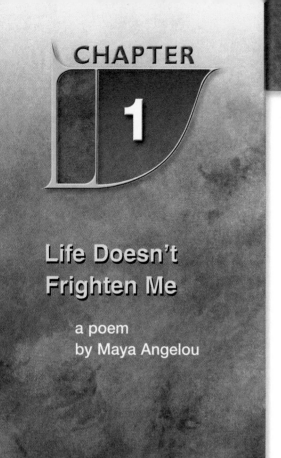

CHAPTER

1

Life Doesn't
Frighten Me

a poem
by Maya Angelou

Objectives

Reading Use images to understand and enjoy poetry.

Listening and Speaking Discuss personal experiences.

Grammar Use prepositional phrases.

Writing Write a poem about a feeling.

Content Science: Learn about the respiratory system.

Use Prior Knowledge

Discuss What Frightens You

Everyone has fears. What frightens you (makes you afraid)?

1. With a partner, make a list of things that frighten you. Think about places, animals, noises, and events.
2. Copy the chart on a piece of paper. Write the words from your list where you think they should go.
3. Draw a picture for one or two of the frightening things.
4. Share your chart and pictures with the class.

Very, Very Frightening	Very Frightening	Frightening	A Little Frightening

Build Background

Nursery Rhymes

Poems for very young children are called nursery rhymes. One famous collection of nursery rhymes is "Mother Goose." Some pictures show the character as a frightening woman.

Tell the class about nursery rhymes you have heard. Compare and contrast nursery rhymes from parts of the United States and other cultures.

Content Connection

Nursery rhymes are one kind of **oral tradition.** They are told out loud by grandparents to parents to children for hundreds of years.

Build Vocabulary

Preview New Vocabulary

The poem in this chapter includes words that name frightening things.

1. Work with a partner to guess the meanings of these words.

| shadow | ghost | frog | snake |

2. Read the dictionary entry for the first word.

> **shad•ow** /ˈʃædoʊ/ *n.* **1** the dark shape formed when someone or something blocks the sun or other light: *The houses made long shadows in the late afternoon.*‖ *At night, scary things hide in the shadows on city streets.*

3. Look up the other words in the dictionary. Read the definition. Use the pronunciation key to help you say each word.

4. Write the words in your Personal Dictionary and look for them as you read the poem.

Personal Dictionary

The Heinle Newbury House Dictionary

Activity Book p. 81

Student CD-ROM

Text Structure

Poem

"Life Doesn't Frighten Me" is a **poem.** Poems let writers share what is important to them. They express their feelings.

As you read "Life Doesn't Frighten Me," look for the distinguishing features of a poem. Notice the speaker's thoughts and feelings.

Poem	
Stanzas	groups of lines
Rhyming Words	words that have the same or similar sounds; they are often used at the ends of lines
Repetition	a repeated idea or theme
Images	words that help you make a picture in your mind

Student
CD-ROM

Reading Strategy

Use Images to Understand and Enjoy Poetry

Poems include words that help readers make pictures in their minds. These images (pictures) allow readers to understand and enjoy a poem better.

1. Read or listen to the audio recording of "Life Doesn't Frighten Me." What images do you see in your mind? Read each line slowly and carefully to help you understand each image.

2. How do these images help you understand and enjoy the poem? Which words help you to make the best images in your mind?

3. Draw a picture of a line from the poem. Make your picture show what the poet is saying in the poem.

Student
CD-ROM

Life Doesn't Frighten Me

a poem by Maya Angelou

Audio

Use Images to Understand and Enjoy Poetry

What images do you make in your mind when you read the words *Big ghosts in a cloud*?

1 Shadows on the wall
Noises down the hall
Life doesn't frighten me at all
Bad dogs barking loud
Big ghosts in a cloud
Life doesn't frighten me at all

Use Images to Understand and Enjoy Poetry

Describe what images you see in your mind after reading this stanza.

2 Mean old Mother Goose
Lions **on the loose**
They don't frighten me at all
Dragons breathing flame
on my **counterpane**
That doesn't frighten me at all.

3 I go **boo**
Make them **shoo**
I make fun
Way they run
I won't cry
So they fly
I just smile
They go wild
Life doesn't frighten me at all.

---

on the loose set free
counterpane a bedspread or quilt
boo a sound made to frighten or surprise

shoo tell someone or something to go away by using motions
way = away

4   Tough guys in a fight
    All alone at night
    life doesn't frighten me at all.
    Panthers in the park
    Strangers in the dark
    No, they don't frighten me at all

Use Images to Understand and Enjoy Poetry

What images do you see in your mind when you read "That new classroom where Boys all pull my hair"?

5   That new classroom where
    Boys all pull my hair
    (Kissy little girls
    with their hair in curls)
    They don't frighten me at all

6   Don't show me frogs and snakes
    And listen for my scream
    If I'm afraid at all
    It's only in my dreams

---

panthers   large, wild cats, usually all black   **strangers**   people that you do not know

7   I've got a magic **charm**
That I keep up my sleeve,
I can walk the ocean floor
And never have to breathe.

8   Life doesn't frighten me at all
Not at all
Not at all
Life doesn't frighten me at all.

Use Images to Understand and Enjoy Poetry

What images stay in your mind after reading this poem?

---

charm   an object that is believed to bring luck

About the Author   Maya Angelou (born 1928)

Maya Angelou faced frightening situations during her childhood. Her family was poor and her parents were divorced. She had to move many times and sometimes lived in places where African-Americans were treated badly. However, people such as Angelou's grandmother taught her how to have courage. Angelou has worked as an actress, a writer, and a teacher. She has also worked for equal treatment of African-Americans.

➤Why did Maya Angelou write this poem? Was it to entertain us or to express herself?

What challenges do you think Maya Angelou faced in becoming an author?

Beyond the Reading

Reading Comprehension

Question-Answer Relationships (QAR)

"Right There" Questions

1. **Recall Facts** Name something that does not frighten the author.
2. **Recall Facts** What is one thing that does frighten the author?

"Think and Search" Questions

3. **Give Reasons** What makes the author not afraid of the frightening things in this poem?
4. **Make Inferences** What might really cause shadows on the wall or noises down the hall?

"Author and You" Questions

5. **Evaluate Ideas** Which of the things in the poem would frighten you the most?

6. **Analyze Illustrations** Why do you think illustrations are placed with the poem instead of photos? How does this help you understand the text?
7. **Analyze Illustrations** How do the style (look and feeling) and elements (parts) of the illustrations help you understand the poem?

"On Your Own" Question

8. **Make Judgments** Are there any things in the poem that you think a person *should* be frightened of?

Activity Book
p. 82

Build Reading Fluency

Echo Read Aloud

Echo reading helps you learn to read with expression. Your teacher reads a line of "Life Doesn't Frighten Me." Then the class reads the same line aloud.

1. Listen to your teacher read the poem.
2. Next, read the same line aloud with expression.
3. Continue listening then reading.

Listen, Speak, Interact

Discuss Personal Experiences

"Life Doesn't Frighten Me" includes real-life situations that you may have experienced.

1. Read the poem aloud with a partner. List frightening things in the poem, such as "Shadows on the wall."
2. Discuss experiences that have frightened you. For example, "There was a hurricane." Compare and contrast your experiences.

3. Present a dramatic interpretation of one of your experiences. Act out the situation that frightened you.

Elements of Literature

Identify Rhyming Words

"Life Doesn't Frighten Me" uses **rhyming words** at the ends of some lines. The ends of rhyming words can sound exactly the same, such as *wall* and *hall*. Sometimes the word endings sound similar, such as *sleeve* and *breathe*.

1. With a partner, find an example in the poem of rhyming words that sound exactly the same at the end. Say the words aloud.
2. Find an example of rhyming words that sound similar at the end. Say the words aloud.
3. Use the pronunciation guide in a dictionary to help you say words you do not know.

4. In your Reading Log, make a chart like the one here. Find examples of each kind of rhyming words and write them in the chart.

Exact Rhyme	Similar Rhyme
wall / hall	sleeve / breathe

Reading Log   Activity Book p. 83   Student CD-ROM

Word Study

Identify Contractions

Contractions are shortened forms of words.

Life <u>doesn't</u> frighten me at all.

The word *doesn't* is a contraction for the words *does not*. The **apostrophe** (') shows where the word *not* has been shortened. It replaces the letter *o*. Notice that the two words become one word.

1. Read the following sentences. Which of these words make up each contraction?

I am   I have   it is   do not

a. They <u>don't</u> frighten me at all.

b. If <u>I'm</u> afraid at all.

c. <u>It's</u> only in my dreams.

d. <u>I've</u> got a magic charm.

2. Write the contractions and the two words that make up the contractions in a chart like the one here.

Contraction	Two Words
doesn't	does not

Activity Book   Student
p. 84   CD-ROM

Grammar Focus

Use Prepositional Phrases

A **prepositional phrase** often answers the question *when, where,* or *how.*

Shadows <u>on the wall</u>

A prepositional phrase is made up of a preposition and an object. Some prepositions are: *about, at, down, for, in, on, over, under, up, with.*

Preposition	Object
in	the closet
on	the wall

1. Read the following lines from the poem. Write the prepositions and the objects in a chart.
  a. Noises down the hall
  b. Big ghosts in a cloud
  c. Dragons breathing flame on my counterpane
  d. Panthers in the park
2. Write your own sentence using a prepositional phrase.

Activity Book   Student   Student
pp. 85–86   Handbook   CD-ROM

From Reading to Writing

Write a Poem About a Feeling

Brainstorm ideas about a feeling you sometimes have. Use these ideas to write a poem. Some feelings are: afraid, happy, sad, angry, surprised, confused.

1. Write your ideas in a web.
2. Use at least two prepositional phrases to tell when and where you feel this. Use the web to write your poem.
3. Use images to help the reader "see" what you are saying.
4. Use rhyming words at the end of the lines.

5. Read your poem aloud to the class. Use expression and gestures to help your classmates understand.

Activity Book
p. 87

Across Content Areas

Learn About the Respiratory System

Your **respiratory system** consists of the **lungs** and the body's air passages. When you breathe in, you **inhale.** When you breathe out, you **exhale.** You breathe in **oxygen,** a gas in the air. In the lungs, the oxygen enters the blood. **Blood** is the red liquid that flows through your body. Blood carries the oxygen to all parts of your body. Oxygen is exhaled as **carbon dioxide,** a compound of carbon and oxygen.

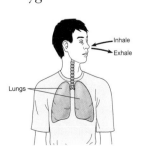

Copy these sentences. Fill in the blanks with the correct words.

blood	exhale	inhale
lungs	oxygen	

1. When you _____ , air fills your _____ .
2. You breathe in a gas called _____ .
3. Your _____ takes the oxygen to parts of your body.
4. When you _____ , carbon dioxide leaves the body.

Activity Book
p. 88

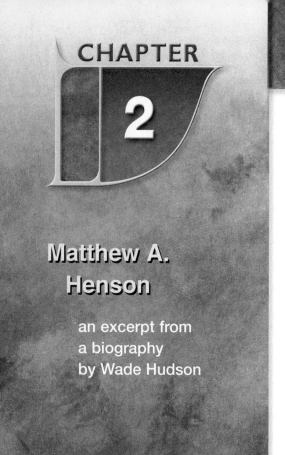

CHAPTER 2

Matthew A. Henson

an excerpt from
a biography
by Wade Hudson

Objectives

Reading Find the main idea and supporting details as you read a biography.

Listening and Speaking Role-play an interview with a character.

Grammar Identify two-word verbs.

Writing Write a short biography.

Content Science: Learn about temperature.

Use Prior Knowledge

Prepare for a Trip

Have you ever taken a trip? Where to? What did you take with you?

What would you take with you on a trip to a very cold place?

1. Copy the chart on a piece of paper.
2. With a partner, brainstorm what you would need to take with you on a trip to a very cold place where there is lots of ice and snow.
3. Share the information in your chart with the rest of the class.

A Trip to a Cold Place
1. Food
2. Sleds and dogs
3.
4.
5.

Build Background

The North Pole

The **North Pole** is the northern-most point of Earth. It is located near the center of the Arctic Ocean. It is made up entirely of frozen ocean. This area does not have any land.

Content Connection

The Inuit are a group of native people who live in Canada near the North Pole.

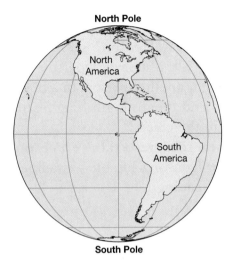

Build Vocabulary

Learn Synonyms with Reference Aids

In "Matthew A. Henson," the people in the story take a long and dangerous trip. Do you know any **synonyms** for the word *trip*? Remember, synonyms are words that have similar meanings.

1. Read the following sentences. The underlined words are synonyms for *trip*.
    a. They sailed on a long <u>voyage</u> from New York City to Canada.
    b. Peary selected Henson and four Inuit guides to make the last leg of the <u>journey</u>.
    c. Congress authorized a medal for all the men on the North Pole <u>expedition</u>.

2. Write the word *trip* and these synonyms in your Personal Dictionary.

3. A **thesaurus** is a reference book for synonyms. As you read, use a thesaurus or another synonym finder to find words with the same meaning as words you don't know. You can also use software such as an electronic or online dictionary or thesaurus. Record these words in your Personal Dictionary.

Personal Dictionary

Activity Book *p. 89*

Student CD-ROM

Text Structure

Biography

"Matthew A. Henson" is a **biography.** A biography is the story of a person's life. It is written by another person. In a biography, you will find the distinguishing features shown in the chart.

As you read, record the events of Matthew Henson's life on a timeline in your Reading Log. Use a timeline like the one below.

Biography	
Dates	when important things happened in the person's life
Actions and Events	important or special things the person did
Descriptions	details about the people and places in the person's life

Reading Log   Student CD-ROM

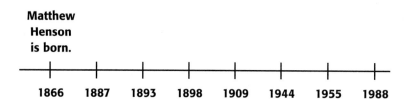

Matthew Henson is born.

1866 1887 1893 1898 1909 1944 1955 1988

Reading Strategy

Find the Main Idea and Supporting Details

The **main idea** of a paragraph (or of a longer part of a reading) is the most important thing that the writer wants you to understand. **Supporting details** are pieces of information that show you that the main idea is true. Here is an example:

> The weather outside was terrible. The temperature was 10°F. The wind was blowing very hard, and it was snowing. I did not want to go out!

Main Idea	Supporting Details
The weather was terrible.	10°F, windy, snowy

1. As you read "Matthew A. Henson," look for the main idea of each long paragraph. You can sometimes find the main idea in the first or last sentence of a paragraph.
2. Write the main ideas and supporting details in your Reading Log.

Reading Log   Student CD-ROM

MATTHEW A. HENSON

an excerpt from a biography
by Wade Hudson

1   The most northern part of the earth has below-freezing temperatures. Ice covers the area. This is the North Pole.

2   In 1893, no one had been to the North Pole. That year Admiral Robert E. Peary and Matthew Henson set out to reach the North Pole. But they were unsuccessful. They tried again in 1898, but failed. In 1909, they set out once more.

3   Peary, Henson, and a group that included explorer Robert Bartlett took off for the Pole. They sailed on a long voyage from New York City to Canada. Next, they set up a base camp at Camp Columbia, Canada. The camp was about 450 miles from the North Pole. In March 1909, the group packed dog sleds with food and supplies. Then they headed over the **polar** sea ice toward the North Pole.

> **Find the Main Idea and Supporting Details**
>
> What is the main idea of this paragraph? Give two supporting details.

4   Some of the men **suffered** from the **harsh** cold weather. They had to return to the camp. Finally, Peary selected Henson and four Inuit guides—Ootah, Seegloo, Egingwah, and Ooqueah—to make the last leg of the journey. It was early April 1909. They were closer than ever to really reaching the North Pole.

Audio

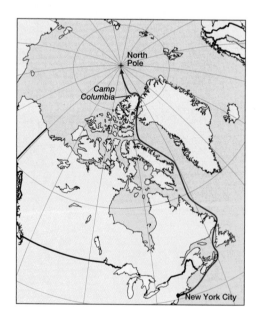

---

polar near one of Earth's poles
suffered felt pain or unhappiness

harsh extreme, very strong

Pack ice near the North Pole.

5   Henson, Peary, and their guides traveled over the ice and snow. Peary's feet were **injured.** He could not walk as quickly as Henson. So Henson and his guides walked ahead—and disaster struck.

6   Along the way, Matthew Henson stepped out on a large cake of ice. *CRACK!* The ice **gave way.** Henson fell into the icy water below. The water temperature was **bitter** cold: **–15 degrees Fahrenheit.** In only a few minutes, Matthew Henson would have frozen to death.

7   Suddenly, there was a tug on Henson's hood. Someone was pulling him from the water. It was Ootah. Quickly, Ootah helped Henson pull off his wet boots and clothes and put on dry ones. Ootah shook the water from the furs Henson wore before the water turned to ice. Then Henson, Ootah, and Seegloo moved on. Admiral Robert E. Peary, Egingwah, and Ooqueah followed. The North Pole was less than thirty-five miles away.

> **Find the Main Idea and Supporting Details**
>
> The main idea of this paragraph can be stated as "Ootah saved Henson's life." Find two details that support this main idea.

8   Henson got closer and closer to the Pole. Finally, he stopped. He looked around. Had he reached the North Pole? Henson set up camp there and waited for Peary.

---

injured hurt
gave way fell down; collapsed

bitter causing pain
–15 degrees Fahrenheit –26 degrees Celsius

Robert Peary's North Pole expedition.

9   When the Admiral arrived, he made **observations** from different points. He returned to the camp and made an **announcement.** The camp was at the exact point of the North Pole. He had Henson and the four guides stand on a ridge and he photographed them. Henson held the American flag. He felt proud. It had been an exciting adventure.

> **Find the Main Idea and Supporting Details**
>
> Read this detail: "He made observations from different points." What main idea does this detail support?

10   Matthew Henson was born in Charles County, Maryland, in 1866. After his mother died, he lived with an uncle in Washington, D.C. Henson always liked adventure. When he was fourteen years old, he signed on as a cabin boy on a ship called the *Katie Hines.* He was a member of the crew for five years.

11   Henson met Peary in 1887, when Henson was working in a clothing store in Washington, D.C. Peary liked Henson right away. Peary offered Henson a job . . . Henson . . . was interested in a trip Peary had planned to Nicaragua. It was a chance for him to travel again. For more than twenty years, the two men took many trips together.

---

observations   things seen or measured

announcement   something said in public

12   On April 7, 1909, the great explorers began their journey back from the North Pole. They were very happy about their victory.

13   Robert E. Peary became famous. Peary was awarded a gold medal by the National Geographic Society. Robert Bartlett was also awarded a medal although he didn't even make the final trip to the North Pole. Matthew Henson was **ignored.**

14   For many years, the white world did not recognize Henson's great **achievement.** The black community, however, presented him with a number of awards. Finally, on January 28, 1944, Congress **authorized** a medal for all the men on the North Pole expedition. A year later, Henson was presented with a silver medal for **outstanding** service to the United States Government.

15   This great explorer died in 1955. On April 6, 1988, his **remains** were reburied with full military honors at Arlington National Cemetery. It was a most **suitable** honor for a great black American.

---

ignored not paid any attention to
achievement something you do that is difficult and important
authorized approved, agreed to

outstanding extra special, more than is expected
remains a dead body
suitable proper, fitting, correct

About the Author   Wade Hudson (born 1946)

Wade Hudson has written many books about African-American heroes for young readers. His wife, Cheryl Willis Hudson, also publishes books about African-Americans. Hudson was born and grew up in Louisiana. He worked for the equal rights of African-Americans before becoming a writer. When he writes, he wants to tell the true story of African-Americans.

➤What is the author's purpose in writing this biography? Is it to entertain, to inform, or to influence?

Beyond the Reading

Reading Comprehension

Question-Answer Relationships (QAR)

"Right There" Questions

1. **Recall Facts** Where is the North Pole?

2. **Recall Facts** Who led the trip that Matthew Henson took to the North Pole?

3. **Recall Facts** What honors did Matthew Henson receive for his journey?

"Think and Search" Questions

4. **Analyze Cause and Effect** What caused Matthew Henson to almost die on the trip?

5. **Recognize Sequence of Events** What steps did Henson's group have to take to reach the North Pole?

6. **Make Inferences** Why do you think that the National Geographic Society did not give Matthew Henson a medal after the 1909 trip?

"Author and You" Questions

7. **Compare Your Experiences** Why do you think that Matthew Henson and Robert Peary liked each other right away? What makes you like someone right away?

8. **Make Inferences** Peary sent Henson ahead after Peary hurt his feet. How do you think Peary felt about Matthew Henson?

"On Your Own" Question

9. **Speculate** How do you think Matthew Henson felt when he was not honored with the other North Pole explorers?

Activity Book
p. 90

Student
CD-ROM

Build Reading Fluency

Repeated Reading

Rereading one paragraph at a time can help increase your reading rate and build confidence.

1. With a partner, read aloud paragraph 1 in "Matthew A. Henson" three times.

2. Did your reading rate increase each time?

3. Next, read paragraph 2 three times.

4. Continue rereading each paragraph.

5. Stop after ten minutes.

Listen, Speak, Interact

Role-Play an Interview with a Character

Select one of the characters in the story you just read.

1. With a partner, role-play an interview. One of you will be the character in the story. The other will be a reporter for a magazine.
2. On a piece of paper, complete an Interview Preparation List like the one here.
3. Role-play the interview. Speak clearly and listen carefully.
4. Ask questions about anything you don't understand.

> **Interview Preparation List**
>
> Date: _____
>
> Name of Character: _____
>
> Name of Reporter: _____
>
> Questions:
>
> 1. Why did you want to join the expedition to the North Pole?
>
> 2. _____
>
> 3. _____
>
> 4. _____
>
> 5. _____

Elements of Literature

Recognize Chronological Order and Transitions

Writers sometimes order events as they happen—starting with the first event and ending with the last. This is called **chronological order.**

Transitions are words or groups of words that connect ideas. They help readers follow the chronological order. Look at these transition words and phrases.

Time	Sequence	Periods of Time
in 1909	first	for five years
on Tuesday	second	in the summer
in the morning	next	last week
	then	
	finally	

1. Reread paragraph 3 of "Matthew A. Henson." Find three examples of transition words or phrases that signal time.
2. List the events in chronological order in your Reading Log.
3. Write three sentences of your own using time words.

Reading Log

Activity Book
p. 91

Student
CD-ROM

Word Study

Recognize Proper Nouns

Proper nouns are the names of people (for example, *Matthew*); important places like cities, countries, and continents (for example, *Sacramento, California*); and some time words (for example, *Tuesday, January*).

The first letter of a proper noun is always written with a **capital letter** (the *t* in *Tuesday* is a capital letter).

Some proper nouns refer to people who are from a certain place, for example: We are **Americans.** *Americans* are people from America.

Add **-n, -an,** or **-ian** to place names to make a proper noun that refers to a person. Copy the chart in your Personal Dictionary and complete it. Capitalize proper nouns.

Country, Region, or Continent	Person
Central America	Central American
Nicaragua	
	African
	Canadian
Europe	
	Asian
	Australian

Personal Dictionary

Activity Book p. 92

Student CD-ROM

Grammar Focus

Identify Two-Word Verbs

Two-word verbs use two words to explain an action.

Matthew Henson <u>set out</u> to reach the North Pole.

The two-word verb *set out* means "left on a trip."

Find sentences with two-word verbs in the following paragraphs. Write the sentences on a piece of paper. Underline both words of the two-word verb.

1. In paragraph 3, find a two-word verb in the first sentence that means "left."
2. In paragraph 7, find a two-word verb that means "continued."
3. In paragraph 10, find a two-word verb that means "joined a group."

Activity Book pp. 93–94

Student Handbook

Student CD-ROM

From Reading to Writing

Write a Short Biography

Write a biography about a famous person or someone in your family or community. Use "Matthew A. Henson" as a model for your writing. Research your biography at the school library, on the Internet, or by talking to people.

1. Introduce the person to the reader. Tell the person's story. Focus on important or special things the person did.
2. Include proper nouns to tell where the person comes from. Be sure to capitalize correctly.

> **Biography**
>
> _____
> (title)
>
> _____ is important because
> (name)
>
> _____ . On , _____
> (reason)   (date)
>
> _____ _____ .
> (name)   (did something)
>
> Next _____ .
>   (event)
>
> Then _____ .
>   (event)
>
> Finally _____ .
>   (event)

Activity Book
p. 95

Across Content Areas

Learn About Temperature

Temperature tells you how hot or cold something is. It is measured in degrees. The degrees are often shown with the symbol ° after the number, such as 75°.

There are two temperature systems, the **Celsius** and the **Fahrenheit** systems.

	Celsius	Fahrenheit
Water freezes	0°C	32°F
Water boils	100°C	212°F

To change from Fahrenheit to Celsius, use this formula:

$$°C = (°F - 32 \times {}^5\!/_9)$$

Can you change 80°F to Celsius? For help with this problem, ask a math teacher or other expert.

Activity Book
p. 96

CHAPTER 3

Anne Frank:
The Diary of a Young Girl

an excerpt from a diary
by Anne Frank

Objectives

Reading Use chronology to locate and recall information as you read a diary.

Listening and Speaking Act out a dialogue.

Grammar Use conjunctions to form compound sentences.

Writing Write a diary.

Content Social Studies: Describe social groups.

Use Prior Knowledge

Explore Differences

You will read a selection about a young girl who was treated badly because she was different. How are people different?

1. With a partner, make a web like the one here.
2. Complete your web with ways that people are different. Add ovals to your web if necessary.
3. As a class, talk about your webs. Discuss ways that people are sometimes treated because they are different.

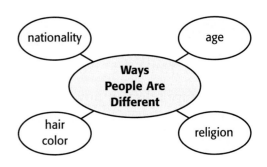

Build Background

World War II

Beginning in the late 1930s, Adolf Hitler, the Chancellor of Germany, invaded many neighboring countries, including Holland. Millions of people in Europe, most of them Jews, were taken to prison camps. Anne Frank, a teenage girl from Holland, and her family lived in a secret hiding place. One thing she took with her was her diary. Anne called her diary "Kitty."

Nazi controlled territories in 1942

Content Connection

SOCIAL STUDIES

After Germany lost World War II in 1945, it was divided into two countries—East Germany and West Germany. Germany was finally reunited in 1990.

Build Vocabulary

Use Context

Sometimes you can learn the meanings of new words by using **context,** or nearby words and sentences.

Use the boldfaced words to help you choose the correct meaning for each underlined word.

1. Margot and I began to **pack** some of our most vital <u>belongings</u> . . . The first thing I put in was **this diary, then hair curlers, handkerchiefs,** . . .

   Belongings probably means
   a. clothes   **b.** possessions

2. We put on <u>heaps of</u> clothes . . . I had on **two vests, three pairs of pants, a dress, on top of that a skirt, jacket,** . . .

   Heaps of probably means
   a. beautiful   **b.** a lot of

Activity Book
p. 97

Student
CD-ROM

Text Structure

Diary

The reading selection is an entry from Anne Frank's diary. A **diary** is a record of daily events. It is usually not meant to be read by others. Private thoughts and feelings are included.

Look for these distinguishing features as you read or listen to the audio recording of Anne Frank's diary.

Diary	
Direct Address	Diary entries sometimes address the diary as if it were a person; for example, "Dear Kitty."
Personal Details	Diary entries often tell how the writer feels.
Informal Writing Style	Diary entries are informal, so they may not always follow all of the rules of grammar or writing.

Student
CD-ROM

Reading Strategy

Use Chronology to Locate and Recall Information

As you read, notice the **chronology**—the order in which events happen. This will help you follow the events in the story and find information in it.

1. Read the first two paragraphs. On which day is Anne writing? Which day is Anne going to tell us about?

2. Now look at the third paragraph. Phrases such as *at three o'clock* and *a bit later* can help you follow the chronology.

3. As you read the selection, notice the chronology. Record important events in your Reading Log.

Reading Log   Student
CD-ROM

Anne Frank:
The Diary of a Young Girl

an excerpt from a diary

by Anne Frank

Audio

Wednesday, 8 July 1942

Dear Kitty,

1   Years seem to have passed between Sunday and now. So much has happened, it is just as if the whole world had turned upside down. But I am still alive, Kitty, and that is the main thing, Daddy says.

2   Yes, I'm still alive, indeed, but don't ask where or how. You wouldn't understand a word, so I will begin by telling you what happened on Sunday afternoon.

3   At three o'clock (Harry had just gone, but was coming back later) someone rang the front doorbell. I was lying lazily reading a book on the **veranda** in the sunshine, so I didn't hear it. A bit later, Margot appeared at the kitchen door looking very excited. "The **S.S.** have sent a call-up notice for Daddy," she whispered. "Mummy has gone to see

> **Use Chronology to Locate and Recall Information**
>
> What day was it when Margot told Anne that their father had received a call-up?

The building where Anne and her family hid.

---

veranda   porch

S.S.   Nazi police

...pack some of our most useful belongings into a school satchel. The first thing I put [in] then hair curlers, handkerchiefs, schoolbooks, a comb, old letters, I put in the craz...

Mrs. Frank and Anne

Mr. Van Daan already." (Van Daan is a friend who works with Daddy in the business.) It was a great shock to me, a **call-up;** everyone knows what that means. I picture **concentration camps** and lonely cells—should we allow him to be **doomed** to this? "Of course he won't go," declared Margot, while we waited together. "Mummy has gone to the Van Daans to discuss whether we should move into our hiding place tomorrow. The Van Daans are going with us, so we shall be seven in all." Silence. We couldn't talk any more, thinking about Daddy, who, little knowing what was going on, was visiting some old people in the Joodse Invalide; waiting for Mummy, the heat and **suspense** all made us very **overawed** and silent.

4   Suddenly the bell rang again. "That is Harry," I said. "Don't open the door." Margot held me back, but it was not necessary as we heard Mummy and Mr. Van Daan downstairs, talking to Harry, then they came in and closed the door behind them. Each time the bell went, Margot or I had to creep softly down to see if it was Daddy, not opening the door to anyone else.

> **Use Chronology to Locate and Recall Information**
>
> Who comes to the Franks' door? In what order do they arrive?

---

call-up   an order to report to the police

concentration camps   camps where the Nazis imprisoned and killed Jews

doomed   likely to face harm or death

suspense   worry about what will happen, especially while waiting

overawed   too shocked to speak; frightened

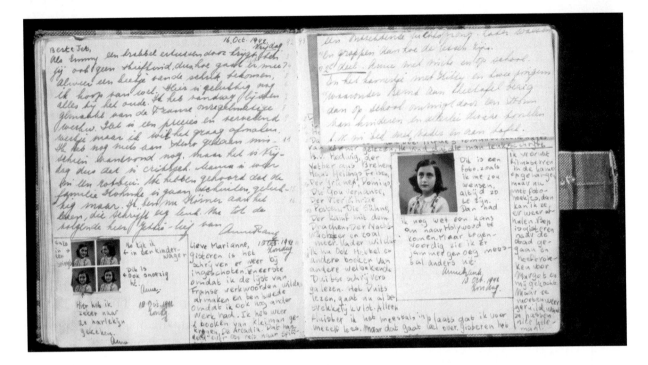

5   Margot and I were sent out of the room. Van Daan wanted to talk to Mummy alone. When we were alone together in our bedroom, Margot told me that the call-up was not for Daddy, but for her. I was more frightened than ever and began to cry. Margot is sixteen; would they really take girls of that age away alone? But thank goodness she won't go, Mummy said so herself; that must be what Daddy meant when he talked about us going into hiding.

6   Into hiding—where would we go; in a town or the country, in a house or a cottage, when, how, where. . . ?

7   These were questions I was not allowed to ask, but I couldn't get them out of my mind. Margot and I began to pack some of our most **vital** belongings into a school **satchel.** The first thing I put in was this diary, then hair curlers, handkerchiefs, schoolbooks, a comb, old letters; I put in the craziest things with the idea that we were going into hiding. But I'm not sorry, memories mean more to me than dresses . . .

> **Use Chronology to Locate and Recall Information**
>
> Why does Anne begin to pack? What will happen next?

---

vital   important to life

satchel   a small bag worn over the shoulder, larger than a purse

Use Chronology to Locate and Recall Information

What day of the week does Anne describe?

8   I was **dog-tired** and although I knew that it would be my last night in my own bed, I fell asleep immediately and didn't wake up until Mummy called me at five-thirty the next morning. Luckily it was not so hot as Sunday; warm rain fell steadily all day. We put on heaps of clothes as if we were going to the North Pole, the **sole** reason being to take clothes with us. No Jew in our situation would have dreamed of going out with a suitcase full of clothing. I had on two vests, three pairs of pants, a dress, on top of that a skirt, jacket, summer coat, two pairs of stockings, lace-up shoes, woolly cap, scarf, and still more; I was nearly **stifled** before we got started, but no one **inquired** about that . . .

9   There was one pound of meat in the kitchen for the cat, breakfast things lying on the table, stripped beds, all giving the impression that we had left helter-skelter. But we didn't care about impressions, we only wanted to get away, only escape and arrive safely, nothing else. Continued tomorrow.

Yours, Anne

---

dog-tired   very tired; feeling like a tired dog
sole   only

stifled   feeling as if there is no air; overheated
inquired   asked

About the Author

Anne Frank (1929–1945)

Anne Frank began her diary in 1942 on her 13th birthday. In 1944, Anne and her family were found by the Nazis. The entire family died in concentration camps except for Mr. Frank. Anne would have turned 16 on her next birthday. After the police took the Frank family, a friend found Anne's diary. Anne's father got it after the war and published it. Millions of people have read Anne's story of life in hiding. Even though Anne lived in fear of the Nazis, she wrote, "I still believe that people are really good at heart . . . I think it will all come right, that this cruelty too will end, and that peace . . . will return again."

➤Do you admire Anne Frank? Why or why not?

Beyond the Reading

Reading Comprehension

Question-Answer Relationships (QAR)

"Right There" Questions

1. **Recall Facts** When do the events in this diary entry take place?
2. **Recall Facts** What are some things that Anne takes with her into hiding?

"Think and Search" Questions

3. **Analyze Cause and Effect** Why do the Franks decide to go into hiding when they do?
4. **Interpret** What does a call-up mean for the Frank family?
5. **Identify** Which member of the Frank family is called up by the police?
6. **Make Inferences** Why does Anne put on so many clothes instead of packing a suitcase? Why would a Jew "in our situation" not carry a suitcase?

"Author and You" Questions

7. **Interpret** Why does Anne say that memories are more important than dresses?
8. **Make Inferences** Why did the family leave their house so messy when they left?

"On Your Own" Questions

9. **Interpret** How do you think Anne felt leaving her home and many of her things behind?
10. **Compare Your Experiences** What things would you take with you if you had to leave home suddenly?

Activity Book
p. 98

Student
CD-ROM

Build Reading Fluency

Reading Chunks of Words Silently

Reading silently is good practice. It helps you learn to read faster.

1. Listen to paragraphs 1 and 2 of "The Diary of Anne Frank" on the Audio CD.
2. Listen to the chunks of words.
3. Silently reread paragraphs 1 and 2 two times.
4. Your teacher or a partner will time your second reading.
5. Raise your hand when you are finished.

Listen, Speak, Interact

Act Out a Dialogue

The **dialogue** of a selection is the exact words that people say to one another. In writing, dialogue is shown with quotation marks.

"That is Harry," I said.

The words *That is Harry* are the words that Anne said. If you write dialogue to act out, you do not need quotation marks.

Anne: That is Harry.

1. Work with a partner. Choose an event that Anne describes in her diary. Write a dialogue about the event to act out.

2. If there is any dialogue with quotation marks in the diary, include it.

3. Listen to the audio recording of the selection to help you learn to distinguish and produce the intonation (changing voice level) of words you will use.

4. Use clues from the text to guess what else the characters said during the event.

5. Perform your dialogue for the class.

Elements of Literature

Understand Tone

Tone is the attitude or feeling that a writer shows in a piece of writing. Tone can be serious or funny, formal or informal.

Copy the following sentences into your Reading Log. Underline the words and phrases (groups of words) that help make Anne's tone informal.

1. Yes, I'm still alive, indeed, but don't ask where or how. You wouldn't understand a word, so I will begin by telling you what happened on Sunday afternoon.

2. I put in the craziest things with the idea that we were going into hiding. But I'm not sorry, memories mean more to me than dresses.

Reading Log   Activity Book   Student
           p. 99   CD-ROM

Word Study

Use the Suffix *-ion*

The suffix *-ion* usually shows that a word is a noun (a person, a place, or a thing).

> These were quest**ion**s I was not allowed to ask . . .

In some cases, you can add *-ion* to a verb to make a noun.

Suffix *-ion*		
Verb	**+ -ion**	**Noun**
impress	-ion	impression
situate	-ion	situation

Notice that some verbs change their spelling when *-ion* is added.

Copy the following sentences in your Personal Dictionary. Fill in the blanks with a noun ending in *-ion*. Use the underlined word to make the noun.

1. The students <u>impressed</u> the teacher. They made a good ＿＿＿ .
2. We are <u>situated</u> in a bad place. We don't like our ＿＿＿ .

Personal Dictionary   Activity Book *p. 100*   Student CD-ROM

Grammar Focus

Use Conjunctions to Form Compound Sentences

A **conjunction** is a word like *and* or *but*. Conjunctions can join two sentences. Use a comma between the two sentences.

Compound Sentence
I'm still alive, but don't ask how.

Two Simple Sentences
I'm still alive.
Don't ask how.

Use *but* when you want to show contrast between two sentences. Use *and* to show a connection.

1. With a partner, reread paragraphs 4 and 7 of the selection.
2. Find two sentences that use the conjunction *but*. Write them on a piece of paper. Then write each one as two separate sentences.

Activity Book *pp. 101–102*   Student Handbook   Student CD-ROM

From Reading to Writing

Write a Diary

Write a diary every day for the next week.

1. Include dates in your diary.
2. Write in the first person, using the pronoun *I* for yourself and the pronoun *you* for the diary.
3. Describe something you did and how you felt each day.
4. Write in an informal tone.

5. Use the conjunctions *but* and *and* to join two sentences into one longer sentence.
6. Use prepositional phrases to tell where something happened.
7. End your diary entry with a closing such as *Yours, Your friend,* or *Love,* plus your name.

Activity Book
p. 103

Across Content Areas

Describe Social Groups

We can describe ourselves in many ways. One way is to describe the social groups that we belong to. Here are some examples:

Social Groups	
nationality	being a citizen of a country (for example, Mexican)
ethnicity	the culture that you feel you belong to (for example, Native American, Hispanic)
religion	your faith (for example, Christian, Buddhist, Muslim, Hindu)
gender	whether you are male or female

Copy the following sentences onto a piece of paper. Fill in the blanks with one of the social groups.

1. My family is from Thailand, so we enjoy eating Thai food and celebrating Thai holidays. Our ____ is Thai.
2. We are Buddhists. Our ____ is Buddhism.
3. Luis is a citizen of Cuba, so his ____ is Cuban.

Activity Book
p. 104

4

Lance Armstrong:
Champion Cyclist

a speech
by President
George W. Bush

Into the Reading

Objectives

Reading Distinguish fact from opinion as you read a speech.

Listening and Speaking Listen to and discuss a speech.

Grammar Use superlative adjectives.

Writing Write a speech.

Content Social Studies: Read a chart.

Use Prior Knowledge

Discuss Ways to Treat Disease

The reading selection in this chapter is a speech addressed to Lance Armstrong. Armstrong is a champion cyclist (bike rider) who had cancer, a serious disease. He was very sick. His doctors did not think he would live.

When people get a disease, they can get help from doctors, from family, and from themselves.

1. Work with a partner. Brainstorm the kinds of help that sick people can get.
2. Copy the chart below on a piece of paper. List your ideas in your chart.
3. Share your information with the rest of the class.

Doctors and Nurses Can . . .	Family and Friends Can . . .	The Sick Person Can . . .
give medicine	visit	have courage

Build Background

The *Tour de France*

The *Tour de France* is a bicycle race held every summer in France. About 200 people enter the race. The race is more than 2,100 miles long (about 3,600 kilometers). The winner is the cyclist who covers the distance in the shortest time. Racers stop along the way to eat, sleep, and rest.

Content Connection

Cyclists in the *Tour de France* ride through the French Alps, mountains that reach a height of 15,771 feet (4,807 meters).

Build Vocabulary

Use Multiple Reference Aids

A **reference** is a source of information such as a dictionary. An **aid** is something that helps you. When you want help for reading, writing, revising, and editing, there are many reference aids that you can turn to.

1. **Glossary:** Some books have a **glossary** at the end that gives the meanings of difficult words.
2. **Encyclopedias:** These books are organized alphabetically and give more information than a dictionary. Many encyclopedias are also on CD-ROM.
3. **Newspapers and Magazines:** These contain current events. They are usually printed daily, weekly, and monthly.
4. **Internet:** This computer network allows you to find information using keywords.

Use two or more of these sources to look up these new vocabulary words: cancer, *Tour de France*, cycling.

Activity Book
p. 105

Student
CD-ROM

Text Structure

Speech

The reading selection is a speech given by President George W. Bush. A speech is written to present to an audience. Sometimes the writer prints the speech for others to read later. Look for the distinguishing features of a speech as you read.

Notice how President Bush uses humor or mentions people in the audience to help the audience feel involved with the topic.

Speech	
Personal Style	A speech may include casual or formal language.
Direct Address	A speech is spoken directly to the audience using the pronoun *you*.
Audience Reaction	A speech may have words in parentheses, such as "(Laughter)," to tell how the audience reacted.

Student
CD-ROM

Reading Strategy

Distinguish Fact from Opinion

When you read, notice the difference between fact and opinion.

1. A **fact** can be proven. As you read, look for facts such as this: "The *Tour de France* takes place in France every summer." You can use reference aids to prove this fact.

2. An **opinion** is a personal view or an idea. It cannot be proven. As you read, look for opinions such as this: "The *Tour de France* is the best sporting event in the world."

Distinguish facts from opinions as you read and listen to the audio recording of the selection.

Student
CD-ROM

LANCE ARMSTRONG: CHAMPION CYCLIST

a speech by President George W. Bush

Prologue

Audio

People who achieve great things are often invited to the White House, where the U.S. President lives. Lance Armstrong won the *Tour de France.* The president made the following speech to introduce Lance Armstrong to guests of the White House.

1   THE PRESIDENT: Please be seated. It's my **privilege** to welcome you all to the White House, and to welcome my friend, a true champ, a great American, Lance Armstrong.

(**Applause.**) America's incredibly proud of Lance, and I know two people who are really proud of him, as well, that's Kristen, his wife, and young Luke. Thank you all for coming, as well. (Applause.)

> ### Distinguish Fact from Opinion
>
> Is the statement "America's incredibly proud of Lance" a fact or an opinion?

2   We're also honored to have Chris Fowler of **ESPN** here. I'm so—thank you for coming, Chris. I was telling Chris a little earlier, it's one of the programs I can watch on TV that doesn't say anything about me at all. (Laughter.)

3   I want to thank the members of my **Cabinet** who are here. Thank you all for coming. I want to thank the members of the **United States Congress and the Senate** who are here. I see a lot from the Texas **delegation** here that are sure proud of you.

---

privilege honor
applause clapping
ESPN a television station that shows sports programs
Cabinet the group of people who advise the president most closely

United States Congress and the Senate the people elected to make U.S. laws
delegation a group of representatives

4   You all know the *Tour de France* is perhaps the most **physically demanding** event in sports. It lasts three weeks, stretches over 2,100 miles, and is often run in both **sweltering** heat and [really] cold weather. In the end, the race is won or lost in the mountains. During five days of climbs that are incredibly steep and **hazardous**—that's when the heart is tested, and that's when Lance Armstrong **excels.**

> **Distinguish Fact from Opinion**
>
> Find a fact in this paragraph.

5   In the hardest part of the race, Lance reveals an unbending will, uncommon **determination** and unquestioned courage. He has shown that courage [in] sport. He has also shown that courage in life.

6   Just a few years ago, Lance was **diagnosed** with cancer. He was weakened by **chemotherapy** treatments and told he had a 50-50 chance of living. He has done more than survive: He has **triumphed.** (Applause.)

---

physically demanding very difficult on your body
sweltering very hot
hazardous very dangerous
excels does the best job
determination the desire to continue even when the task is hard

diagnosed identified by a doctor that you have a disease
chemotherapy a treatment for cancer
triumphed succeeded greatly

7   One observer commented that when you survive cancer, the French Alps start to look like speed bumps. (Laughter.)

8   Lance's story from cancer diagnosis to a third straight victory in the last *Tour de France* is one of the great human stories. It is a story of character and it is a story of class.

9   Germany's Jan Ullrich, the 1997 *Tour de France* **champion,** is Lance Armstrong's chief **competitor.** The two of them were leading during a critical stage of this year's *Tour de France* when Ullrich lost control of his bicycle, missed a turn and ended up in a ditch. When Lance saw what happened, he slowed down in order to allow his chief competitor to recover. It was, as Lance said, the right thing to do . . .

> **Distinguish Fact from Opinion**
>
> Is the statement that Jan Ullrich won the *Tour de France* in 1997 a fact or an opinion? Explain your answer.

---

champion   a winner, especially of many prizes

competitor   a person you race against

10 Lance Armstrong is a vivid reminder that the great **achievements** of life are often won or lost in the mountains, when the climb is the steepest, when the heart is tested. There are many children in this audience who are showing similar determination in their fight with cancer and other serious illnesses. You face tough challenges and you **embrace** life day by day. You're showing courage on your own journey, and all of us are **inspired** by your example as well.

Ladies and gentleman, it is my honor to present to you a son of Texas, a great American champion, and an extraordinary human being: Lance Armstrong. (Applause.) 11

Epilogue

Lance Armstrong won his fourth *Tour de France* in 2002. After this win, he said, "Regardless of one victory, two victories, four victories, there's never been a victory by a cancer survivor. That's a fact that hopefully I'll be remembered for."

---

achievements successes
embrace put all your energy into
inspired given hope and energy to try hard

About the Author — George W. Bush (born 1946)

George W. Bush, the forty-third president of the United States, is the son of the forty-first president, George H. W. Bush. George W. Bush became president in 2000. He grew up in Texas and was governor of Texas from 1994 until he became president. Bush had an oil business and also owned part of the Texas Rangers baseball team before he began working in politics. Bush wants people to feel that he is someone like them: "I want the folks to see me sitting in the same kind of seat they sit in."

➤ Why did President Bush give this speech? To entertain, to inform, or to persuade people? Support your answer with a sentence from the speech.

Beyond the Reading

Reading Comprehension

Question-Answer Relationships (QAR)

"Right There" Questions

1. **Recall Facts** Who is giving this speech?
2. **Recall Facts** Who is the speech about?

"Think and Search" Questions

3. **Interpret** How has Lance Armstrong shown his strengths as a cyclist?
4. **Character Traits** What does the story about Lance Armstrong waiting for Jan Ullrich tell you about Armstrong's character?

"Author and You" Questions

5. **Make Judgments** Do you agree with President Bush's opinion about Lance Armstrong? Why or why not?

6. **Make Inferences** Why does President Bush say that it was a triumph that Lance Armstrong won the *Tour de France*?
7. **Reflect** How does someone such as Lance Armstrong encourage other people?

"On Your Own" Questions

8. **Speculate** Why do you think that presidents pay attention to people like Lance Armstrong?
9. **Compare Your Experiences** How do you think Lance Armstrong felt as President Bush spoke? Think of a time when you have felt like that.

Activity Book
p. 106

Student
CD-ROM

Build Reading Fluency

Adjust Your Reading Rate

When you read a speech, you can learn to adjust your reading rate. Pause and read as if you are speaking to an audience.

1. Listen to paragraphs 1–3 of the speech on the Audio CD.

2. Silently read paragraphs 1–3.
3. With a partner, take turns reading aloud, as if you are giving the speech.
4. Did you adjust your reading rate?

Listen, Speak, Interact

Listen to and Discuss a Speech

One way to understand a speech is to listen to it and discuss it with someone.

1. Listen to the recording of this speech. Focus on the speaker's message. Listen also to gain information about the subject of the speech. Ask your teacher to help you clarify words and ideas you do not understand.

2. Summarize your understanding of the speech for a partner. Then listen to your partner's summary. Compare your summary with your partner's.

3. Discuss the speech. Talk about the speaker's perspective. What are his opinions of Lance Armstrong? What facts support his opinions?

Elements of Literature

Identify Style, Tone, and Mood in a Speech

Style is the particular way something is written. For example, a style can be informal (using everyday words) or formal (using unusual words).

Tone is the writer's attitude toward the subject. For example, does the writer show respect, disapproval, or support of the topic?

Mood is the feeling the writer wants the audience to get from the speech. Happiness, sadness, and anger are examples of moods.

1. Make a chart like the one below in your Reading Log.

2. Read and listen to President Bush's speech again. Complete the chart with at least one description for each element.

3. What effect did the speech have on you as you read or listened to it? What mood or feeling did you have?

Reading Log   Activity Book   Student
                    p. 107   CD-ROM

Style, Tone, and Mood of President Bush's Speech		
The style is _____ .	The mood is _____ .	The tone is _____ .

Word Study

Interpret Figurative Language

Writers use **figurative language** to make writing vivid and exciting. In figurative language, meanings go beyond the usual definitions in a dictionary.

President Bush uses figurative language in his speech. The underlined words are figurative. What do they mean?

1. Lance Armstrong is a <u>son</u> of Texas.
   a. He was born and raised in Texas.
   b. He really likes Texas.

2. That's when the <u>heart</u> is tested.
   a. That's when you need courage.
   b. That's when you have a heart problem.

3. You <u>embrace</u> life day by day.
   a. You hug your friends every day.
   b. You love and enjoy your life.

Activity Book
p. 108

Student
CD-ROM

Grammar Focus

Use Superlative Adjectives

Use **superlative adjectives** to compare three or more people, places, or things.

Ana thinks that science, math, and English are hard. But math is **the hardest** of the three.

There are two ways to form superlative adjectives.

Superlative Adjectives	
Most Short Adjectives: adjective + -est	**Long Adjectives:** most + adjective
hard + -est = the hardest	the most difficult

1. Find three examples of superlative adjectives using -*est* or *most* in paragraphs 4, 5, and 10.

2. Write one sentence using the superlative form of a short adjective and one sentence using the superlative form of a long adjective.

Activity Book
pp. 109–110

Student
Handbook

Student
CD-ROM

From Reading to Writing

Write a Speech

Write a three-paragraph speech about someone you know who has shown courage.

1. Use informal, everyday language. However, be sure you use correct grammar.
2. Address your audience directly using the word *you.*
3. Use words that set a tone. You can be humorous or serious, or both.
4. Use superlative adjectives, such as *smartest* or *most interesting,* to create a mood of appreciation for the subject of your speech.
5. Practice your speech aloud. Listen carefully for a smooth flow of ideas.

6. Present your speech to the class.

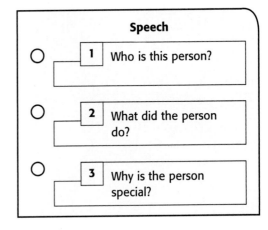

Activity Book
p. 111

Across Content Areas

Read a Chart

The chart below shows the **altitudes** (measures of height) of the highest mountains in four areas in the world.

In the **metric system,** height can be measured in *meters* (m.). In the **English system,** it can be measured in *feet* (ft.).

1. What are the names of the mountains on the chart? Where are they?
2. Find the name of the mountain in the U.S. How high is it?
3. How high is Mt. Blanc in meters? How high is it in feet?

Country	France	Argentina	Nepal	U.S.
Mountain Range	the Alps	the Andes	the Himalayas	the Rocky Mountains
Highest Mountain	Mt. Blanc	Mt. Aconcagua	Mt. Everest	Mt. Elbert
Altitude	4,807 m. 15,771 ft.	6,960 m. 22,028 ft.	8,848 m. 29,028 ft.	4,399 m. 14,433 ft.

Activity Book
p. 112

Earthquake

an excerpt from a memoir
by Huynh Quang Nhuong

Objectives

Reading Draw conclusions and give
support as you read a memoir.

Listening and Speaking Discuss
emergencies.

Grammar Identify pronoun referents.

Writing Write a memoir.

Content Social Studies: Read a map.

Use Prior Knowledge

Brainstorm Qualities of Natural Disasters

You are going to read a selection about
an earthquake. An earthquake is a natural
disaster. A disaster is an event that causes a
lot of damage. A natural disaster happens
by nature. It is not caused by people.

1. Look at this list of natural disasters.

2. Choose at least two of the natural
disasters that you know about.

3. On a piece of paper, complete a
cluster map like the one here. Add
more ovals if necessary.

4. Share your ideas with the class.

Natural Disasters
earthquake
hurricane
flood
snowstorm
tornado

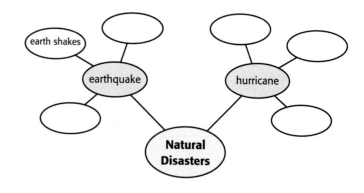

Build Background

Vietnam

Vietnam is a country in Southeast Asia. About 70 percent of the people in Vietnam are farmers. Most Vietnamese farmers grow rice as their main crop. In 1954, Vietnam was divided into two countries: North Vietnam and South Vietnam. The two countries went to war. The war ended in 1975, and Vietnam became one country again.

Content Connection

About 70 million people live in Vietnam.

Build Vocabulary

Use the Dictionary

In "Earthquake," some animals are frightened because they sense that an earthquake is coming. Find out how they acted.

1. Look up the underlined words below in a dictionary. Write the words and their definitions in your Personal Dictionary.
   a. bellow
   b. jump frantically in a net
   c. whine

2. Match the parts of the sentences to describe what each animal did.

The buffalo (a large animal like a cow)	jumped frantically as if caught in a net.
The fish	bellowed fearfully.
The dog	whined.

Personal Dictionary

The Heinle Newbury House Dictionary

Activity Book p. 113

Student CD-ROM

Text Structure

Memoir

The reading selection is a **memoir.** A memoir tells about people and events that the writer remembers. Look at the chart. It shows the features of a memoir.

Memoir	
Personal Pronouns	*I, me, we,* or *us*
Interesting Facts and Memories	people and events
Structure	a beginning, a middle, and an end
Feelings	the writer's feelings and perspectives about the events and people in the memoir
Setting	usually a long time ago

Student
CD-ROM

Reading Strategy

Draw Conclusions and Give Support

When you **draw a conclusion,** you make a true statement based on the information in the reading or from your own experience.

When you **give support,** you provide details and examples that explain your conclusion.

1. Read paragraph 1 of "Earthquake."

2. You can draw the conclusion that the animals and the people in the story lived closely together. You can support this because the animals "often warned" the people about danger. They had done this before.

3. As you read "Earthquake," continue to draw conclusions. Give support for your conclusions.

Student
CD-ROM

Earthquake

an excerpt from a memoir
by Huynh Quang Nhuong

Audio

1   **Domestic** animals living very close to the jungle often **preserve** their natural **instincts.** Most of the time our animals felt rather than saw danger and often warned us of the presence of enemies.

2   One afternoon we were not out in the field working because of the Lunar New Year holiday. The sky above our **hamlet** was clear, but the **atmosphere** became very heavy. Tank and our other buffaloes remained in the shed, eating. Suddenly they stamped their feet very hard and bellowed fearfully. We looked around and saw chickens and ducks run into bamboo bushes to hide, and in the ponds, fish of all sizes jumped frantically as if they were caught in a net. Our watchdog crawled under a bed and whined.

---

domestic   kept in the house or for the family's use

preserve   keep, still have

instincts   ways of acting that an animal or person can do without learning or thinking about

hamlet   a small village

atmosphere   the air

Draw Conclusions and Give Support

What conclusion can you draw about the animals? Give support for your conclusion.

Draw Conclusions and Give Support

What is Tank's role in the herd of buffalo? What support is there for this conclusion?

3   We quickly opened the door of the shed and let Tank and the other buffaloes out. At first Tank led his small herd to the garden; then he changed his mind and moved them to the banana grove behind the house. We then ran to the **bomb shelter,** and the watchdog followed us. About three minutes later a powerful earthquake shook the whole area.

4   The **deafening** noise made by trees falling, rocks crashing down the mountains, and houses **collapsing** was terrifying. When it was over and we **emerged** from our shelter, we saw that both the house and the shed were **demolished.** Most of the fruit trees in the garden were either broken or **uprooted** by fallen boulders. We realized that if Tank and the other buffaloes had stayed in the

---

bomb shelter a building or an underground cave made to keep people safe during a bomb explosion

deafening loud enough to make you deaf or hurt your hearing

collapsing falling down

emerged came out of

demolished destroyed, broken

uprooted torn out of the ground with the roots

garden, they could easily have been killed, because five of our eight huge mango trees had been knocked down. All the houses on the southern side of the hamlet were gone, but nobody got hurt. The **casualties** were limited to a few cattle that had been crushed by falling rocks.

5   That evening we cleared part of the garden of broken branches to make a place for our family and cattle to spend the night. It was **relatively** safe for us and for them to be in the garden, because a thick **hedge** surrounded it. Earthquakes like this one had struck our village before. But after those disasters, people had not built shelters for themselves or their domestic animals. Then wild beasts, attracted by the smell of **unburied** dead animals, had come to the hamlet and caused much damage.

---

casualties   injuries
relatively   fairly, mostly

hedge   a tall border of thick plants
unburied   not yet put under the ground

Draw Conclusions and Give Support

Is the family comfortable in the garden? What conclusion can you draw? What support can you give?

6   While my father and my cousin **barricaded** the entrance of the garden with broken branches, my mother and I built a **bonfire.** The fire would help keep **predators** away and at the same time keep us warm—all our blankets were buried under heavy **debris.** There wasn't much space in the garden. We were **hemmed in** by enormous fallen trees, three water buffaloes, five goats, and a watchdog. There would also have been several hogs, but they determinedly made holes in the hedge and went back to their **half-demolished** sty.

---

barricaded covered, closed up
bonfire a large fire
predators animals that eat other animals or people

debris remains of something broken
hemmed in surrounded by
half-demolished partly destroyed

Draw Conclusions and Give Support

Why does the author enjoy sleeping outdoors? Give support from what you know about young people.

7   This was the first time I had slept in the open air, and despite **circumstances,** I thoroughly enjoyed it. Tank and the other **domestic** animals, unlike wild **beasts,** liked the fire very much. They lay down as close as possible to it and stayed awake, while we people tried to sleep to escape the terrible day. But worry kept us **wakeful,** so my father, my mother, and my cousin sat up near the fire and talked about what they would do in the next few days. While they discussed how to build a new house and where to get the money to **finance** their project, I stayed with Tank.

---

circumstances the situation
domestic related to home life
beasts animals

wakeful unable to sleep
finance pay for

8   I leaned against Tank's shoulder and gazed into the sky to count the number of giant fruit bats passing by. The warmth of his shoulder, the **regularity** of his breathing, the beat of his heart, and the **enormity** of his body made me feel safe and comfortable. The lonely call of **nocturnal** birds, the occasional roaring of tigers in the nearby jungle—these belonged to the **insecure** and **unpredictable** dark world outside our garden. Little by little I drifted into a gentle sleep.

---

regularity   evenness, in a regular pattern
enormity   very large size
nocturnal   awake and active at night; sleeping in the day

insecure   unsafe
unpredictable   unsure, impossible to know what to expect

About the Author   Huynh Quang Nhuong (born 1946)

Huynh Quang Nhuong writes about his boyhood in Mytho, Vietnam, in his book *The Land I Lost.* He tells about the place where he grew up. Mr. Huynh served in the South Vietnamese army. After the war, he came to the United States and became a citizen. He now lives in Missouri. Mr. Huynh wants his books to please people in both of his homelands: Vietnam and the United States. He says, "I am the first Vietnamese to write fiction and nonfiction in English. I hope my books will make people from different countries happy . . . Good literature unites people."

➤What challenges do you think the author faced in writing *The Land I Lost?*

Beyond the Reading

Reading Comprehension

Question-Answer Relationships (QAR)

"Right There" Questions

1. **Recall Facts** Where are the animals during the earthquake?
2. **Recall Facts** Where does the family spend the night after the earthquake?

"Think and Search" Questions

3. **Recognize Sequence of Events** What happens before the earthquake?
4. **Make Inferences** Why does Tank take the buffaloes to the garden and then to the banana grove?
5. **Compare and Contrast** How is the southern side of the hamlet different after the earthquake?
6. **Paraphrase Text** How would you tell someone what the selection is about in your own words?

"Author and You" Questions

7. **Make Connections** Why does the author's family want to rebuild their home?
8. **Analyze Cause and Effect** Why do you think Tank's presence makes the author feel better?

"On Your Own" Questions

9. **Predict** What do you think the author's family will do now?
10. **Understand Characters' Experiences** How would you feel sleeping next to a buffalo?

Activity Book
p. 114

Build Reading Fluency

Rapid Word Recognition

It helps to practice reading words with silent letters. Rapidly recognizing these words will help increase your reading speed.

1. With a partner, review the words in the box.
2. Next, read the words aloud for one minute. Your teacher or partner can time you.

often	heavy	were	one	were
rather	one	heavy	were	one
one	sky	rather	often	sky
were	were	each	rather	often
sky	rather	heavy	sky	heavy

3. How many words did you read in one minute? Was it more than on page 98?

Listen, Speak, Interact

Discuss Emergencies

"Earthquake" describes an emergency that Huynh Quang Nhuong and his family faced. An emergency is a bad or dangerous situation that requires immediate attention.

1. What kinds of emergencies do you know about?
2. With a partner, choose one kind of emergency, for example, a car accident, a fire in a house, or a person getting sick suddenly.

3. Create a list of steps to take in this kind of emergency. Practice reading your list aloud to your partner. Speak clearly and with an informative, or helpful, tone to describe each step. Share your list with the rest of the class.

In Case of Fire
Step 1: *Get out of the building.*
Step 2: _____
Step 3: _____
Step 4: _____

Elements of Literature

Recognize Foreshadowing

Foreshadowing gives clues about what is going to happen in a narrative. In "Earthquake" Huynh Quang Nhuong uses foreshadowing to show that something bad is going to happen. For example, in the sentence "Our watchdog crawled under a bed and whined," the dog's behavior is foreshadowing.

1. Find two more examples of foreshadowing in paragraph 2. Hint: Look for foreshadowing in the descriptions of the weather and the behavior of the animals.
2. Write the examples in your Reading Log.

Reading Log

Activity Book
p. 115

Student
CD-ROM

Word Study

Form Compound Words

Compound words are formed by combining two words into one larger word. For example, the word *earthquake* is made of two words: *earth + quake*.

You can sometimes learn the meaning of a compound word by looking at the meanings of the smaller words. Look at the chart.

Word	Word	Compound Word
earth: the planet we live on	quake: to shake	earthquake: a shaking of the earth

1. Use the chart to figure out the meaning of *uprooted*.
2. Find another example of a compound word in paragraph 2 of the reading. Can you guess its meaning? Look it up in a dictionary to check your guess.
3. What other compound words do you know? Match up the words to make compound words.

snow   work
home   book
text   storm

The Heinle Newbury House Dictionary

Activity Book
p. 116

Student CD-ROM

Grammar Focus

Identify Pronoun Referents

Pronouns stand for nouns.

My father, my mother, and my cousin sat near the fire and talked about what <u>they</u> would do.

In the sentence above, *they* stands for the nouns *my father, my mother, and my cousin.* We can also say that *my father, my mother, and my cousin* is the **referent** for *they.*

Read each sentence and find the referent for each underlined pronoun.

1. Fish of all sizes jumped frantically as if <u>they</u> were caught in a net.
2. Tank led his herd to the garden; then <u>he</u> changed his mind.
3. If Tank and the other buffaloes had stayed in the garden, <u>they</u> could easily have been killed.

Activity Book
pp. 117–118

Student Handbook

Student CD-ROM

From Reading to Writing

Write a Memoir

Write a three-paragraph memoir that describes an event from your past.

1. In the first paragraph, tell about an event and why it is interesting to your audience.
2. In the second paragraph, give details that make this event interesting.
3. In the third paragraph, tell your audience about your thoughts and feelings about the event.

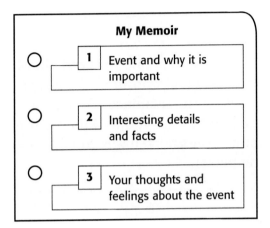

Activity Book
p. 119

Across Content Areas

Read a Map

There are many earthquakes in a part of the world called the Ring of Fire. Look at the map of the Ring of Fire and answer the questions below.

1. The blue area in the middle of the map is an ocean. Which ocean is it?
2. Which continents do you see to the east?
3. Which continents do you see to the west?
4. Which continents does the Ring of Fire touch?

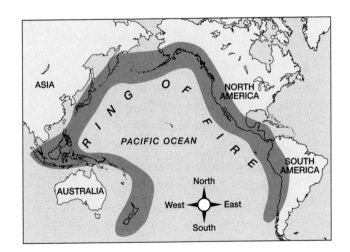

Activity Book
p. 120

Listening and Speaking Workshop

Present a Biographical Narrative

> **Topic**
>
> Choose someone you read about or know about who showed courage. Focus on the sequence of events in the person's life and how the person found courage. Tell why you admire the person.

Step 1: Use a timeline to get organized.

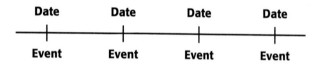

Step 2: Be specific and present facts.

Answer the following questions to present the major ideas of your narrative.

1. *Who* shows courage?
2. *What* challenge or problem does this person face? (Describe specific actions and feelings of the character.)
3. *Where* do the main events take place? (Describe the setting.)
4. *When* do the sequence of events in this person's life take place? (Use dates and times.)

Step 3: Use an attention-grabbing opening.

Use one of these suggestions for your opening:

1. Ask a question.
2. Say something funny.
3. Make a dramatic statement.
4. Refer to an authority and use quotations.

Step 4: Prepare some visuals to add interest.

1. Use a timeline on a poster, a picture from the Internet, or a drawing of your own to show information you found. Help your listeners interpret the visuals.
2. If possible, use a computer presentation to help you sequence the events.

Step 5: Practice your biographical narrative.

1. After you have one idea for an opening, put each group of additional ideas on a note card.
2. Practice with a partner.
3. Answer the questions on the Active Listening and Speaking Checklists.
4. Revise your report based on feedback.
5. Practice your talk to include stops or pauses to show visuals.

Active Listening Checklist

1. I liked ____ because ____ .

2. I want to know more about ____ .

3. You stayed on the topic. Yes / No

4. I understood the major ideas of your narrative. Yes / No

5. Your nonverbal messages helped me to understand ____ .

Speaking Checklist

1. Did I speak too slowly, too quickly, or just right?

2. Did I speak loudly enough?

3. Was my voice too high, too low, or just right?

4. Did I use visuals to make the speech interesting?

5. Did I look at the audience?

Step 6: Present.

Use nonverbal messages such as gestures and body language. This will help listeners understand your presentation. Speak slowly and clearly. Smile!

Viewing Workshop

Compare and Contrast Visual and Electronic Media with Written Stories

Compare Points of View

View a video, a television, or an Internet biography about someone you read about in this unit.

1. What information did you learn about the subject of the biography? Where was the person born? What was the challenge? How was the person courageous?

2. Compare and contrast the video, television, or Internet version with the reading selection in this unit. Were the attitudes toward the person the same or different in the two presentations?

3. Evaluate which presentation gives you the most information about the subject of the biography. Explain your ideas.

4. Find out two new facts about the person.

Further Viewing

Watch the *Visions* CNN Video for Unit 3. Do the Video Worksheet.

CNN Video

Writer's Workshop

Response to Literature

Writing Prompt

Decide what *you* think courage means. Write a definition of courage in response to the selections that you have read and the material that you have viewed.

Step 1: Research.

1. Create a list of questions about courage.
2. Gather information from books that you have read or from TV shows and movies that you have viewed. Discuss with family and friends their experiences with courage. Write your ideas on note cards.
3. Evaluate your research to check if you found answers to your questions. Frame new questions you would like to research answers to.

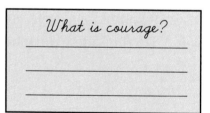

What is courage?

What is courage?

Step 2: Write a draft.

1. Review your ideas and plan the order of your definition.
2. Use the Definition Checklist below to help you.

> ✓ **Definition Checklist**
>
> 1. Include an introduction that states your definition of courage.
>
> 2. Write at least three main paragraphs that include a supporting idea about courage.
>
> 3. Give two or three details such as facts or examples to support the main idea in each paragraph.
>
> 4. End with a conclusion that summarizes your thoughts on courage.

3. Use superlative adjectives to make comparisons. For example, compare the courage of people you know about.
4. Write a list of sources (places where you gathered information). For example, write the titles of books, TV shows, and movies you used.
5. Use the correct format for citing your sources. See your Student Handbook.

Step 3: Revise your work.

1. Use a resource such as the Editing Checklist in your Student Handbook to check your work.
2. Refer to reference sources you used for research to help you clarify ideas and revise text. Also ask your teacher to help you clarify and revise your work.
3. Reread your draft and ask yourself these questions:
   a. Is my definition of courage clear?
   b. Do my transitions lead readers from one paragraph to the next?
   c. Is my main point convincing?
4. Collaborate with a partner. Read each other's work. Note on a piece of paper any strong and weak points in your partner's draft. Give your partner ideas about how to revise and organize the definition.
5. Give the notes to your partner. Use the Peer Editing Checklist in your Student Handbook. Discuss the strong and weak points in each of your papers. Make any changes you feel are necessary.

Step 4: Edit and proofread.

1. Proofread your revised definition. Make sure you have used correct punctuation, spelling, and grammar.
2. Use the Editor's Checklist in your Student Handbook.
3. If possible, use a computer to write your paper. Use software such as an online dictionary or thesaurus to check your work.

4. Ask your teacher to help you edit your work for correct punctuation, spelling, and grammar. Use the spelling and grammar checks on your computer.

Step 5: Publish.

Make an anthology, or collection, of the class's work. Follow these steps:

1. Collect everyone's work. Write a table of contents listing each paper's title, author, and page number.
2. Title the collection *Visions of Courage.* Design an illustrated cover with your class drawings or photos that show courage.
3. Analyze your classmates' published work as models for writing. Review them for their strengths and weaknesses.
4. What strategies did you and your classmates use to write? How did you and your classmates express ideas?
5. Set goals as a writer based on your writing and the writing of your classmates.

The Heinle Newbury House Dictionary

Student Handbook

Projects

These projects will help you develop your ideas about courage. Work alone, with a partner, or with a group of classmates. If you need help, ask a teacher, a parent, or your librarian.

Project 1: Give a Speech

What are some reasons why people today need to have courage? Choose a topic, such as saying "No" to smoking, and prepare a speech to your class about why people would need courage to face this situation. Write five questions about the topic and courage.

1. Gather information.
   a. Talk to the school librarian and five other adults. Ask each of them the five questions.
   b. Visit some Internet news sites. Read articles on the topic you have chosen.
2. Write a speech about what you learn. Make visuals to help your listeners understand your points. Refer to Chapter 4 and use George W. Bush's speech as a model.
3. Check your written speech for word choice and tone. Does your speech explain why we need courage?
4. Give your speech to the class. If possible, make an audio or a video recording of it so that you can share your speech with your family.

Project 2: Design a Web Page or an Art Exhibit

Think about what you have learned about courage in this unit. Use that information to make a Web page, an art exhibit, or a technology presentation.

1. Find pictures that show courage. Use the Internet or look in art books from the school library.
2. Gather speeches that people have made about courage. Look in books of collected speeches. Use tables of contents and headings to find speeches about courage.
3. Find short quotes about courage. Look in books or CD-ROMs that include quotes (such as *Bartlett's Familiar Quotations*). Use the keyword *courage* to search the index.
4. For a Web page or technology presentation, design the quotes you found in special type.
5. For an art exhibit, write the speech or quotation text on a poster board. Label each image and include where you found it. You may also record the text on audio. Play the audio as viewers look at the images.
6. Share your presentation with the class or other classes in your school.
7. Compare and contrast your work with the reading selections. How does your presentation show courage in a similar or different way to the selection?

Further Reading

The books below tell how people have shown courage in their lives. Read one or more of them. In your Reading Log, record how courage was displayed in the books you read. Write your thoughts and feelings about what you read. Answer these questions:

1. How do the characters show courage?
2. Do the characters show similar or different types of courage?

The Diary of Anne Frank: The Definitive Edition
by Anne Frank, Bantam Books, Inc., 1997. Anne describes her life in hiding during World War II. This newly published edition includes 30 percent more material than the original.

Lance Armstrong
by Kimberly Garcia, Mitchell Lane Publishers, Inc., 2002. Being the four-time champion of the *Tour de France* is only one of Lance Armstrong's accomplishments. In this biography, Garcia describes Armstrong's battle against cancer.

Out of the Dust
by Karen Hesse, Scholastic Inc., 1999. Fifteen-year-old Billie Jo lives on a wheat farm in Oklahoma during the Great Depression. She struggles to rebuild her relationship with her father after an accident kills her mother. Billie Jo finds the courage to repair her life in this unique story told completely in free-verse poetry.

A Single Shard
by Linda Sue Park, Clarion Books, 2002. This book takes place in twelfth-century Korea. In a journey against great odds, Tree-Ear, an orphan boy, pursues his dream of becoming a potter. He learns how courage helps achieve a goal.

The Unknown Shore: The Lost History of England's Arctic Colony
by Robert Ruby, Henry Holt & Co., Inc., 2001. England first attempted to settle the New World on an island off the coast of the Canadian Arctic known as Meta Incognita ("Unknown Shore"). This book tells the story.

Charlotte's Web
by E. B. White, HarperTrophy, 1999. In this classic barnyard book, small but valiant Charlotte uses courage and her sharp wit to save Wilbur from being killed.

Miracle's Boys
by Jacqueline Woodson, Penguin Putnam, 2000. Tyree, Charlie, and Lafayette are three orphaned brothers raising themselves after their father drowns and their mother dies of diabetes.

Reading Log

Heinle Reading Library

UNIT 4

Discoveries

Louis Pasteur experimenting for the cure of hydrophobia in his laboratory,
Adrien Emmanuel Marie, print. 1885.

View the Picture

1. What could the person in this picture be discovering?
2. What are some discoveries you have made?

In this unit, you will read a story, a poem, a nonfiction narrative, a tale, and a biography that center on people and their discoveries. You will share their excitement. You will learn about the features of these writing forms and how to write them yourself.

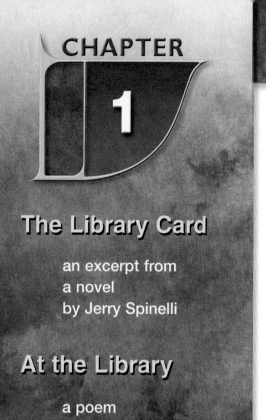

CHAPTER 1

The Library Card

an excerpt from
a novel
by Jerry Spinelli

At the Library

a poem
by Nikki Grimes

Objectives

Reading Compare and contrast as you read an excerpt from a novel and a poem.

Listening and Speaking Take notes, organize, and summarize.

Grammar Identify sentences with relative clauses.

Writing Write a story.

Content Language Arts: Use the library.

Use Prior Knowledge

Explore Sources of Information

Where do you go when you need answers to questions? How do you know which source to use for certain questions?

1. Make a chart like the one shown. List the kinds of information you can find from each source.
2. Talk as a group about what information you can find in each of these sources.
3. Is there a library in your school or community? Have you been there? Tell your class about it.

Library	
Internet	
Teacher/Expert	

Build Background

Public Libraries

Hundreds of years ago, books were rare and expensive. Only wealthy people owned books and had libraries. Today, almost every town or city in the United States has at least one public library. If you live in the town, you can get a library card. With a library card, you can borrow books, videos, and other materials for free.

A Library Card

Content Connection

Librarians are people who work in libraries. They help you find the book or information that you are looking for.

Build Vocabulary

Use Repetition to Find Meaning

Writers often say something and then mention it again using different words. You can use this repetition to learn words.

1. Copy the following sentences in your Personal Dictionary.
   a. The bug was called <u>cicada</u>, also seventeen-year locust.
   b. The whole idea made him <u>tingly</u>. He looked at his arm. He had goosebumps.
   c. The ceiling was spinning, he was <u>woozy</u>.

2. Circle the part of the sentence that repeats the meaning of the underlined word.

3. Look up any words that you do not know in a dictionary. Write the words and their definitions in your Personal Dictionary.

Personal Dictionary

The Heinle Newbury House Dictionary

Activity Book p. 121

Student CD-ROM

Text Structure

Fiction and Poem

"The Library Card" is a work of **fiction.** It tells a made-up story about made-up people.

Look for these elements of fiction as you read "The Library Card."

Fiction	
Characters	the people in the story
Plot	the events that happen in the story
Sequence of Events	the order of the events; there is a beginning, a middle, and an end

"At the Library" is a **poem.**

Poem	
Rhyme	the last words of some lines have the same ending sound
Vivid Language	expressive nouns, verbs, and adjectives help the reader form images
Repetition	sentence structures are repeated

Look at these elements of a poem as you read "At the Library."

Student
CD-ROM

Reading Strategy

Compare and Contrast

To **compare** is to see how two or more things are the same. To **contrast** is to see how they are different. For example, think about a public library and a school library.

Compare: Both libraries have books.
Contrast: The public library is for everyone. The school library is only for the students at the school.

1. As you read "The Library Card," look for things to compare and contrast in the selection. Look at the descriptions of different animals and insects that the main character reads about. How are they the same or different?

2. As you read "At the Library," look for things to compare and contrast with "The Library Card." For example, "Who is the main character? How does the character feel about books?"

3. Write your ideas in your Reading Log.

Reading Log

Student
CD-ROM

THE LIBRARY CARD

an excerpt from a novel
by Jerry Spinelli

AT THE LIBRARY

a poem
by Nikki Grimes

Audio

The Library Card
an excerpt from a novel by Jerry Spinelli

Prologue

In this excerpt you will read about a boy named Mongoose. He is a street-smart teenager who lives in New York City. One day he finds the shell of a bug called a locust. He also finds a mysterious blue library card. Mongoose goes to the library that same day to find out more about the strange insect.

> **Compare and Contrast**
>
> How is the card in the boy's hand the same as or different from the way he remembers it being?

1   He had passed the library so many times in his life, hundreds, but he had never gone inside. He was not even sure it was for kids.

2   He pulled the blue card from his pocket. He had put it there after picking it up from the floor that morning. For the first time he took a good look at it. One side was blank. The other side was . . . blank too! He kept turning it over and over. He could have sworn it said LIBRARY CARD when he had looked at it on the roof.

3   It was just a blue, blank scrap.

4   And yet still, somehow, he knew it was a library card.

5   Problem was, he wasn't sure how it worked. He thought maybe it was like a ticket, giving the holder **admittance,** as to a basketball game. Finding no ticket-taker at the door, he entered, walked up three steps, turned a corner, and found himself facing a counter with a lady behind it.

6   When the lady looked up and saw him coming, she smiled as if she knew him. Was he supposed to know her? He walked up to the counter and showed her the card. He felt silly showing a blank card. "You collecting tickets?" he said.

---

admittance   the right to enter

Compare and Contrast

How is using a library card the same as or different from using a ticket to get into a basketball game?

7   She took the card. She looked at it, then into his eyes. The silly feeling **vanished.** "No," she said, "this is not to let you in. It's to let a book out." She reached across the counter and slid the card into his coat pocket. "Now, how may I help you?"

8   Mongoose told the lady about the big bug.* She nodded and went away for a minute. She returned with a book.

9   "You'll find what you need in here," she said. She handed him the book. She smiled. "Good reading."

10   As he left the library, he stuck the book under his coat and in his **waistband.** He sprinted home.

11   Only behind the closed door of his room did he take out the book. It was called the *I Wonder.* He found what he wanted on page twenty-three. The bug was called cicada, also seventeen-year locust. Mongoose read on. He learned that this cicada bug comes down from the tree as a baby worm and buries itself in the ground for seventeen years. And when it comes out—**presto!** It's a big bug that sheds its skin—eyes and all—and that's what Mongoose had found.

12   Amazing.

13   Imagine being in the dark—underground—for seventeen *years.*

14   And when you come out you're different than when you went in.

* The shell of a strange insect Mongoose found that day.

---

vanished disappeared

waistband   the part of a skirt or pair of pants that fits
    around the waist

presto   quickly, suddenly

15   And then you crawl out of your own skin!

16   The whole idea **boggled** him, made him tingly. He looked at his arm. He had goosebumps.

17   The chair he sat in no longer felt safe. He moved to the floor, his back against the wall. He started paging back to the start of the book—he knew books should be read from beginning to end—but he kept getting **ambushed.** Pictures and words and numbers drew his eyeballs to them like flies to flypaper.

18   He read about a bird that stays in the air for up to four years.

19   And a bird, called the tickbird, that **hitches** a ride on the back of a rhino.

20   And an insect—none other than the common old cockroach—that can walk around for two weeks with its head cut off.

21   And a fish that climbs trees.

22   And another bird that fights its enemies by vomiting on them.

Compare and Contrast

How are Mongoose's feelings different from his feelings at the beginning of the story?

---

boggled amazed, confused

ambushed attacked from a hidden position; in the reading *ambushed* is used to mean *distracted*

hitches hitchhikes, or asks for a ride

23　　And an eel that's electric, that can turn on a lightbulb.

24　　And the mole rat. The book called it the world's ugliest animal, and it was right. He had to spend an hour on the picture of the mole rat alone.

25　　And a worm that can stretch itself up to ninety feet.

26　　Mongoose slid full-body to the floor. The ceiling was spinning, he was woozy.

27　　His mother came in. She frowned down at him. "How long have you been in here?"

28　　"Don't know," said Mongoose truthfully.

29　　"You know you missed dinner four hours ago? You know it's nine o'clock?"

30　　"You know there's a fish that climbs trees?"

31　　Mrs. Hill looked down at her son, on his back on the floor, eyes closed, a look on his face she could not recall ever seeing before. And a book in his hand. About tree-climbing fish she knew nothing, but she did know that if there were such a thing, it surely was not as rare as the sight of her youngest son holding a book. And missing a meal.

Compare and Contrast

How are Mrs. Hill's feelings about Mongoose the same as or different from her feelings about him before she came into the room?

About the Author

Jerry Spinelli (born 1941)

Jerry Spinelli has been writing since he was a teenager. He has written many novels that use his own experiences as a child growing up. Spinelli's books often look at the difficult choices young adults have to make. Spinelli says, "Don't tell my English teachers, but not much planning goes into my novels. . . . There's no outline telling me how to get from here to there, because I have found that there is no way to know what is inside the story until I am in there myself."

► What strategies does the author use to compose his novels?

Audio

At the Library
a poem by Nikki Grimes

Compare and Contrast

How are the speaker's reading experiences similar to or different from Mongoose's in "The Library Card"?

I flip the pages of a book and slip inside,
where **crystal** seas await and **pirates** hide.
I find a **paradise** where birds can talk,
where children fly and trees prefer to walk.
Sometimes I end up on a city street.
I recognize the brownskin girl I meet.
She's skinny, but she's strong, and brave, and **wise**.
I smile because I see *me* in her eyes.

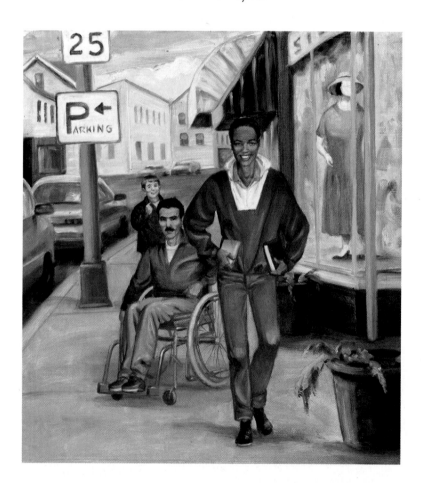

---

crystal   clear and sparkling
pirates   people who steal ships and planes and the cargo they carry

paradise   a perfect place where everything is just the way you want it to be
wise   having good judgment

About the Author

Nikki Grimes (born 1950)

Nikki Grimes moved around a lot as a child. Her family faced difficult times. During this challenging period, she always discovered a friend in books. But Grimes felt unhappy that very few books contained girls like herself—African-American girls from families with problems. She decided to write some herself. Grimes said, "'When I grow up,' I thought, 'I'll write books about children who look and feel like me.'"

➤ Do you think that Nikki Grimes is the girl in the poem?
What challenges did Nikki Grimes face to become a writer?

Beyond the Reading

Reading Comprehension

Question-Answer Relationships (QAR)

"Right There" Questions

1. **Recall Facts** Has Mongoose ever been inside the library before?
2. **Recall Facts** What does the librarian do?
3. **Recall Facts** What kind of book does Mongoose check out?

"Think and Search" Questions

4. **Make Inferences** What information does Mongoose most want to get from the library book?
5. **Connect** Why does Mongoose not understand how a library card works?
6. **Compare and Contrast** In what ways are the two reading selections in this chapter the same and different?

"Author and You" Questions

7. **Make Inferences** Why does Mongoose's silly feeling vanish when the librarian looks into his eyes?
8. **Understand Figurative Language** Why does Mongoose feel "ambushed" by the information in the book?
9. **Evaluate** In "At the Library," why do you think the speaker smiles about seeing a young girl who seems like her?

"On Your Own" Question

10. **Compare Your Experiences** Mongoose did not know how to behave in a library. Have you ever been in a similar situation? Describe it.

Activity Book
p. 122

Student
CD-ROM

Build Reading Fluency

Reading Chunks of Words Silently

Reading silently is good practice. It helps you to learn to read faster.

1. Listen to the audio recording of paragraphs 1–2 of "The Library Card."
2. Listen to the chunks of words.
3. Silently reread paragraphs 1–2 two times.
4. Your teacher or a partner will time your second reading.
5. Raise your hand when you are finished.

Listen, Speak, Interact

Take Notes, Organize, and Summarize

Both selections in this chapter are about the joy of reading.

1. Choose something that you really enjoyed reading. Tell your partner about it. What was it about? Why did you like it?
2. As your partner speaks, listen carefully to gain information. Take notes.
3. Organize your notes in outline form.
4. Write a summary of your partner's talk.

> **Outline**
>
> Book: "Strange Animals"
>
> I. *What it was about:*
> a. Frogs
> B. Worms that can stretch
> II. *Why she liked it:*
> a. She likes science.
> B. It had great pictures.
> C. She learned a lot.

Elements of Literature

Recognize a Writing Style

Writers use **style** (the way they use language) to express themselves.

1. Look at paragraphs 19–25 of "The Library Card." Notice that the writer begins several sentences with the word *and.* Each *and* that the writer uses suggests "And there's more!" This lets us know that Mongoose feels amazed and excited.
2. Skim the reading (read quickly) to find another place in the selection where the author does the same thing.
3. With a partner, read paragraphs 19–25. Use an excited tone of voice to match the writer's style.
4. Make a section in your Reading Log called "Uses of style to show emotion." Write some of the *and* sentences from paragraphs 19–25 in your log. As you discover other similar uses of style write them in this section of your Reading Log.

Reading Log   Activity Book *p. 123*

Student CD-ROM

Word Study

Understand Historical Influences on English Words

English often has two words for the same idea. One word is often scientific or formal and is often from Latin. The other is usually informal and is from Old English.

1. Read each of these sentences from "The Library Card." Look at the underlined word. The word after the sentence means the same thing.
   a. Mongoose told the lady about the big <u>bug</u>. (insect)
   b. The bug was called <u>cicada</u>. (seventeen-year locust)
   c. And another bird that fights its enemies by <u>vomiting</u> on them. (throwing up)
2. Copy the chart in your Personal Dictionary.

3. Use the dictionary to locate the origin of the words in the first column. Find the Latin root for each word. Write it next to the English word.

From Latin	From Old English
insect	bug
vomit	throw up
employer	boss
autumn	fall (the season)

Personal Dictionary

The Heinle Newbury House Dictionary

Activity Book p. 124

Student CD-ROM

Grammar Focus

Identify Sentences with Relative Clauses

A **clause** is a group of words that has a subject and a verb. In a complex sentence, there is more than one clause. One of the clauses can be a **relative clause.**

A relative clause is introduced by a relative pronoun such as *that*. This kind of clause describes something in the main clause. Relative clauses are *not* complete sentences.

He read about a **bird** that stays in the air
for up to four years.

1. Look in paragraphs 18–23 on pages 230–231 for relative clauses starting with *that*.
2. Identify the relative clause and tell which word it describes.
3. Write your own sentence containing a relative clause beginning with *that*.

Activity Book pp. 125–126

Student Handbook

Student CD-ROM

236 **Unit 4** Discoveries

From Reading to Writing

Write a Story

Write a story to show what reading can mean to a person.

1. Make sure your story has a beginning, a middle, and an end.
2. Base your story on one main character. This can be a made-up person.

3. In the story, tell how the person feels about reading. Use the character's actions and words to help you show this. Use your writing style to show the character's feelings.
4. Include relative clauses with *that* to describe.

Activity Book
p. 127

Across Content Areas

Use the Library

Most libraries have a computerized **catalogue,** which is a list of all the books in a library. You type in a search word, for example, *insects.* All the books that are about that word come up in a list.

This information tells you where to find the book. If you need help, ask a librarian. Librarians are there to help you.

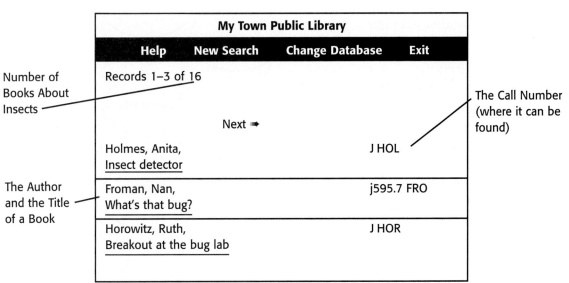

Number of Books About Insects

The Call Number (where it can be found)

The Author and the Title of a Book

Activity Book
p. 128

Into the Reading

Discovering the Inca Ice Maiden

a nonfiction narrative
by Johan Reinhard

Objectives

Reading Use graphic sources of information as you read a nonfiction narrative.

Listening and Speaking Describe personal accomplishments.

Grammar Identify *be* + adjective + infinitive.

Writing Write a first-person nonfiction narrative.

Content Social Studies: Understand the atmosphere and altitude.

Use Prior Knowledge

Share Knowledge About Mountains

What do you know about mountains?

1. With a partner, discuss what you know about mountains. Use the following questions as a guide:
   a. What is a mountain?
   b. Look at a map. Name some mountains in the United States or in another country.
   c. Why do people climb mountains?
2. Copy the web on a piece of paper. Add words that describe mountains.

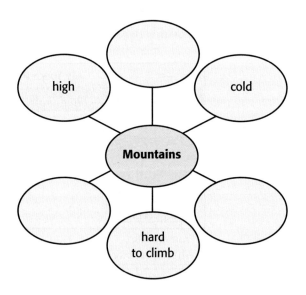

high

cold

Mountains

hard to climb

Build Background

Inca Culture

The Inca people lived in the Andes Mountains in South America. They formed the Inca empire. An empire is a group of nations ruled by an emperor, or leader. The Inca empire grew strong until the Spanish took control in 1532. The Incas were known for their beautiful arts and crafts as well as buildings and temples. Today, we still find items left behind by the Incas, such as jewelry, clothing, and pottery.

Content Connection

Anthropologists are scientists who study people and their culture.

Build Vocabulary

Understand Key Words and Related Words

Key words are the most important words in a narrative. **Related words** are words or phrases that are connected to the key words.

1. Copy the chart in your Personal Dictionary.
2. As you read "Discovering the Inca Ice Maiden," write additional related words that are associated with the key words in the chart.

Key Words	Related Words
volcano	erupting
mountain	summit
mountain climbing	ice ax

Personal Dictionary

Activity Book
p. 129

Student CD-ROM

Text Structure

Nonfiction Narrative

"Discovering the Inca Ice Maiden" is a **nonfiction narrative.** It describes real events as they happened. Look for the elements in the chart in a nonfiction narrative.

As you read this nonfiction narrative, look for the facts the author provides.

Nonfiction Narrative
Facts answer the following questions:
• Who?   • Where? • What?   • Why? • When?   • How?

Student
CD-ROM

Reading Strategy

Use Graphic Sources of Information

In this selection, there are several **graphic sources of information.** There are illustrations, a map, and a timeline. Graphic sources of information can help you understand a reading. They can also give information that is *not* in the reading.

1. Look at the illustration on page 241. What does it tell you about the story? Where does it take place? Can you guess what the story is about?

2. As you read the selection, use the graphics as a source of information. Use them to locate and learn information.

Student
CD-ROM

Discovering the Inca Ice Maiden

a nonfiction narrative
by Johan Reinhard

1   *Sabancaya became increasingly active during 1990, **erupting** about half a dozen times a day—every day of the year. The erupting volcano **spewed** clouds of dark ash up into the sky. Wind carried the ash over Sabancaya's higher neighbor, the volcano Ampato, which is inactive. Eventually Ampato's snow-capped summit was covered with dark ash, which slowly began absorbing the sun's rays, causing the snow to melt.*

2   *After four years the weight of the melting snow caused a section of Ampato's highest summit to collapse into its **crater**.*

Use Graphic Sources of Information

How does the illustration on this page help you understand the collapse of Mt. Ampato?

3   *Within this mix of falling ice and rock was a cloth-wrapped bundle.*

4   *When the bundle smashed against an icy outcrop about 200 feet below, an outer cloth was torn open—and 500-year-old Inca artifacts were strewn over the rugged landscape.*

Audio

5   *But the most important part of the bundle remained intact as it came to rest on top of the ice . . .*

6   I'd climbed more than a hundred volcanoes in the Andes mountains without ever seeing an active volcano up close. From the top of Ampato, I would be able to look down and see Sabancaya erupting. I was as excited as my Peruvian assistant, Miguel Zárate, and I started our climb out of the village of Cabanaconde, heading toward Ampato. On September 5, we made a small base camp at 16,300 feet.

---

erupting   exploding
spewed   pushed out with force

crater   a large hole in a volcano

7   During our first **ascent** of Ampato on September 6, we made our way up the northern slope. We thought this would be a fairly simple **route,** but, as we neared the top, ice **pinnacles** blocked our way. They had been formed by **erosion** caused by the sun and wind.

8   We had to break through a mile of ice pinnacles to reach one of the lower summits at 20,400 feet. Much to our surprise, just as we were about to reach it, we saw a long layer of grass **encased** in the ice. We were puzzled. How did so much grass get here? Grass could not grow at this altitude!

9   We climbed the rest of the way to the summit and found that it was rounded and covered with grass, the "grass site." Pieces of Inca pottery and textiles, rope, chunks of wood, and even leather and wool sandals were scattered about. Flat **slabs** of rock had been carried from over a thousand feet below to make flooring. One slab still had a rope around it. The rock floor had been covered with thick layers of grass, to make a resting place.

> ### Use Graphic Sources of Information
>
> Look at the illustration. What kinds of things did the Inca people use?

10   [The climbers were unable to reach the summit that day because it was too late. They went back to their camp.]

11   . . . The next morning we crossed over the "grass site" at 20,400 feet and made our way through and around ice pinnacles inside Ampato's crater until we were about 200 feet below the summit . . . The frozen rock was steep and slippery . . . Finally I was just able to get over the worst part by pulling myself up with my ice ax.

---

ascent   going upward
route   a path of travel
pinnacles   pointed formations on a mountain peak

erosion   a natural process in which material is moved on Earth's surface
encased   enclosed
slabs   thick, flat pieces of something

12   I pulled Miguel up, too, and the rest of the way was a simple scramble up over ice and rock to the **ridge** top . . .

13   I stopped to take notes while Miguel continued along the ridge. He whistled, and I looked up to see him with his ice ax raised.

14   When I reached him, he pointed without saying a word: Even from 40 feet away, it was possible to see reddish feathers sticking out near the top of the ridge. We had both seen feathers like this on Inca statues at other sites, and so we knew instantly they would most likely be from a feathered headdress.

15   Although the feathers were only about 10 feet down from the top, the slope was steep and slippery—a mix of gravel and sand over ice. A slip would have meant certain death. Miguel . . . climbed down to uncover a statue made of a rare seashell, with a reddish feathered headdress. Nearby, also covered with gravel, were two more statues, one gold and one silver.

> **Use Graphic Sources of Information**
>
> How does the illustration help you understand the danger that Miguel was in?

16   Their **textiles** were so well **preserved,** they looked new. The feathers that had been exposed were still in good condition. This meant that the gravel in which the statues had been buried had fallen away only days before. Indeed, the statues could have fallen farther down the slope at any moment . . . We then climbed down off the ridge and scrambled our way around beneath it . . . A little farther we saw what looked to us like a **mummy bundle** lying on the ice.

---

ridge   a long, narrow, high piece of land
textiles   cloths, fabrics made by weaving
preserved   kept in good condition

mummy   a dead body that has been kept in very good condition
bundle   things close together, usually tied

17   It seemed so unlikely to find a mummy out in the open, we literally couldn't believe our eyes. Miguel said, "Maybe it's a climber's backpack . . ." As we drew closer, I knew from the stripes on the cloth that it was probably a mummy bundle . . . The bundle containing the victim had been buried in the structure that had collapsed when part of the summit ridge crashed into the crater . . . I grew more excited as I remembered that only three frozen mummies had been recovered in all of South America.

18   Descending toward it, we found fragments of a torn textile. A seashell, two cloth bags containing food offerings (**maize** kernels and a maize cob), **llama** bones, and pieces of Inca pottery were **strewn** about on the slope above the bundle.

Use Graphic Sources of Information

Use the text and the illustration to summarize what Reinhard and Miguel found.

19   After I photographed these items, Miguel used his ice ax to cut loose the bundle from the ice.

20   He turned it on its side for a better grip. Both of us were momentarily stunned as the body turned.

21   We looked straight into the face of a young girl.

22   She was the first *frozen* female mummy found in South America!

---

maize corn
llama a South American animal, like a small camel, used to carry loads

strewn scattered

23   I wondered what to do next. If we left the mummy behind in the open, the sun and the volcanic ash would cause further damage. Climbers might find her and take her and the other **artifacts** as souvenirs or to sell. The ground was frozen rock hard, and it was impossible to bury the mummy. A heavy snowfall could cover the summit and make recovery impossible . . .

24   I decided that we should try to carry the mummy and the statues down the mountain. This would be difficult under the best **circumstances.** Unfortunately, we were both feeling weak, and I had an upset stomach . . .

25   Brushing aside a feeling of **dread,** we wrapped the bundle in plastic and attached it to my backpack. We had to scramble for a mile around the ice pinnacles inside the crater to link up with the route back to camp.

26   This was one of the hardest things I've ever done. My backpack was so heavy that any slip meant a hard fall, and I crashed to the ground a dozen times. I could only get back on my feet by propping myself against the ground with my ice ax and lunging upward. Every fall meant precious minutes lost.

27   Instead of its getting easier once we were out of the crater, the way became more dangerous . . . Finally I realized it was foolish to continue. We left the mummy **amidst** some ice pinnacles at 19,900 feet.

28   It took us two hours to descend to our tent 700 feet below and crawl exhausted into our sleeping bags.

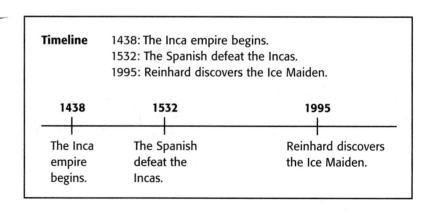

Use of Graphic Sources of Information

Read and interpret (to understand) the timeline. Around what time did the Ice Maiden live? How does the timeline help you know this?

Timeline   1438: The Inca empire begins.
            1532: The Spanish defeat the Incas.
            1995: Reinhard discovers the Ice Maiden.

1438	1532	1995
The Inca empire begins.	The Spanish defeat the Incas.	Reinhard discovers the Ice Maiden.

---

artifacts objects produced by human workmanship
circumstances conditions that affect something else

dread a strong fear of something in the future
amidst surrounded by

Epilogue

29   The next day, Reinhard went back to get the mummy. He and Zárate took it to the city of Arequipa where specialists gathered to study it. In 1996, the mummy was sent to the United States for further study. The Ice Maiden is now back in Arequipa, and scientists continue to learn from her. For example, they have discovered that:

30   The girl lived around A.D. 1470. She was about 14 years old when she died. She had normal skeletal growth, no bone disease, and she had no **malnutrition.**

---

malnutrition   a sick condition caused by lack of food

About the Author   Johan Reinhard (born 1943)

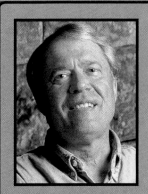

Johan Reinhard was born in Joliet, Illinois. He studied anthropology at the University of Arizona and at the University of Vienna in Austria. Since 1980, Reinhard has worked in the mountains of South America. He has discovered more than 50 burial sites there. Reinhard has written five books and has published many articles about his adventures.

➤Why do you think Johan Reinhard wrote about his discovery of the Inca Ice Maiden? To entertain, to inform, or to persuade?

Beyond the Reading

Reading Comprehension

Question-Answer Relationships (QAR)

"Right There" Questions

1. **Recall Facts** What active volcano is near Ampato?
2. **Recall Facts** Who is Miguel Zárate?
3. **Recall Facts** What tool helped the climbers reach the summit?

"Think and Search" Questions

4. **Explain** Why was it difficult for the climbers to continue up the northern slope?
5. **Identify** What did the climbers find growing near the summit? Why was this strange?
6. **Analyze Cause and Effect** What happened to Ampato when Sabancaya erupted?
7. **Analyze Cause and Effect** What might have happened to the mummy if Reinhard and Zárate had left it on the mountain?

"Author and You" Questions

8. **Explain** Explain how the author's description of the mountain helps you understand the setting of the narrative.
9. **Describe** Describe how you think the author felt after finding the mummy.
10. **Analyze Tone** What is the tone of the text? Humorous, serious, or excited? What do you think is the author's attitude toward the events in the text?

"On Your Own" Question

11. **Find Differences** Identify several differences between where the Inca lived and where you live.

Activity Book
p. 130

Student
CD-ROM

Build Reading Fluency

Read to Scan for Information

You must adjust your reading rate to read fast when you scan. Scan to look for the title and boldfaced (darkened) key words in "Discovering the Inca Ice Maiden." Write the answers to these questions on a piece of paper.

1. What is the title of the reading?
2. What are the key words?

Listen, Speak, Interact

Describe Personal Accomplishments

In "Discovering the Inca Ice Maiden," Johan Reinhard describes his accomplishments. He explains how he climbed a mountain and how he discovered the mummy.

1. Work with a partner. Discuss how you accomplished something in the past. Clarify your ideas with examples: *I got an A in math. I studied hard.* Then answer the following questions:

a. What did you learn from this accomplishment?

b. What difficulties did you face?

c. How did it change you?

2. Discuss something you would like to accomplish in the future. Answer the following questions:

a. Why would you like to accomplish this?

b. Has it been done before?

c. How are you going to accomplish this?

Elements of Literature

Understand First-Person Point of View

Johan Reinhard, the author of the reading selection, is the narrator (teller) of the story. He uses the pronouns *I, me, we,* and *us.* This kind of story is written in **first-person point of view.**

In grammar, the pronouns *I, me, we,* and *us* are called *first-person pronouns.* That is why we call this point of view *first person.*

There are two people in "Discovering the Inca Ice Maiden," Johan Reinhard and Miguel Zárate.

1. Read paragraph 6 of the story. Notice the use of the pronouns *I* and *we.*

	Johan Reinhard	Miguel Zárate	Both
Author			
Character			
Narrator			
I			
We			

2. Copy the chart. Which words on the left refer to Johan Reinhard, Miguel Zárate, or both? Put an "X" in the correct column.

Activity Book
p. 131

Student
CD-ROM

Word Study

Spell -*ed* Forms of Verbs

You know that you can add -*ed* to regular verbs to make the past tense.

erupt + ed → erupt**ed**

Look at the chart. Sometimes you need to make a spelling change before adding -*ed*.

1. Reread paragraph 16. Find four examples of past tense verbs that end with -*ed*.
2. Write the verbs on a piece of paper. Circle the endings.

If the verb ends in a vowel, add **-d.** describe → describe**d**
If the verb ends in *consonant* + **y,** change the **y** to **i** and add **-ed.** carry → carr**ied**
For a one syllable verb that ends in *consonant* + *vowel* + *consonant,* double the final consonant and add **-ed.** slip → sli**pped**

Activity Book   Student
p. 132   CD-ROM

Grammar Focus

Identify *Be* + Adjective + Infinitive

You can sometimes use a form of *be* + an adjective + an infinitive to describe the infinitive's action. An **infinitive** is the word *to* followed by the simple form of a verb.

The ground was frozen rock hard, and it <u>was impossible to bury</u> the mummy.

1. Reread paragraph 27. Find a sentence that uses *be* + adjective + infinitive.
2. Write the sentence on a piece of paper. Label the form of *be*, the adjective, and the infinitive.

Subject	*Be*	Adjective	Infinitive
It	is was	impossible difficult	to bury.
We	are were	puzzled	to see it.

Activity Book   Student   Student
pp. 133–134   Handbook   CD-ROM

From Reading to Writing

Write a First-Person Nonfiction Narrative

Write a first-person nonfiction narrative about a place you have visited. Write three paragraphs. Use "Discovering the Inca Ice Maiden" as a model.

1. Answer these six questions before you begin:
   a. Where is the place?
   b. When were you there?
   c. Who was there?
   d. What was there?
   e. Why did you go there?
   f. How did you react to it?

2. Provide details. Describe some of your activities during the trip. Describe some of your thoughts and feelings during the trip. Discuss how you felt after the trip was over.

3. Use the past tense form of verbs.

Activity Book
p. 135

Across Content Areas

Understand the Atmosphere and Altitude

The **atmosphere** is the air that surrounds Earth. The atmosphere changes depending on how high you are.

At **sea level** (the height of the land right by the ocean), the atmosphere is thick. There is a lot of oxygen to breathe. On a high mountain, the atmosphere gets thinner. There is less oxygen in the air.

We use sea level as a starting point to measure **altitude** (the height of land or a flying airplane). Sea level is at 0 meters (0 feet) altitude. Mt. Everest, the highest mountain in the world, has an altitude of 8,848 meters (29,028 feet) above sea level. When people climb Mt. Everest, they take bottles of oxygen with them.

Copy these sentences on a piece of paper. Complete each one with the word *atmosphere, sea level,* or *altitude.*

1. A city on a mountain has a higher _____ than a city by the ocean.
2. The _____ was so thin that it was hard to breathe.
3. Denver, Colorado, is 5,280 feet above _____ .

Activity Book
p. 136

CHAPTER 3

The Art of Swordsmanship

a folktale
by Rafe Martin

Reading Use dialogue to understand character as you read a folktale.

Listening and Speaking Participate in a dramatic read-aloud.

Grammar Use adverbs to show time.

Writing Write a tale.

Content The Arts: Learn about art in everyday objects.

Use Prior Knowledge

Evaluate Learning Experiences

Think about how you learn math. Then think about how you learn to ride a bicycle. How are these learning experiences the same or different?

1. Choose one skill from each list in the chart. Think about how you learned each skill.
2. Tell a partner how you learned the skills.
3. As a class, discuss the difference between skills you learn by someone explaining them to you and skills you learn through practice.

Learn how to:	Learn how to:
• find your way around town	• add fractions
• organize your schoolbooks	• tell a verb from a noun
• throw a ball	• cook
• ride a bicycle	• tie your shoes

Build Background

Swordfighting

For hundreds of years, people used swords as weapons. Swords are metal and have sharp edges that make them dangerous weapons. Today, fencing is an Olympic sport based on swordfighting.

Content Connection

The different types of fighting arts that came from Asia are called the **martial arts.** Some popular forms are karate, judo, kung fu, and tai chi. Many of the martial arts are practiced without using any weapons.

Build Vocabulary

Identify Related Words

Sometimes a group of unfamiliar words will share a root word. If you know the meaning of the root word, you can guess the meaning of the larger words. In this reading selection, several words are about swords and using swords.

1. Write the following sentences on a piece of paper:
   a. Once a young man named Manjuro sought out the greatest <u>swordmaster</u> in the country.
   b. How long will it take me to become a master <u>swordsman</u>?
   c. Time went on but Manjuro received no training in <u>swordsmanship</u>.
2. Circle the root word that is shared by all of the underlined words.
3. Then use the remaining part of the word to tell what you think each underlined word means. Check your work in a dictionary.

The Heinle Newbury House Dictionary

Activity Book
p. 137

Student CD-ROM

Text Structure

Folktale

"The Art of Swordsmanship" is a **folktale.** It tells a special kind of story. Folktales were originally told orally (out loud). Folktales are usually passed down to us by word of mouth. This is called the *oral tradition*. Look at the chart. It shows some features of a folktale.

Many folktales come from different regions and cultures. Read or listen to the selection. Compare and contrast the selection to other folktales you have heard from different regions and cultures.

Folktale	
A Time-Related Beginning	Folktales come from a long time ago. The story usually begins, "Once upon a time" or "Once."
Simple Plots and Settings	The events in a folktale might have taken place anywhere and at any time.
A Lesson	Folktales teach something or show how to behave.

Student CD-ROM

Reading Strategy

Use Dialogue to Understand Character

The **dialogue** of a story is the exact words the characters say. In a story, you can identify dialogue by the quotation marks ("...") around the words. Dialogue can tell you something about the speaker's **character.** Character is the combination of features that make a person different from others. This includes how he or she thinks, feels, and acts.

1. Listen as your teacher reads aloud the first page.

2. Pay special attention to what the characters say to each other.
3. Describe Manjuro's character by what he says.
4. Take notes on words he says that support your opinion.

Student CD-ROM

The Art of
Swordsmanship

a folktale

by Rafe Martin

1 Once a young man named Manjuro sought out the greatest **swordmaster** in the country, a man named Banzo, wanting to become his student.

2 "How long," Manjuro asked, "will it take me to become a **master** swordsman?"

3 Banzo replied, "Your entire life."

4 "I can't wait that long," said Manjuro. "What if I become your **devoted** servant, how long then?"

5 "Maybe ten years," said Banzo.

6 "That's still too long," said Manjuro. "What if I work even harder, day and night? How long then?"

7 "Thirty years, then," Banzo said.

8 "Thirty years!" exclaimed Manjuro. "First you tell me ten, and then thirty. How can that be?"

Use Dialogue to Understand Character

Describe Manjuro's character. What does he say to support your description?

---

swordmaster a person very skilled in using a sword

master an expert

devoted loyal

9   "A man in such a hurry seldom learns quickly," said Banzo.

10 Understanding that he was being **reprimanded** for **impatience,** Manjuro agreed to become Banzo's servant. "However long it takes," he **vowed,** "I will become a great swordsman!"

Use Dialogue to Understand Character

What words tell you that Manjuro's attitude has changed?

11 But to his **dismay,** for the first year he did nothing but sweep and clean, chop wood, wash dishes, cook, carry water, and other such household tasks. He never got a chance to even look at a sword, much less handle one! "I will be patient," Manjuro said to himself. "Surely Banzo is just testing my determination." But the second year was the same as the first. As was the third. Time went on but Manjuro received no training in swordsmanship.

---

reprimanded criticized, scolded
impatience a lack of patience; an inability to wait

vowed promised
dismay disappointment

Use Dialogue to Understand Character

How does Manjuro feel at this point?

12   Finally Manjuro became quite upset. "I'd better leave," he thought. "I'm not learning a thing and time is going by." A short time later, while Manjuro was working in the garden, Banzo quietly approached him and thwacked him with a wooden sword. Whack! The next day Banzo again surprised Manjuro and whack! hit him again. Soon Manjuro became **alert** at all times—cooking, cleaning, chopping wood—for, whack! he never knew when Banzo might strike again with the **blunt** wooden sword.

---

alert watchful

blunt not sharp

13   **Gradually,** something **extraordinary** began to happen. As the sword descended, Manjuro instantly and **instinctively** blocked the oncoming blow with a pot lid, a broom, or a piece of wood. **Sharpened** naturally by the constant and unexpected attacks of Banzo, Manjuro had become a talented swordsman! No one could overcome him now—not even the great swordsman Banzo himself.

14   And so, Manjuro went on to become even greater than his teacher.

---

gradually a little at a time
extraordinary unusual, special

instinctively naturally, as if by instinct
sharpened made very skilled

About the Author — Rafe Martin (born 1946)

Rafe Martin's mother read folktales to him before he could read himself. At that time, many people in Martin's large family had recently come to the United States. He heard all of their stories whenever the family gathered. He noticed that each person added a special piece to the stories. Martin says, "Those who hear or read . . . words [in a story] can see, can feel and live, a whole life in their minds."

➤ What was the author's purpose in writing this folktale? To entertain? To inform? To persuade? To teach a lesson?

Beyond the Reading

Reading Comprehension

Question-Answer Relationships (QAR)

"Right There" Questions

1. **Recall Facts** Who is Manjuro?
2. **Recall Facts** Who is Banzo?
3. **Recall Facts** What does Manjuro do for the first years that he works for Banzo?
4. **Analyze Cause and Effect** What is one thing that Manjuro offers to do in order to shorten his training time as a swordmaster?

"Think and Search" Questions

5. **Interpret** What does Banzo mean when he says that working harder will make Manjuro's lesson take longer?
6. **Make Inferences** Why does Banzo whack Manjuro with the wooden sword?

"Author and You" Question

7. **Evaluate** Do you agree with the statement that a man in a hurry seldom learns as quickly?

"On Your Own" Question

8. **Make Judgments** Do you think that Banzo's teaching method is a good one? What could be some bad results of this method?

Activity Book
p. 138

Student
CD-ROM

Build Reading Fluency

Repeated Reading

Rereading one paragraph at a time can help increase your reading rate and build confidence in reading dialogue.

1. With a partner, read paragraph 1 in "The Art of Swordsmanship" two times.

2. Did your reading rate increase the second time you read?
3. Next, read paragraph 2 two times.
4. Continue rereading each paragraph.
5. Stop after ten minutes.

Listen, Speak, Interact

Participate in a Dramatic Read-Aloud

A dramatic read-aloud helps you understand a selection. You can gain confidence by dramatically using **pitch, tone,** and **volume** as you read aloud.

Use Your Voice
Pitch—low or high
Volume—loud or soft
Tone—angry, sad, happy, or friendly

1. Form groups of three. Decide who will be the narrator and the two characters.
2. Practice reading the story aloud with expression.
3. Take turns reading aloud in front of your classmates.

Elements of Literature

Examine Character Traits and Changes

Authors create characters through what the characters say, think, and do. These actions show **character traits**—what the characters are like. Some traits are intelligence, kindness, and honesty. Authors also often cause their characters to change in a story.

The Art of Swordsmanship	
Character	
Dialogue Words	
Actions	
Thoughts	
Appearance	
Change	

1. Use dialogue and details in the folktale to understand the character traits of Manjuro and Banzo.
2. Create a chart like the one here in your Reading Log. Choose one character and complete the chart.

Reading Log

Activity Book
p. 139

Student
CD-ROM

Word Study

Find Word Origins and Prefixes

Many English words have their **origins** (where they come from) in other languages. To find out the origins of words, look in a large dictionary.

Prefixes are word parts added to the beginnings of words. Some prefixes also come from other languages.

Prefix	Origin	Meaning	Prefix + Root
1. extra-	Latin	outside of or beyond	extraordinary
2. im-	Latin	not	impatience
3. in-			
4. un-			

1. Copy the chart into your Personal Dictionary. Complete it with two more words from paragraph 13.
2. Use a large dictionary to locate the origins of the prefixes.

Personal Dictionary

Activity Book p. 140

Student CD-ROM

Grammar Focus

Use Adverbs to Show Time

When writers want to tell the reader *when* something happened, they often use **adverbs** or **adverb phrases** near the beginning of a sentence.

<u>Once</u> a young man named Manjuro sought out the greatest swordmaster.

The word *once* places Manjuro's story in the past.

1. Here is a list of some adverbs and adverb phrases that tell *when* something happened:

once	ten years ago	finally
the next day	soon	

2. Find the adverbs showing time in paragraph 12. Write the sentences on a piece of paper.
3. For each example, underline the adverb or adverb phrase.

Activity Book pp. 141–142

Student Handbook

Student CD-ROM

From Reading to Writing

Write a Folktale

Write a folktale about something extraordinary that has happened to you or to someone else. Use the questions in the box to help you collect information.

1. Make sure your folktale has a beginning, a middle, and an end.
2. Use dialogue to show the character traits of the people.
3. Start your folktale with "Once upon a time . . ." Start sentences with adverbs or adverb phrases to show time.

> Where did the events happen?
> When did the events happen?
> Who is the main character?
> What does the character look like?
> How does the character act?
> What does the character do?
> What lesson does the character learn?

4. Draw a visual, such as a picture, to go with your story.
5. Read your tale to the class.

Activity Book
p. 143

Across Content Areas

Learn About Art in Everyday Objects

Many useful objects are also works of art. Read the sentences. They tell about other objects that can be works of art.

1. The museum had **pottery.** People used the pottery to carry water.
2. The floors of the king's palace were covered with **carpets** from Persia.
3. Much of the **furniture** in the palace was made of wood that was carved by hand.
4. The dress was made of special **fabric.** The fabric had pictures painted on it.

Now match each word with the correct photo.

a. **carpet** c. **fabric**
b. **furniture** d. **pottery**

Activity Book
p. 144

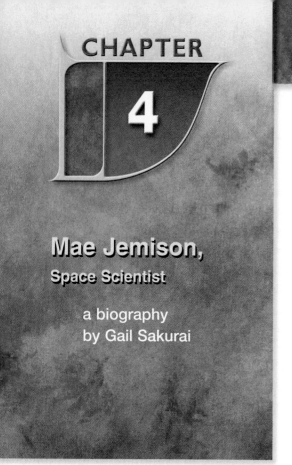

CHAPTER 4

Mae Jemison,
Space Scientist

a biography
by Gail Sakurai

Objectives

Reading Find the main ideas and supporting details as you read a biography.

Listening and Speaking Discuss your goals.

Grammar Use and punctuate dependent clauses with *although* and *when*.

Writing Write a short biography.

Content Science: Understand gravity.

Use Prior Knowledge

Discuss Astronauts

An astronaut is a person who goes into outer space. What do you know about astronauts and outer space?

1. With a partner, brainstorm answers to this question. Record your ideas on a chart.
2. As a class, make a list of everyone's ideas on the board.
3. Ask a science teacher to visit your classroom. Find out which ideas on your list are correct.

Astronauts	Outer Space
train for a long time	no air

Build Background

The United States Space Shuttle

A space shuttle is a vehicle that carries astronauts into space. Space shuttles take off like rockets but land on Earth like airplanes. In 1981, the United States sent up its first space shuttle. The space shuttle carries astronauts into space to do scientific studies. These astronauts study outer space, Earth's weather, and how the human body responds to weightlessness.

Content Connection

SCIENCE

The space shuttle carries materials for the construction of a permanent International Space Station, where scientists will live and work.

Build Vocabulary

Adjust Reading Rate

Adjusting your reading rate (changing how fast you read) can help you understand the meanings of new words.

1. **Unfamiliar Words** Read more slowly. Take time to read each word in a sentence carefully. Reread sentences that have unfamiliar words.

2. **Familiar Words and Sentences** Use the text you already understand to help you find the meanings of unfamiliar words.

3. **Glosses** Use glosses if they are included. A gloss gives a short definition of an unfamiliar word. Glosses in this book appear at the bottom of the selection pages.

Activity Book
p. 145

Student
CD-ROM

Text Structure

Inductive Organization

"Mae Jemison, Space Scientist" is a biography that organizes information **inductively. Inductive** texts begin with specific facts that lead to a general conclusion. They are organized the following way:

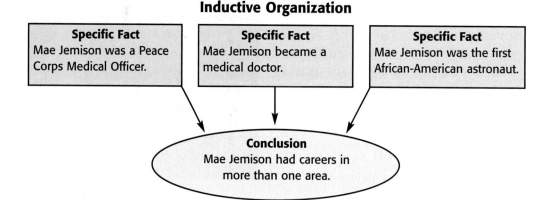

Inductive Organization

Specific Fact	Specific Fact	Specific Fact
Mae Jemison was a Peace Corps Medical Officer.	Mae Jemison became a medical doctor.	Mae Jemison was the first African-American astronaut.

Conclusion
Mae Jemison had careers in more than one area.

Student CD-ROM

Reading Strategy

Find the Main Ideas and Supporting Details

The **main ideas** in a biography are the important parts of a person's life. The **supporting details** include all the information that helps you understand the main idea.

Main Idea	The space shuttle *Endeavour* thundered into the morning sky above Kennedy Space Center.
Supporting Detail	Higher and higher it soared over the Atlantic Ocean.

1. As you read each paragraph, ask yourself what it is mostly about. If you are not sure, try this. Take a sentence out of the paragraph. If the paragraph is unclear without it, you have found the main idea. It is the sentence you took out.
2. Look for supporting details in the rest of the paragraph. Each detail will answer a question such as *how, what, who, when, where,* or *why.*

Student CD-ROM

MAE JEMISON,
SPACE SCIENTIST

a biography
by Gail Sakurai

1   The space shuttle *Endeavour* **thundered** into the morning sky above Kennedy Space Center. Higher and higher it soared over the Atlantic Ocean. A few minutes later, *Endeavour* was **in orbit** around the Earth.

> **Find the Main Ideas and Supporting Details**
>
> What is the main idea of this paragraph?

2   Aboard the **spacecraft,** astronaut Mae Jemison could feel her heart pounding with excitement. A wide, happy grin split her face. She had just made history. She was the first African-American woman in space. The date was September 12, 1992 . . .

3   Mae's dream didn't come true overnight. It happened only after many long years of hard work, training, and preparation . . . Her parents, Charlie and Dorothy Jemison, were helpful and **supportive** of all of Mae's interests. "They put up with all kinds of stuff, like science projects, dance classes, and art lessons," Mae said. "They **encouraged** me to do it, and they would find the money, time, and energy to help me be involved."

Audio

---

thundered   made a noise like thunder

in orbit   on a path in space that leads around Earth

spacecraft   a machine that flies in space

supportive   giving support; helping to make happen

encouraged   acted in ways that helped something happen

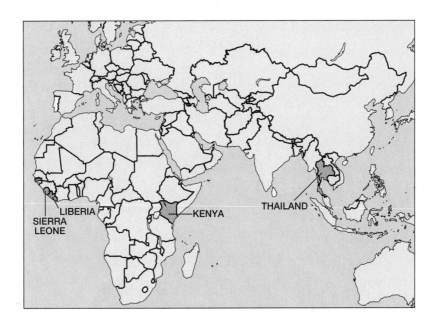

4   Other adults were not as encouraging as Mae's parents. When Mae told her kindergarten teacher that she wanted to be a scientist, the teacher said, "Don't you mean a nurse?" In those days, very few African-Americans or women were scientists. Many people, like Mae's teacher, couldn't imagine a little black girl growing up to become a scientist. But Mae refused to let other people's limited imaginations stop her from following her dreams.

5   Mae loved to work on school science projects. She spent many hours at the public library, reading books about science and space . . . She knew that she wanted to be an astronaut. Although all the astronauts at that time were white and male, Mae wasn't **discouraged** . . .

Find the Main Ideas and Supporting Details

How does the detail that Jemison spent many hours at the public library reading about science and space support the main idea of this paragraph?

6   Mae went to college, and then to medical school. She traveled to several countries as part of her medical training . . . She helped provide basic medical care for people in rural Kenya and at a Cambodian **refugee** camp in Thailand . . .

---

discouraged likely to give up

refugee a person who has left his or her homeland because of war, poverty, or hunger

7   Although she had settled into a career as a doctor, . . . Mae decided to join the Peace Corps, an organization of volunteers who work to improve conditions in **developing nations.**

8   She spent more than two years in West Africa as the Peace Corps Medical Officer for Sierra Leone and Liberia . . .

9   When her **tour of duty** in the Peace Corps was over, Mae returned home and **resumed** her medical practice. She also started taking engineering classes.

10   Mae had not forgotten her dream of traveling in space . . . She applied to the National Aeronautics and Space Administration (NASA), which is responsible for U.S. space exploration . . . She was accepted into the astronaut program in June, 1987. She was one of only fifteen people chosen from nearly two thousand **qualified applicants!** . . .

> **Find the Main Ideas and Supporting Details**
>
> What is the main idea of this paragraph?

---

developing nations   countries with less wealth and technology
tour of duty   time you have agreed to serve

resumed   started again
qualified   trained in the correct way
applicants   people who want and apply for a job

11   At the end of her training, . . . Mae officially became a mission **specialist** astronaut. "We're the ones people often call the scientist astronauts," Mae explained. "Our responsibilities are . . . to do the experiments once you get into orbit . . . and . . . do . . . space walks . . ."

12   Although Mae was a **full-fledged** astronaut, she still had to wait four more years before she went into space . . . But on September 12, 1992, the long wait was over . . . On that day Dr. Mae Jemison earned her place in the history books as the first African-American woman in space. Mae said, "My participation in the space shuttle mission helps to say that all peoples of the world have astronomers, physicists, and explorers."

> **Find the Main Ideas and Supporting Details**
>
> What is one detail that supports the main idea that Mae Jemison finally made it into space?

13   *Endeavour's* mission was **devoted to** scientific research. Mae was responsible for several key experiments . . . She **investigated** a new way of controlling space motion sickness. Half of all astronauts experience space sickness during the first few days in space. They often feel dizzy and nauseated. Astronauts can take medicine to control space sickness, but the medicine can make them tired.

---

specialist   someone with special training in a particular area
full-fledged   completely trained

devoted to   focused on
investigated   explored, studied

14   To carry out the space sickness experiment, Mae used "biofeedback" techniques. Biofeedback uses **meditation** and relaxation to control the body's functions. Mae wore special **monitoring** equipment to record her heart rate, breathing, temperature, and other body functions. If she started to feel ill, she would meditate . . . The purpose of the experiment was to see if Mae could avoid space sickness without taking medication. The results of the experiment were not **conclusive,** but space researchers still hope to use biofeedback in the future.

> ### Find the Main Ideas and Supporting Details
>
> Is the main idea of this paragraph in the first or last sentence?

15   Mae was also in charge of the frog experiment. Early in the flight, she **fertilized** eggs from female South African frogs. A few days later, tadpoles **hatched.** She then watched the tadpoles carefully. Her goal was to find out if the tadpoles would develop normally in the **near-zero gravity** of space.

"What we've seen is that the eggs were fertilized and the tadpoles looked pretty good," said Mae. "It was exciting because that's a question that we didn't have any information on before."

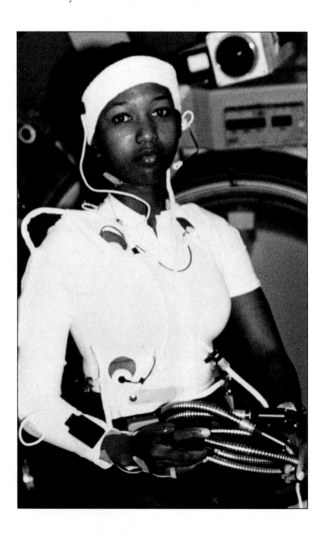

---

meditation   a period of focused deep thought and quiet thinking
monitoring   keeping track of, watching
conclusive   sure, complete, final

fertilized   started the development of new life
hatched   came out of an egg
near-zero gravity   almost no gravity

16   On September 20, 1992, at 8:53 A.M., *Endeavour* landed at Kennedy Space Center. The crew had spent more than 190 hours (almost eight days) in space. They had traveled 3.3 million miles and had completed 127 orbits of Earth! . . .

17   Mae Jemison had made her childhood dream come true. She was ready for new challenges . . . On March 8, 1993, she permanently **resigned** from the astronaut corps.

18   Mae formed her own company called The Jemison Group, Inc. The Jemison Group's goal is to develop ways of using science and technology to improve the quality of life. Mae's company makes a special effort to improve conditions in poor and developing countries . . .

> ### Find the Main Ideas and Supporting Details
> Name a detail that supports the main idea about The Jemison Group, Inc.

19   Besides her work with The Jemison Group, Mae spends much of her time traveling around the country, giving speeches, and encouraging young people to follow their dreams. Mae Jemison believes in the motto:

20   "Don't be limited by others' limited imaginations."

---

resigned   gave up her job

About the Author

Gail Sakurai (born 1952)

Gail Sakurai started to write stories because she loved to read. She was only eight when she wrote her first story. Many of Sakurai's books are nonfiction books about people or important parts of history. She also enjoys retelling folktales. Sakurai feels that it is hard to find the time for writing. Yet she does not let that stop her. Sakurai says, "My childhood dream came true with the publication of my first book in 1994—only twenty-nine years later than originally planned."

➤ What challenges did Gail Sakurai face in writing and publishing her books?

Beyond the Reading

Reading Comprehension

Question-Answer Relationships (QAR)

"Right There" Questions

1. **Recall Facts** What experiments does Mae Jemison do in space?
2. **Recall Facts** Which of Mae Jemison's jobs does the biography focus on?

"Think and Search" Questions

3. **Find the Main Idea** Why is Mae Jemison's work as an astronaut especially important?
4. **Recognize Sequence of Events** What was Mae Jemison's job before she became an astronaut?
5. **Note Steps in a Process** What steps did Mae Jemison have to take to get into space?

"Author and You" Questions

6. **Draw Conclusions** Why do you think Mae Jemison set up a company that uses science to help people living in developing countries?
7. **Form Questions** Based on the information and knowledge you have, what additional questions would you ask Mae Jemison?

"On Your Own" Questions

8. **Compare Your Own Experiences** Mae Jemison reached an important goal. How do you feel when you reach a goal?
9. **Evaluate** Do you agree with Mae Jemison's motto? Why or why not?

Activity Book p. 146

Student CD-ROM

Build Reading Fluency

Reading Silently

Reading silently is good practice. It helps you learn to read faster.

1. Listen to the audio recording of paragraphs 1 and 2 of "Mae Jemison, Space Scientist."
2. Listen to the chunks of words as you follow along.
3. Reread paragraphs 1 and 2 silently two times.
4. Your teacher or partner will time your second reading. Raise your hand when you are finished.

Listen, Speak, Interact

Discuss Your Goals

When you set a goal for yourself, you choose something that you want to happen in the future, and you work to make it happen. For example, getting a good job is a goal for many young people.

Mae Jemison worked hard for a long time to reach her goal of becoming an astronaut. The author tells about what Jemison studied and what jobs she had to prepare her for space.

1. With a partner, reread the biography aloud. Record ways Jemison worked to reach her goal.
2. Talk about goals each of you has worked hard to reach. List them in a chart like the one below.
3. Share your goals with your partner and the steps you took to reach your goals.

Goals	Steps to Reach the Goals
learn to skateboard	ask my friend for help practice every day

Elements of Literature

Recognize Flashbacks

The biography "Mae Jemison, Space Scientist" begins when Mae Jemison is an adult. Then the selection goes back in time to tell stories about Jemison's childhood. In a **flashback,** the author describes earlier events.

In your Reading Log, put the following events in chronological (time) order—the order in which they happened.

a. Jemison goes into space on September 12, 1992.
b. Jemison's kindergarten teacher tells her to become a nurse.
c. Jemison goes to medical school.
d. Jemison works on school science projects.

Reading Log

Activity Book
p. 147

Student
CD-ROM

Word Study

Identify Greek and Latin Word Origins

Many English words and spellings come from other languages and cultures. Knowing the meanings of some Greek and Latin word forms, or **roots,** can help you figure out English words.

1. Copy a chart like the one below into your Personal Dictionary.
2. Look up the word origins and their meanings in the dictionary.
3. Complete the chart.

Word	Root	Origin	Root Meaning	English Definition
astronaut	astro	Latin	star	person who flies into space (to the stars)
	naut	Latin	sailor	
physicist	phys			
television	tele			
	vision			
discover	cover			

Personal Dictionary

The Heinle Newbury House Dictionary

Activity Book p. 148

Student CD-ROM

Grammar Focus

Use and Punctuate Dependent Clauses with *Although* and *When*

Gail Sakurai begins several sentences with a clause that starts with **although** or **when.**

> Although all of the astronauts at that time were white and male,
> (dependent clause)

> Mae wasn't discouraged.
> (main clause)

Dependent clauses are not complete sentences. They must be used with a main clause.

You must always use a comma after a dependent clause when it comes at the beginning of a sentence.

1. Find other sentences in the selection that include dependent clauses with *although* or *when.*
2. Write a sentence that begins with a clause containing *although* or *when.* Use correct punctuation.

Activity Book pp. 149–150

Student Handbook

Student CD-ROM

From Reading to Writing

Write a Short Biography

1. Choose a person who is important to you in some way.
2. Gather information by talking to the person or by using reference materials and resources in the library and on the Internet.
3. Make sure all facts, dates, and details are correct.
4. Begin your biography with a moment from the person's adult life. Then use a flashback to explore how that person grew up and was educated.
5. Include important parts of the person's life. Do not describe everything that the person ever did. Show your readers the most important parts of the person's life.

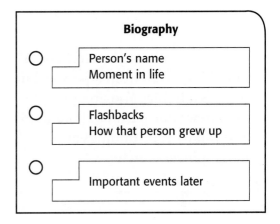

Activity Book
p. 151

Across Content Areas

Understand Gravity

When you read scientific texts, look for **definitions, explanations,** and **examples.** Read the following article. Then find an example of each.

Activity Book
p. 152

Gravity

Gravity is the force that attracts one object to another. If an object is very large, like Earth, its attraction is very strong. If you jump into the air, you fall back down because Earth's gravity pulls you down.

The larger an object is, the greater its gravitational pull is. The sun is much larger than Earth, so it has much more gravity.

Astronauts in space float in the air. This is because the astronauts do not have the same gravitational force pulling them to Earth as when they are on (or closer to) Earth.

Apply and Expand

Listening and Speaking Workshop

Report a Biographical Sketch About a Person's Hobby

Topic

A biographical sketch is about one thing or event in a person's life, such as a hobby. You are going to interview your partner about a hobby and report your findings as a biographical sketch.

Step 1: Prepare a list of questions.

1. *Who* are you? (Get your partner's name, age, and grade in school.)
2. *Where* do you live? (City, state, neighborhood)
3. *What* do you like to do? (Hobby—could be a sport, singing, collecting something)
4. *With whom* do you do the hobby? (Family and friends, alone)
5. *What* do you like most about your hobby?

Step 2: Conduct your interview.

1. Make sure your partner knows the questions ahead of time.
2. Use note cards for each question to help you stay on track. Make notes about what your partner says.
3. Allow your partner enough time to answer without interruption.
4. Ask for more details if necessary.

5. State the purpose of the interview before you begin.
6. If possible, record your interview on audio or video.

✔ Active Listening Checklist

1. I liked _____ because _____ .
2. I understood the purpose of the biographical sketch. Yes / No
3. I understood the major ideas. Yes / No
4. I needed you to clarify _____ .

✔ Speaking Checklist

1. Did I speak too slowly, too quickly, or just right?
2. Did I speak loudly enough for the audience to hear me?
3. Did I produce the correct intonation patterns? (Was my voice too high, too low, or just right?)
4. Did I show respect and act politely?

Step 3: Be attentive and polite.

1. Look at your partner when he or she is speaking.
2. Show interest in the answers.
3. Thank the person when you are finished.

Step 4: Prepare and give your biographical sketch.

1. Review the notes you took and organize the information in a logical way. If you recorded the interview, listen to it to be sure that your information is correct.

2. Ask your teacher to help you distinguish your intonation patterns. This will help you determine if your voice is too low or too high.
3. On a new set of note cards, write the three or four key points that you want to make.
4. Practice your report. Give it to your partner. Ask him or her to check your facts. Use the Presentation Checklist in your Student Handbook.
5. Give your biographical sketch to the class.

Viewing Workshop

Interpret Important Ideas from Maps

View a Historical Atlas

At the school library, find a historical atlas. View maps from different time periods. Use the Internet or CD-ROM encyclopedias to view exploration maps. Choose two maps to study further. For each map, answer the following questions:

1. What does the map show? What is its title?
2. What time period does the map cover?
3. How are the places on the map different?

4. What kind of special information does the map explain? It might explain exploration routes, crops grown in certain places, where and when battles were fought.
5. Does the legend help you understand the map?

Further Viewing

Watch the *Visions* CNN Video for Unit 4. Do the Video Worksheet.

CNN Video

Writer's Workshop

Write to Inform: Write an E-mail

Writing Prompt

You want to tell a friend about the best book you have ever read. Write an e-mail message to recommend it to him or her.

Step 1: Brainstorm.

1. What book interests you?
2. Make a short list of specific things about the book that interest you.
3. What effect did it have on you?

Step 2: Arrange your ideas in logical order.

1. What is the most important idea?
2. What is the least important idea?

Step 3: Write a draft.

Paragraph 1: The Opening

1. Tell your friend that you are writing to tell about a great book.
2. Name the title and the author, and tell why you like the book.
3. Use a tone and a style to show why you like this book best.

Paragraph 2: The Body

1. State your main idea clearly and add details for support.
2. Use "first" for your first detail.

Paragraph 3: The Closing

1. The last paragraph is the closing.
2. Repeat the opening with new words.
3. Write your name at the end.

```
To: Julie
Cc:
Subject: A Great Book


Julie,

I wanted to tell you about a
great book. It's about _____
and the title is _____
by _____. I liked it because
_____.
I think you'll like it too.

The book has wonderful characters
and a great plot. First

_____
_____.

I hope you'll get this book out
of the library and tell me what
you think.

Miguel
```

Step 4: Revise your e-mail.

1. Use resources such as the Editor's Checklist in your Student Handbook to check your work.
2. Refer to the book you are writing about to clarify ideas and details. Ask your librarian or teacher if you need help.
3. Be sure your main idea and supporting details are clear. Include details that support your opinion of the book.
4. Collaborate with a partner. Read and review each other's work. Can you organize and combine sentences better?

Step 5: Edit your e-mail

1. Use your software's spelling and grammar checks.
2. Edit spelling mistakes and typing errors. Make sure you correctly spell words that sound the same but are spelled differently. For example, *there, their,* and *they're.*
3. Check for capitalization, apostrophes, and punctuation.
4. Can you combine any of your sentences with *although* or *when*?
5. Can you combine any of your sentences with relative clauses?

Step 6: Send your e-mail.

1. Ask your teacher to help you send your e-mail. If possible, send it to a classmate.
2. Did you receive any e-mail messages from your classmates? What did you learn about the books they have read?

Student
Handbook

Projects

These projects will help you further explore what you know about discoveries. Work alone, with a partner, or with a group. Remember to ask adults for help when you need it.

Project 1: Make a Future-Discovery Poster

Think of discoveries that would make life easier, safer, healthier, or more enjoyable. Make a poster of one of your ideas.

1. Choose the discovery that you like best. Think of a name or a short phrase to describe your discovery.
2. Write reasons why this discovery helps people. These are the benefits of the discovery.
3. Ask your partner to tell you if your ideas are clear.
4. For your discovery, list its name and its benefits.
5. Illustrate your discovery. You can show what the discovery looks like, you can show its benefit, or you can show someone using it.
6. Talk about the items and why you think they would be important.

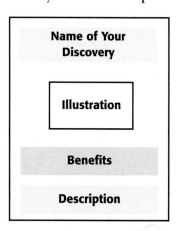

Project 2: Make Discoveries About Your Community

1. Work with a group. Divide the research into categories such as community history, services, sports, arts, buildings, and ways to have fun. Each person or pair should choose one of the categories. Think of two questions to answer for each category.
2. Brainstorm ways to get information. For example, you might scan the phone book, look at your community's Web site, talk to a town official, or read books about local history.
3. Revise your questions if you need to. Then continue to research answers.
4. Look for the information. Organize and summarize what you find in a chart like the one shown.
5. Send the chart to a chamber of commerce in your community or region. What is their reaction?

Category	Information
sports	baseball team plays four nights a week at Newtown Stadium

Further Reading

The books listed below explore the theme of discovery. Read one or more of them. In your Reading Log, record the discoveries described in each book. Write your thoughts and feelings about what you read. Take notes on your answers to these questions:

1. What new discoveries did this book describe?
2. What similar discoveries have you made in your life?

The Library Card
by Jerry Spinelli, Scholastic, Inc., 1998. This book includes four short stories about four different teenagers who find a mysterious blue library card. The main characters in the stories discover the joy of reading—a discovery that changes their lives.

Find Where the Wind Goes: Moments from My Life
by Dr. Mae Jemison, Scholastic, Inc., 2001. In her autobiography, Dr. Mae Jemison tells about her experience in becoming the first African American woman in space.

Tuck Everlasting
by Natalie Babbitt, Farrar, Straus & Giroux, Inc., 1986. The Tuck family has the secret to eternal life. Winnie, a girl in their town, discovers their secret. Through her discovery, Winnie learns the true meaning of life and death and why eternal life may not be as desirable as she once believed.

The Tiger Rising
by Kate DiCamillo, Candlewick Press, 2001. Rob Hurton and his friend Sistine discover a tiger trapped inside of a cage in the woods behind the motel where Rob lives. Rob and Sistine's attempt to free the tiger starts the emotional healing process for Rob, who has just recently lost his mother.

Jason's Gold
by Will Hobbs, HarperTrophy, 2000. In 1897, gold was discovered in Canada's Yukon Territory. This story mixes fiction and facts about the Klondike gold rush to tell the story of 15-year-old Jason and his dog King as they make an incredible 10,000-mile journey.

Travels with a Tangerine: A Journey in the Footnotes of Ibn Battutah
by Tim Mackintosh-Smith, Welcome Rain Publishers, 2002. In 1325, Ibn Battutah began a 29-year pilgrimage from his home in Tangiers to Mecca. This book describes the first stage of his pilgrimage as he travels from Tangiers to Constantinople.

Popular Science: Science Year by Year: Discoveries and Inventions from the 20th Century That Shape Our Lives
by Popular Science Magazine, Scholastic, Inc., 2001. The nation's leading science magazine has compiled a book of the greatest scientific inventions of the twentieth century. Inventions include electric guitars, toasters, television, computers, and bubble gum.

Reading Log

Heinle Reading Library

UNIT 5

Communication

Rock engravings at Petroglyph National Monument,
Danny Lehman, Photographer. ca. 1000–1600.

View the Picture

1. How does this picture show communication?
2. How do you communicate with other people?

   In this unit, you will read a story, biography, play, textbook article,
and pictorial narrative. Each reading selection focuses on
communication. You will learn about the features of these writing
forms and how to write them yourself.

CHAPTER 1

How Tía Lola Came to ~~Visit~~ Stay

an excerpt from a novel
by Julia Alvarez

Objectives

Reading Predict what will happen in a narrative.

Listening and Speaking Role-play dialogue.

Grammar Recognize the present perfect tense.

Writing Write a narrative with dialogue.

Content Social Studies: Read a weather map.

Use Prior Knowledge

Discuss Different Cultures and Languages

The people of a culture are often connected through language. Research how many different languages the students in your class can speak.

1. Make a chart like the one below.
2. Ask students, "Which languages do you speak?" Record the answers on your chart.

3. Make a class chart with everyone's answers. Take turns interpreting the chart: "Six people speak Chinese."
4. Discuss what you know about the languages and the countries where they are spoken.

Name	Chinese	English	Hmong	Spanish	_____
Sergio	X	X			

Build Background

The Dominican Republic

The Dominican Republic is a country on the Caribbean island of Hispaniola. Hispaniola is between the Caribbean Sea and the Atlantic Ocean. The weather in the Dominican Republic is warm and tropical.

The people of the Dominican Republic speak Spanish. Almost half of the Dominican population works on farms.

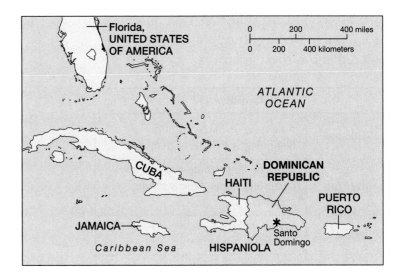

Content Connection

The Dominican Republic shares Hispaniola with Haiti. Haitians speak Creole and French.

Build Vocabulary

Use Context Clues

You can learn the meaning of a new word by looking for clues in the same sentence or the next sentence. For example, you will find in the reading selection that *tía* is the Spanish word for *aunt*.

Use context clues to guess the meanings of the underlined words in the following sentences.

1. I won't have much to say to her except "¡*Adiós*!" Goodbye!
2. "*Te quiero mucho*," she closes, just as Miguel has done. I love you lots.
3. Juanita <u>blubbers</u> tearfully and follows their mother out of the room.

Activity Book
p. 153

Student
CD-ROM

Text Structure

Narrative

"How Tía Lola Came to ~~Visit~~ Stay" is **narrative** writing. It tells a story. A narrative has these features:

Narrative	
Structure	A narrative is made up of a beginning, a middle, and an end.
Dialogue	Dialogue in a narrative shows how characters speak directly to one another.
Details	Details make a narrative real, interesting, and entertaining.

1. As you read or listen to the recording of the selection, notice what you learn about the characters from the dialogue. Notice what you learn from the story details.
2. How do the characters use language to reflect their culture or region?

Student CD-ROM

Reading Strategy

Predict

As you read or listen to the audio recording of the selection, **predict** what will happen next. When you predict, you make a guess about the future. You can do this based on your knowledge of what has already happened.

1. Read the title and look at the pictures. What do you think the selection is about? Write your prediction in your Reading Log.
2. Read page 290. What will happen next? Why do you think so? Write your prediction in your Reading Log.

3. Check your prediction after you read page 291. Is it answered there? Were you correct?
4. Continue to predict as you read the selection.

Reading Log   Student CD-ROM

How Tía Lola Came to ~~Visit~~ Stay

an excerpt from a novel by Julia Alvarez

Audio

Prologue

Miguel and his younger sister, Juanita, are dealing with two big changes in their lives: their parents have ended their marriage, and they have moved with their mother from New York City to Vermont. Their mother is sad about ending the marriage, but she is happy that her Tía (Aunt) Lola is coming to visit. Miguel is not sure that he likes the idea.

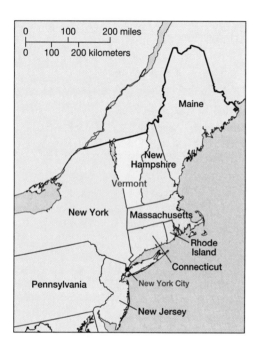

1   "Why can't we just call her *Aunt* Lola?" Miguel asks his mother. Tomorrow their aunt is coming from the Dominican Republic to visit with them in their new home in Vermont. Tonight they are **unpacking** the last of the kitchen boxes before dinner.

2   "Because she doesn't know any English," his mother explains.

3   "*Tía* is the word for aunt in Spanish, right, Mami?" Juanita asks. When their mother's back is turned, Juanita beams Miguel a know-it-all smile.

4   Their mother is gazing sadly at a blue bowl she has just unpacked. "So you see, Miguel, if you call her Aunt, she won't know you're talking to her."

5   That's fine, Miguel thinks, I won't have much to say to her except "*¡Adiós!*" Goodbye! But he keeps his mouth shut. He knows why his mother is staring at the blue bowl, and he doesn't want to upset her in the middle of a **memory.**

6   "So, please, Miguel," his mother is saying, "just call her Tía Lola. Okay?"

Predict

How do you think Miguel will greet Tía Lola? Make a prediction based on what Miguel is saying here.

---

unpacking   taking things out of a box or suitcase

memory   thoughts about something from the past

7   Miguel kind of nods, kind of just **jerks** his head to get his hair out of his eyes. It can go either way . . .

8   [Juanita] begins asking questions about Tía Lola because it makes their mother happy to talk about her favorite aunt back on the island where she was born. "How old is she, Mami?"

9   "Who?"

10   "Tía Lola, Mami, *Tía Lola que viene mañana,*" Juanita says in Spanish. It also makes their mother happy when they use Spanish words. *Tía* for "aunt." *Mañana* for "tomorrow." Tía Lola who comes tomorrow. "Is she real old?"

11   "Actually, nobody knows how old Tía Lola is. She won't tell," their mother says. She is smiling again. Her eyes have a **faraway** look. "She's so young at heart, it doesn't matter. She'll be fun to have around."

12   "Is she married?" Juanita asks. Mami has told them they have **tons** of cousins back on the island, but are any of them Tía Lola's kids?

Predict

Make a prediction about how Tía Lola will look and what she will be like. What clues does Juanita's mother give you to make a prediction?

---

jerks moves quickly
faraway from a long distance

tons a lot

13 "I'm afraid Tía Lola never did get married," Mami sighs. "But, kids, do me a favor. Just don't ask her about it, okay?"

14 "Why not?" Juanita wants to know.

15 "It's a **sensitive issue,**" her mother explains.

16 Juanita is making her I-don't-understand-this-math-problem face. "But why didn't she get married?"

17 Miguel speaks up before his mother can answer. He doesn't know how the thought has popped into his head, but it suddenly pops out of his mouth before he can stop it. "She didn't get married so she wouldn't have to **get divorced** ever."

18 Mami blinks back tears. She stands quickly and leaves the room.

19 Miguel studies the beans pictured on the outside of the can his mother has picked for dinner. One little bean has on a Mexican hat.

20 "You made Mami cry!" Juanita **blubbers** tearfully and follows their mother out of the room.

21 Miguel finds himself alone in a drafty kitchen with all the dirty bowls and plates to wash and the table to wipe. As he cleans up at the sink, he glances out the window at the frosty world outside. Up in the sky, the moon is just the tiniest silver sliver. It looks as if someone has gobbled up most of it and left behind only this bit of light for Miguel to see by.

22 For the first time since he heard the news, he is glad his aunt is arriving tomorrow. It might be nice to have a fourth person—who is still talking to him—in the house, even if her name is Tía Lola.

Predict

Check your prediction about Miguel. Predict how he will greet her.

---

sensitive issue   a topic that is hard to talk about
get divorced   end a marriage

blubbers   cries loudly

◇◇◇◇

23   The next morning at the airport, Miguel's mother cannot find a parking space. "You kids, go in so we don't miss your aunt. I'll join you as soon as I find a spot."

24   "I'll help you," Miguel offers.

25   "Miguel, *amor,* how can you help me? You don't have a license. The **cops'll** take you in if they catch you driving," his mother **teases.**

26   As nervous as Miguel is feeling about his aunt's visit and his new school and their move to Vermont, he thinks he wouldn't mind spending the next year all by himself in jail.

27   "*Por favor,* honey, would you go inside with your sister and look for Tía Lola?" His mother's **sweetened-up** voice is like a handful of chocolate chips from the package in the closet. Impossible to resist.

28   "*¡Los quiero mucho!*" she calls out to both children as they clamber out of the car.

29   "Love you, too," Juanita calls back.

30   The crowd **swarms** around them in the small but busy terminal.

Predict

Will Miguel go inside with his sister to find Tía Lola?

---

cops'll   cops (police officers) will
teases   makes fun of

sweetened-up   very sweet
swarms   moves in a large group

31   Juanita slips her hand into Miguel's. She looks scared, as if all that Spanish she has been showing off to their mother has just left on a plane to South America. "You think we'll **recognize** her?" she asks.

Predict

How do you think Miguel and Juanita will find Tía Lola?

32   "We'll wait until somebody who looks like *she's* looking for *us* comes out of the plane," Miguel says. He sure wishes his mother would hurry up and find a parking spot.

33   Several businessmen rush by, checking their watches, as if they are already late for whatever they have come for. Behind them, a grandma puts down her shopping bag full of presents, and two little boys run forward and throw their arms around her. A young guy turns in a slow circle as if he has gotten off at the wrong stop. A girl hugs her boyfriend, who kisses her on the lips. Miguel looks away.

34   Where is this aunt of theirs?

35   The crowd **disperses,** and still their aunt is nowhere in sight. Miguel and Juanita go up to the counter and ask the lady working there to please page their aunt. "She doesn't know any English," Miguel explains, "only Spanish."

36   The woman in the blue suit has so many **freckles,** it looks as if someone has spilled a whole bag of them on her face. "I'm sorry, kids. I took a little Spanish back in high school, but that was ages ago. I'll tell you what. I'll let you **page** your aunt yourself."

---

recognize   see someone and know who it is
disperses   moves away in different directions

freckles   brown spots on a person's skin
page   use a loudspeaker to call someone or make an announcement

Predict

Do you think Juanita will page her aunt? What do you know about Juanita that can help you make this prediction?

37 "She'll do it," Miguel **nudges** his sister forward. Even though he is older, Juanita is the one who is always showing off her Spanish to their father and mother.

38 Juanita shakes her head. She looks scared. She looks about to cry.

39 "There's nothing to be scared of," Miguel **encourages,** as if he himself has paged his aunt every day of his life.

40 "That's right, sweetie," the woman agrees, nodding at Juanita. But Juanita won't **budge.** Then, turning to Miguel, the woman suggests, "Seeing as she's scared, why don't you do it instead?"

41 "I don't speak Spanish." It isn't **technically** a lie because he doesn't know enough to speak Spanish in public to a whole airport terminal.

42 "You do, too," Juanita **sniffles.** "He knows but he doesn't like to talk it," she explains to the airline lady.

43 "Just give it a try," the freckled lady says, opening a little gate so they can come behind the counter to an office on the other side. A man with a bald head and a tired face and earphones sits at a desk turning dials on a machine. The lady explains that the children need to page a lost aunt who does not speak any English.

44 "Come here, son." The man beckons to Miguel. "Speak right into this microphone. Testing, testing." He tries it out. The man adjusts some knobs and pushes his chair over so Miguel can stand beside him.

---

nudges pushes gently
encourages helps someone to do something
budge move

technically exactly
sniffles speaks while crying

45   Miguel looks down at the microphone. He can feel his stomach getting **queasy** and his mind going blank. All he can remember of his Spanish is Tía Lola's name and the word for "hello."

46   "*Hola, Tía Lola,*" Miguel says into the microphone. Then, suddenly, the **corny** words his mother says every night when she tucks him into bed, the ones she has just called out when he and Juanita climbed out of the car, **pop out.** "*Te quiero mucho.*"

47   Juanita is looking at him, surprised. Miguel scowls back. "It's the only thing I remember," he mutters. With all the stuff popping out these days, he's going to have to get a **brake** for his mouth.

Predict

Do you think Tía Lola will hear or understand Juanita's language? How will Tía Lola react? Make predictions based on what you know about Tía Lola.

48   "I remember more!" Juanita **boasts.** She steps forward, her fears forgotten, and speaks into the microphone. "*Hola, Tía Lola,*" she says in a bright voice as if she is on TV announcing sunny weather tomorrow. "*Te esperamos por el mostrador.*" She and Miguel will be waiting by the counter. "*Te quiero mucho,*" she closes, just as Miguel has done. I love you lots.

49   As Miguel and his sister walk out of the office, they hear a **tremendous** shout. It isn't a shout in Spanish, and it isn't a shout in English. It's a shout anyone anywhere would understand.

50   Someone is **mighty** pleased to see them.

51   On the other side of the counter stands their aunt Lola. You can't miss her! Her skin is the same soft brown as theirs. Her black hair is piled up in a bun on her head with a pink **hibiscus** on top. She wears bright red lipstick and above

---

queasy sick to one's stomach
corny too obvious, not sophisticated
pop out come out on its own
brake the part of a machine that makes it stop

boasts brags, makes oneself look good
tremendous very big or loud
mighty very, in a strong way
hibiscus a bright, tropical flower

her lips she has a big black beauty mark. On her colorful summer dress, parrots fly toward palm trees, and flowers look ready to **burst** from the fabric if they can only figure out how.

52 Behind their aunt, their mother is approaching in her hiking boots and navy-blue parka, her red hat and mittens. "Tía Lola!" she cries out. They hug and kiss and hug again. When Tía Lola pulls away, the beauty mark above her upper lip is gone!

53 "Those two," Tía Lola is saying in Spanish to Miguel's mother as she points to him and Juanita, "those two gave me my first welcome to their country. *¡Ay Juanita! ¡Ay Miguel!*" She **spreads** her arms for her niece and nephew. "*Los quiero mucho.*"

Predict

How do you think Tía Lola will like living with them?

54 It is a voice impossible to resist. Like three handfuls of chocolate chips from the package in the closet . . . For the moment, Miguel forgets the recent move, his papi and friends left behind in New York. When Tía Lola wraps her arms around him, he hugs back, just as hard as he can.

---

burst come out, break open

spreads opens wide

About the Author — Julia Alvarez (born 1950)

Julia Alvarez came to the United States from the Dominican Republic when she was ten years old. She liked to read so that she would not feel alone. When she was in high school, she knew she wanted to be a writer. She said, "What made me into a writer was coming to this country . . . losing a culture, a homeland, a language, a family . . . I wanted a portable homeland. And that's the imagination."

➤ What do you think Julia Alvarez's purpose was in writing this story? What challenges did she face? What strategies did she use?

Beyond the Reading

Reading Comprehension

Question-Answer Relationships (QAR)

"Right There" Questions

1. **Identify** Who is Tía Lola?
2. **Recall Facts** Where is Tía Lola from?
3. **Recall Facts** Who went to the airport to meet Tía Lola?

"Think and Search" Questions

4. **Draw a Conclusion** Why would Tía Lola not understand the word *aunt* in English?
5. **Draw a Conclusion** Why are Miguel and Juanita afraid to page their aunt in the airport?
6. **Understand Motivation** Why did Miguel say, "*Te quiero mucho!*" over the microphone when he was trying to find his aunt?

"Author and You" Questions

7. **Draw an Inference** Why do you think Miguel's words in paragraph 17 make his mother cry?
8. **Draw an Inference** Why does the world look "frosty" to Miguel on page 292?

"On Your Own" Questions

9. **Draw an Inference** Why do you think Miguel is nervous about his aunt's visit?
10. **Speculate** Do you think that Miguel will like Tía Lola? Why or why not?
11. **Speculate** Why do you think that Miguel doesn't like to speak Spanish?

Activity Book
p. 154

Build Reading Fluency

Reading Silently

Reading silently is good practice. It helps you learn to read faster. This is an important way to become a fluent reader.

1. Listen to the audio recording of paragraph 1 of "How Tía Lola Came to V̶i̶s̶i̶t̶ Stay."
2. Listen to the chunks of words as you follow along.
3. Reread paragraph 1 silently two times.
4. Your teacher or partner will time your second reading.

Listen, Speak, Interact

Role-Play Dialogue

The characters in "How Tía Lola Came to ~~Visit~~ Stay" use **dialogue.** Dialogue is the words that the characters speak. Quotation marks go around what the people say. Look at this example of dialogue:

"Why not?" Juanita wants to know.

"It's a sensitive issue," her mother explains.

1. With two partners, read aloud the dialogue in paragraphs 1–6, on page 290. Role-play the characters. One person reads Miguel's dialogue, one reads Juanita's dialogue, and one reads Mami's dialogue.

2. Perform your dialogue for the class. Use this checklist to help you.

Speaking Checklist
1. Speak loudly enough for the audience to hear.
2. Speak slowly and clearly.
3. Produce the correct intonation patterns of words and sentences.
4. Speak with feeling.
5. Look at the audience.
6. _____

Elements of Literature

Recognize Point of View

Every story has a **point of view.** The point of view is the way the person narrates (tells) the story. "How Tía Lola Came to ~~Visit~~ Stay" is told from the **third person** point of view. Who tells the story in third person point of view? Study the chart to find out. Copy the chart into your Reading Log.

Point of View	
First Person	A character tells the story using the words *I, me, we,* and *us.*
Third Person	Someone else tells the story using the words *he, she,* and *they.*

Reading Log   Activity Book
                    p.155

Student
CD-ROM

Word Study

Use the Prefixes *un-* and *im-*

Prefixes are word parts added to the beginning of words. They change the meaning of a word. Two common prefixes are:

un-: means "not" or the "opposite of"

Example: The kids were <u>un</u>happy about the move to Vermont.

im-: means "not"

Example: Juanita thought Miguel was <u>im</u>polite.

1. Make a chart like the one here in your Personal Dictionary.
2. Read paragraphs 4 and 27 of the reading selection and find other words with the prefixes *un-* and *im-*. Write the words in your chart.

Prefix	Word	New Word
un-	happy	unhappy
im-	polite	impolite

3. Look up other words starting with *un-* and *im-* in your dictionary. You can also use an electronic dictionary on a CD-ROM. Write the words and their meanings in your Personal Dictionary.

Personal Dictionary   The Heinle Newbury House Dictionary   Activity Book p. 156   Student CD-ROM

Grammar Focus

Recognize the Present Perfect Tense

Writers use the **present perfect tense** when they describe a past action that has an effect on the present. It is formed with *has* or *have* and the past participle of a verb.

> Mami <u>has cooked</u> lunch for Miguel and Juanita.

The effect is on the present: Lunch is ready for them to eat now.

Find sentences in paragraphs 4, 12, 17, and 21 that use the present perfect tense.

Activity Book pp. 157–158   Student Handbook   Student CD-ROM

From Reading to Writing

Write a Narrative with Dialogue

Write a story about someone coming to visit your family. Use the list of questions to plan the main parts of your story. Answer each question on the list.

1. Include details about your family, your home, and your visitor.
2. Use quotation marks to show dialogue.
3. Be sure your story has a beginning, a middle, and an end.
4. Use the third person point of view.
5. Be sure you have correctly spelled words that sound the same but are spelled differently. For example, *they're, there,* and *their.*

The Visitor
• **Who** is coming to visit? • **How** is the visit special? • **Why** is the visitor coming? • **When** is the visitor coming? • **What** happens? • **Where** is your home and **where** is the visitor coming from?

Activity Book
p. 159

Across Content Areas

Read a Weather Map

A **weather map** gives information about the weather on a specific day.

A **legend** tells you how to read a map. Find the legend at the bottom of the map. Find the **symbols** (pictures that stand for ideas) for rain and snow.

1. What color is used for the hottest temperature?
2. What color is used for the coldest temperature?
3. Name one state where it is raining.

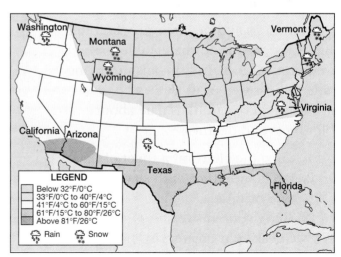

LEGEND
Below 32°F/0°C
33°F/0°C to 40°F/4°C
41°F/4°C to 60°F/15°C
61°F/15°C to 80°F/26°C
Above 81°F/26°C
Rain   Snow

Activity Book
p. 160

Into the Reading

Helen Keller

an excerpt from a biography
by George Sullivan

The Miracle Worker

an excerpt from a play
by William Gibson

Objectives

Reading Compare and contrast as you read a biography and a play.

Listening and Speaking Interpret lines from a play.

Grammar Recognize and use past progressive verbs.

Writing Write a scene from a play.

Content Science: Learn about some causes of diseases.

Use Prior Knowledge

Recall Facts About Blindness and Deafness

Blindness and deafness are disabilities. Blindness means not being able to see well or at all. Deafness means not being able to hear well or at all.

What do you think is true about blindness and deafness?

1. Copy the chart on a sheet of paper.
2. Decide whether each statement is true or false.
3. Share your answers with a partner. Check your answers in the school library or on the Internet.

Blindness and Deafness		
	True	**False**
1. People who are blind can read books.		
2. People who are blind or deaf cannot go to school.		
3. People who are deaf can learn to speak a language.		
4. People who are blind cannot have jobs or live alone.		
5. Some people who are deaf communicate by using a hand language.		

Build Background

Helen Keller

Helen Keller was born in Tuscumbie, Alabama, in 1880. She was a smart and friendly child who learned to speak very early. When Helen was one and a half years old, she became very sick. Doctors think she may have had scarlet fever.

Helen got better from her fever but lost her sight and hearing. She lived in darkness and silence. Helen struggled very hard to tell others what she needed and what she was feeling. The struggle often made her angry, and she became a difficult child.

SCIENCE

Content Connection

People who get scarlet fever today usually take penicillin. Penicillin is an **antibiotic** that kills **bacteria** (tiny living things that can cause diseases).

Build Vocabulary

Find Synonyms for Action Verbs

"The Miracle Worker" includes **action verbs** to describe what is happening.

1. With a partner, look at the underlined words in the following sentences. Choose the **synonym** (a word with a similar meaning) for each word from the box.

turns	reaching	breaks	soaks

   a. The water tumbling half into and half around the pitcher <u>douses</u> Helen's hand.
   b. Helen scrambles back onto the porch, <u>groping</u>, and finds the bell string.
   c. Helen <u>whirls</u> to the pump, pats it, holds up her palm, and Annie spells into it.
   d. Helen drops the pitcher on the slab under the spout, it <u>shatters</u>.

2. Check your work in a dictionary or synonym finder.
3. Write the words and their synonyms in your Personal Dictionary.

 Personal Dictionary

 The Heinle Newbury House Dictionary

 Activity Book *p. 161*

 Student CD-ROM

Text Structure

Biography and Drama

The first reading selection, "Helen Keller," is a **biography** (a story of a person's life). The second selection, "The Miracle Worker," is a **drama** (a play).

As you read, look for the features of a biography and a drama.

Biography	
Events	Biographies describe important events in the person's life.
Point of View	Biographies are usually told in the third-person point of view.
Facts	Biographies include information and facts that are true.

Drama (Play)	
Playwright	The author of a play is called a playwright.
Stage Directions	Stage directions tell actors where to move, what actions to make, and how to speak.
Characters	The name of the character who is speaking is before each line of dialogue.
Acts	Plays are divided into sections called acts.
Scenes	Acts can be divided into scenes. Each scene is a different place or time.

Student
CD-ROM

Reading Strategy

Compare and Contrast

You are going to read two selections. Both describe the same moment in Helen Keller's life. As you read, compare and contrast the selections.

1. View the pages of both selections. How do they look different?
2. Read the first paragraph of each selection. How are they the same? Do they include the same facts? Do they have different information?
3. Make a Venn Diagram in your Reading Log to record the similarities and differences you find in the two selections.

Reading Log

Student
CD-ROM

Helen Keller

an excerpt from a biography by George Sullivan

The Miracle Worker

an excerpt from a play by William Gibson

Audio

Helen Keller
an excerpt from a biography by George Sullivan

Prologue

When Helen Keller was seven years old, her parents brought Annie Sullivan to their home. Annie came to teach Helen. She had studied at a school for the blind. When Annie first came to the Keller's home, she taught Helen the manual alphabet. This means she formed the letters of the alphabet with her fingers. She did this in the palm of Helen's hand so that Helen could feel the letters. For a long time, Helen enjoyed this game, but she did not understand that the letters Annie formed made words. She did not realize that words stood for things, people, and feelings.

Compare and Contrast

What has happened to Helen's behavior? How does it compare to how she acted before?

1   About two weeks after Helen and Annie had moved into "The Little House," Annie wrote a joyful letter to a friend at the Perkins Institution. "My heart is singing for joy this morning. A miracle has happened! . . . The wild little creature of two weeks ago has been **transformed** into a gentle child. She is sitting by me as I write, her face serene and happy, **crocheting** a long red chain of Scotch wool.

2   "She lets me kiss her now," Annie's letter continued, "and when she is in a particularly gentle mood, she will sit in my lap for a minute or two . . .

3   "The great step—the step that counts—has been taken."

4   The "great step" would soon lead to an event that some people would call a miracle.

5   Day after day, Annie spelled words into Helen's hand. Helen would then take Annie's hand and spell each word back. It was like a

---

transformed   changed in an important way

crocheting   making cloth by looping thread with a hooked tool

game to Helen, and she enjoyed it. But she did not **link** the words to the things they stood for. B-R-E-A-D was just a series of letters to Helen. She did not know that it meant a baked food.

6 "She has no idea yet," Annie Sullivan wrote, "that everything has a name."

7 One day, Helen and Annie began their daily spelling lesson. Helen was in a restless mood. She was being difficult that day. Annie decided that they should take a break. They headed for the water pump at the back of the main house.

8 Helen described what then happened in *The Story of My Life.* "Someone was drawing water and my teacher placed my hand under the spout. As the cool stream **gushed** over one hand, she spelled into the other the word water, first slowly, then rapidly. I stood still, my whole attention fixed upon the motions of her fingers.

9 "Suddenly, I felt [as if] somehow the **mystery** of language was **revealed** to me. I knew then that W-A-T-E-R meant the wonderful cool something that was flowing over my hand."

10 After Helen had spelled out "water" several times, she dropped to her knees and pointed to the ground and asked for its name. She pointed to the pump and asked for its name. Suddenly, she pointed to Annie and asked for her name. Annie slowly spelled out T-E-A-C-H-E-R. From that time on, Annie was "Teacher" to Helen.

Compare and Contrast

What did Helen know at the beginning of this page? What did she know at the end?

---

link   connect
gushed   flowed quickly and in a large stream

mystery   something hard to understand
revealed   shown

11   Now Helen was eager to learn. "Everything had a name," she wrote, "and each name gave birth to a new thought.

12   "I learned a great many new words that day," Helen continued. "I do not remember what they all were. But I do know that mother, father, sister, teacher were among them. . . .

13   "It would have been difficult to find a happier child than I was as I lay in my crib at the close of that **eventful** day and lived over the joys it had brought me, and for the first time longed for a new day to come."

---

eventful   worth remembering, important

About the Author — George Sullivan (born 1927)

George Sullivan has written more than 250 books, mostly for young readers. He has written about sports and history. Sullivan has written biographies about interesting people. He enjoys taking photographs and includes these in many of his books. Sullivan said, "I'm always being asked where I get the ideas for my books. That's never been a problem for me. The ideas spring from my curiosity about people, places, and events."

➤ Why do you think George Sullivan wrote this book? To entertain, to inform, or to persuade? What strategies does he use to write?

The Miracle Worker
an excerpt from a play by William Gibson

1 (ANNIE *has pulled* HELEN *downstairs again by one hand, the pitcher in her other hand, down the porch steps, and across the yard to the pump. She puts* HELEN'S *hand on the pump handle,* **grimly**.)

2 **Annie:** All right. Pump.

3 (HELEN *touches her cheek, waits uncertainly.*)

4 No, she's not here. Pump!

5 (*She forces* HELEN'S *hand to work the handle, then lets go. And* HELEN *obeys. She pumps till the water comes, then* ANNIE *puts the pitcher in her other hand and guides it under the spout, and the water tumbling half into and half around the pitcher douses* HELEN'S *hand.* ANNIE *takes over the handle to keep water coming, and does automatically what she has done so many times before, spells into* HELEN'S *free palm:*)

6 Water. W, a, t, e, r. *Water.* It has a—*name*—

7 (*And now the miracle happens.* HELEN *drops the pitcher on the* **slab** *under the spout, it shatters. She stands transfixed.* ANNIE *freezes on the pump handle: there is a change in the sundown light, and with it a change in* HELEN'S *face, some light coming into it we have never seen there, some struggle in the depths behind it; and her lips tremble, trying to remember something the muscles around them once knew, till at last it finds its way out, painfully, a baby sound buried under the* **debris** *of years of dumbness.*)

8 **Helen:** Wah. Wah.

9 (*And again, with great effort*)

10 Wah. Wah.

11 (HELEN *plunges her hand into the* **dwindling** *water, spells into her own palm. Then she gropes* **frantically,** ANNIE *reaches for her hand, and* HELEN *spells into* ANNIE'S *hand.*)

12 **Annie** [*whispering*]: Yes.

13 (HELEN *spells it again.*)

Compare and Contrast

How is this description of Helen's discovery different from the description in the first reading, "Helen Keller"?

---

grimly unhappily, perhaps a little angrily
slab a large, flat piece of stone or concrete
debris garbage

dwindling getting smaller and smaller
frantically in a panic, hurrying

14   Yes!

15   (HELEN *grabs at the handle, pumps for more water, plunges her hand into its* **spurt** *and grabs* ANNIE'S *to spell it again.*)

16   *Yes!* Oh, my dear—

17   (*She falls to her knees to clasp* HELEN'S *hand, but* HELEN *pulls it free, stands almost* **bewildered,** *then drops to the ground, pats it swiftly, holds up her palm,* **imperious,** ANNIE *spells into it:*)

18   Ground.

19   (HELEN *spells it back.*)

20   Yes!

21   (HELEN *whirls to the pump, pats it, holds up her palm, and* ANNIE *spells into it.*)

22   Pump.

23   (HELEN *spells it back.*)

24   Yes! Yes!

25   (*Now* HELEN *is in such an excitement she is* **possessed,** *wild,* **trembling,** *cannot be still, turns, runs, falls on the porch steps, claps it, reaches out her palm, and* ANNIE *is at it instantly to spell:*)

26   Step.

27   (HELEN *has no time to spell back now, she whirls groping, to touch anything,* **encounters** *the* **trellis,** *shakes it, thrusts out her palm, and* ANNIE *while spelling to her cries wildly at the house.*)

28   Trellis. Mrs. Keller! Mrs. Keller!

29   (*Inside,* KATE *starts to her feet.* HELEN *scrambles back onto the porch, groping, and finds the bell string, tugs it; the bell rings, the distant chimes begin tolling the hour, all the bells in town seem to break into speech while* HELEN *reaches out and* ANNIE *spells* **feverishly** *into her hand.* KATE *hurries out, with* KELLER *after her;* AUNT EV *is on her feet, to peer out the window; only* JAMES

Compare and Contrast

Compare this description of Helen to what you learned about Helen in the first reading. Do you know more about her?

---

spurt   a big burst

bewildered   confused

imperious   having an attitude; acting superior or better than someone else

possessed   held by, unable to get away from the feeling

trembling   shaking

encounters   finds

trellis   a wooden structure for plants

feverishly   with excitement

remains at the table, and with a napkin wipes his damp brow. From up right and left the servants—VINEY, the two Negro children, the other servant—run in, and stand watching from a distance as HELEN, ringing the bell, with the other hand encounters her mother's skirt; when she throws a hand out, ANNIE spells into it:)

30 Mother.

31 *(KELLER now **seizes** HELEN'S hand, she touches him, **gestures** a hand, and ANNIE again spells:)*

32 Papa–she *knows!*

33 *(KATE and KELLER go to their knees, **stammering,** clutching HELEN to them, and ANNIE steps **unsteadily** back to watch the threesome, HELEN spelling wildly into KATE'S hand, then into KELLER'S, KATE spelling back into HELEN'S; they cannot keep their hands off her, and rock her in their clasp.*

Compare and Contrast

How is the mood or feeling at the end of the play the same or different from the biography?

34 *Then HELEN gropes, feels nothing, turns all around, pulls free, and comes with both hands groping, to find ANNIE. She encounters ANNIE'S thighs, ANNIE kneels to her, HELEN'S hand pats ANNIE'S cheek impatiently, points a finger, and waits; and ANNIE spells into it:)*

35 Teacher.

36 *(HELEN spells it back, slowly; ANNIE nods.)*

37 Teacher.

---

seizes grabs
gestures makes a motion that suggests a particular meaning, such as a wave

stammering unable to complete words, usually from being full of strong feelings
unsteadily as if shaky on one's feet or likely to fall over, perhaps moving from side to side or stumbling

About the Author   William Gibson (born 1914)

William Gibson is best known for his drama about Helen Keller and Annie Sullivan. He wrote *The Miracle Worker* in 1957 as a script for television. The script was later changed to work as a stage play and a film.

► Why do you think that William Gibson gave the title *The Miracle Worker* to this play?

Beyond the Reading

Reading Comprehension

Question-Answer Relationships (QAR)

"Right There" Questions

1. **Recall Facts** What is the relationship between Helen and Annie?
2. **Recall Facts** In "Helen Keller," what problem does Annie have with Helen?
3. **Recall Facts** In both reading selections, what is the first word that Helen connects to the thing it names?

"Think and Search" Questions

4. **Connect** How does Helen learn that W-A-T-E-R spells *water?*
5. **Recognize Distinguishing Features** Name one feature from "Helen Keller" that helps you identify it as a biography.
6. **Understand Literary Terms** In "The Miracle Worker," what is an example of stage directions?

"Author and You" Questions

7. **Evaluate** Do you think Annie Sullivan was a good teacher? Why or why not?
8. **Make an Inference** How did Helen feel as she learned her first words?
9. **Draw Conclusions** Why do you think Helen was so excited by her discovery?

"On Your Own" Question

10. **Connect with Your Own Experiences** Tell about a time when you have been very excited about learning something.

Activity Book
p. 162

Build Reading Fluency

Adjust Your Reading Rate

When you read a play, you can learn to adjust your reading rate. Pause and read like you are speaking to a person.

1. With a partner, choose parts in "The Miracle Worker."
2. Read the parts with expression.
3. Choose your favorite part of the play.
4. Read it aloud in front of the class.
5. Did you adjust your reading rate?

Listen, Speak, Interact

Interpret Lines from a Play

"The Miracle Worker" tells the actors what to do through dialogue and stage directions.

1. With a partner, reread the play. Choose two examples of stage directions and the dialogue that goes with them.

2. Act out (perform) the dialogue. One of you will play Annie, and the other will play Helen.
3. Videotape your performance, if possible.
4. Share your interpretation with the class. Talk about how you acted out the dialogue and stage directions.

Elements of Literature

Analyze Stage Directions

Stage directions are an important part of a play. They tell readers how the characters act. Most of the text in "The Miracle Worker" is stage directions. Look at the following text from the reading:

5 (. . . ANNIE takes over the handle to keep water coming, and does automatically what she has done so many times before, spells into HELEN'S free palm:)

6 Water. W, a, t, e, r. *Water*. It has a— *name*—

The stage directions in paragraph 5 show what Annie does as she says the words in paragraph 6.

Look at the following examples. Choose the correct dialogue to go with the stage directions.

1. (JENNIFER *is sad. She walks toward her mother with her head down.*)
   a. **Jennifer:** Mom, guess what? I won the essay contest!
   b. **Jennifer:** I didn't have a good day today. I lost the essay contest.
2. (MOM *wipes* JENNIFER's *tears and hugs her. She speaks softly.*)
   a. **Mom:** That's OK. You still did a good job. You can try again next year.
   b. **Mom:** That's great! We should celebrate!

Activity Book
p. 163

Student
CD-ROM

Word Study

Use the Suffix -ly

You learned earlier that one common suffix is **-ly.** It makes an adjective into an adverb. **Adverbs** describe a verb and tell more precisely *how* an action happened.

> **grimly** means "in a grim way"

> She puts Helen's hand on the pump handle, grimly.

The word *grimly* answers the question: How did Annie put Helen's hand on the pump? She did it in a grim (serious) way. Both of the selections in this chapter have examples of vivid and precise adverbs ending in *-ly*.

1. In your Personal Dictionary, make a chart and list other words ending in *-ly* from paragraph 8 of "Helen Keller" and paragraphs 5, 7, 11, and 17 of "The Miracle Worker."
2. Write the verb that each *-ly* word describes.

Adverb	Verb It Describes
grimly	puts

Personal Dictionary   Activity Book p. 164   Student CD-ROM

Grammar Focus

Recognize and Use Past Progressive Verbs

The **past progressive tense** describes an action from the past that was in progress. Here is an example from the first reading selection:

> W-A-T-E-R meant the wonderful cool something that <u>was flowing</u> over my hand.

The water continued to flow. Notice that the past progressive verb has a helping verb. The helping verb can be *was* or *were.*

1. Find two more examples of past progressive verbs from paragraphs 7 and 8 of "Helen Keller."
2. On a piece of paper, write your own sentence using a past progressive verb. Underline the past progressive verb. Circle the helping verb.

Activity Book pp. 165–166   Student Handbook   Student CD-ROM

From Reading to Writing

Write a Scene from a Play

Write a **scene** from a play. Focus your scene on a discovery you have made.

1. Show what happens in the story through the characters' actions.
2. Use past continuous verbs.
3. Use adverbs to describe *how* actions are completed.
4. Share your written scene with a partner. Read your scene aloud, with each of you taking different roles.

> **Scene 1**
>
> *Carlos:* Hey! Let's turn down this street and see if we can find our way home.
>
> (CARLOS points down the street and looks at his friend, BEN.)
>
> *Ben:* I don't know what the street is on the other side.

Activity Book
p. 167

Across Content Areas

Learn About Some Causes of Diseases

Microorganisms are very small living things. Some can cause diseases.

Bacteria are single cell microorganisms. Bacteria can cause diseases like scarlet fever and cholera. Medicines called **antibiotics** can kill bacteria.

Viruses are another type of microorganism. They can cause flu and chicken pox. Scientists have developed **vaccines** that prevent some viruses from making us sick.

Write the answers to these sentences on a piece of paper.

1. Antibiotics can be used to cure diseases caused by _____ .
   a. bacteria   **b.** viruses
2. An example of a disease caused by a virus is _____ .
   a. cholera   **b.** flu
3. How could you find more information about one of the diseases listed in the article?
   Look _____ .
   a. in an encyclopedia
   b. on the Internet
   Both **a** and **b**

Activity Book
p. 168

Hearing:
The Ear

an excerpt
from a textbook

Objectives

Reading Represent text information in an outline as you read an excerpt from a textbook.

Listening and Speaking Discuss how sound waves travel.

Grammar Recognize subject and verb agreement in the present tense.

Writing Write to inform.

Content The Arts: Learn about the voice.

Use Prior Knowledge

Listen to Learn

1. Close your eyes and sit quietly for one minute. Listen to all of the sounds you hear. Make a mental list of the sounds. A mental list is a list that is in your mind and not written down.

2. Open your eyes. Copy the chart below on a piece of paper. Write down the sounds you heard.
3. Compare your list with your classmates'. Did everyone hear the same things?
4. Discuss what helps you to listen better.

Sounds in the Classroom	Sounds in the School	Sounds Outdoors
foot tapping	door closing	siren

Build Background

The Ear

The human ear is made up of three main parts: the outer ear, the middle ear, and the inner ear. The outer ear is what you see on the outside of your head plus the ear canal. The ear canal connects the outer ear to the middle ear. A tube in the middle ear opens when your ears "pop" in an airplane or elevator. Hearing occurs in the inner ear.

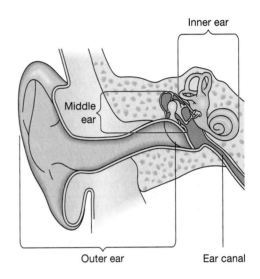

Inner ear

Middle ear

Outer ear

Ear canal

Content Connection

Sound pressure is measured in **decibels.** Sounds over 85 decibels (such as big city traffic) can cause damage to hearing.

Build Vocabulary

Identify Science Vocabulary

As you read "Hearing: The Ear," you will see words that you may not know. Here are ways to learn new science words.

1. **Glosses** Check the glosses at the bottom of each page to find definitions.
2. **Dictionary** Check a dictionary for definitions.
3. **Graphics in a Science Textbook** Check the drawings, photographs, and labels. Important terms are used as headings so you can find them.

As you read, write definitions for the science vocabulary in your Personal Dictionary.

Personal Dictionary

The Heinle Newbury House Dictionary

Activity Book *p. 169*

Student CD-ROM

Text Structure

Textbook

"Hearing: The Ear" comes from a science **textbook,** a book written specifically to teach students. Look for these features of a textbook as you read:

Textbook	
Headings	"titles" of major sections; capital letters are used for the first word and important words
Subheadings	"titles" that divide major sections into smaller sections; capital letters are used for the first word and important words
Graphics	ways of showing information with drawings, charts, and other features
Specific Details and Examples	information that helps you understand the points the textbook is making

The Parts of the Ear

The Outer Ear

Xxxx xxxxxxx x xxxxxxxxx xxxxxxx xxx. Xxx xxxxxxxxx xxxx xxxx xxxxxxxxxxx xxx xxxxx. Xxx xxxxxxxxxx xxxxxx x xxxxxxxxxxxxx xx xxxxxxx xxxx xxxxxxxxxxx xxxx xxxx xxxxx. Xxxxx xxxxxx xxxxxx xxxxxxxxxx. Xxxxx xxxxxx xxxxxx. Xxx xxxxxxxxxx xxxxxx x xxxxxxxx.

The Middle Ear

Xxxx xxxxxxx x xxxxxxxxxx xxxxxxx xxx. Xxx xxxxxxxxx xxxx xxxx xxxxxxxxxx xxx xxxxx. Xxx xxxxxxxxxx xxxxxx x xxxxxxxxxxxxx xx xxxxxxx xxxx xxxxxxxxxxx xxx.

The Inner Ear

Xxxx xxxxxxx x xxxxxxxxxx xxxxxxx xxx. Xxx xxxxxxxxx xxx xxxxx xxxxxxxxxx xxx xxxxx. Xxx xxxxxxxxxx xxxxxx x xxxxx xxxxxxx xx xxxxxxx xxxx. Xxxxx xxx xxxxxx xxxxxx xxx xxxxxxx xxxx xxxx xxxx.

Student
CD-ROM

Reading Strategy

Represent Text Information in an Outline

One way to learn as you read a textbook is to write an **outline** of the information. In an outline, you list the major parts of what you are reading. Then you list the important facts about that part.

You can use the subheadings and the words in **bold** in a text to help you with your outline. Use **Roman numerals** (I, II, III) for the major parts.

As you read "Hearing: The Ear," write an outline of the information.

Outline

I. Sound Waves
   A. Vibrations produce sounds.
   B. Vocal cords vibrate to produce voice.
   C. etc.
II. Ears for Hearing and Balance
   A. Outer ear funnels sound waves to eardrum.
   B. etc.

Student
CD-ROM

Hearing: The Ear

an excerpt
from a textbook

Hearing: The Ear

How do your ears work?

1   Next time you watch television, close your eyes and listen. What do you hear? Besides the sounds from the television, you might hear people talking in the kitchen and cars on the street. But what exactly are these sounds? And how do you hear them?

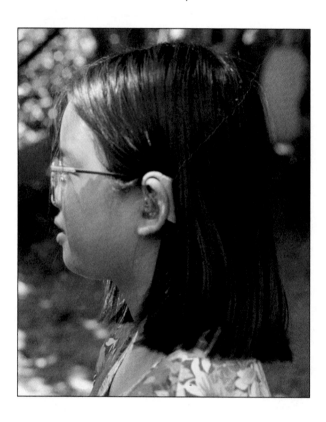

Audio

Sound Waves

2   You can find out what sound is by carefully stretching a rubber band tightly and plucking it with your finger. The plucking causes the rubber band to move back and forth, or vibrate, very quickly. At the same time, the rubber band makes a humming sound. If you touch the rubber band to keep it from vibrating, the hum stops, too.

> **Represent Text Information in an Outline**
>
> What is the name of the subheading for this section?

3   **Vibrations** produce sounds. You hear the sound of a drum when you hit a drum head and make it vibrate. You hear sounds from a TV or radio when parts inside the speakers vibrate. People hear your voice when the **vocal cords** in your throat vibrate.

4   Some things vibrate, or move back and forth, very slowly. Slow vibrations make low sounds, like the boom of a bass drum or a fog horn. **Rapid** vibrations make high sounds, like the sound of a guitar string or a high note in music.

---

vibrations   the movement created when something moves back and forth very quickly

vocal cords   the part of the throat that vibrates to help a person speak

rapid   very quick

5   Sound is a form of energy that moves in waves. For example, you give the strings of a guitar energy when you pluck them. This energy makes the strings move back and forth. Then, gas **molecules** in the air next to the strings begin to vibrate too. They bump against other molecules, and make them vibrate. In this way, sound waves move through the air.

6   Many of the sounds you hear travel through the air. But sound waves also travel through **liquids** and **solids.** When you go swimming, you can hear sounds underwater because sound waves move through water. You can even hear yourself crunch foods such as celery because sound waves move through the bones in your head!

> ### Represent Text Information in an Outline
>
> What important fact from this paragraph should you include in your outline?

7   The sounds you hear in one ear are a little different from the sounds you hear in the other ear. Because you have two ears, you can tell that sounds are coming from different places.

8   **Sound engineers,** who make compact discs and tapes, record music and other sounds in **stereo.** The engineers use at least two differently placed **microphones** to record the music. When you play the music through two stereo speakers, sounds for the left ear come through one speaker, and sounds for the right ear come through the other speaker.

---

molecules   tiny particles of material such as water or air

liquids   matter that is fluid and is not a gas or a solid; water is an example of a liquid

solids   matter that is not a liquid or a gas; a piece of wood is a solid

sound engineers   people who record music using machines to blend and control the sounds

stereo   using two or more channels

microphones   small machines that make sounds louder

Ears for Hearing and Balance

9   Your ears are much more than flaps on the sides of your head. The most important parts of your ears are inside your head. Find the ear parts in the picture, as you read about how the ear works.

> **Represent Text Information in an Outline**
>
> Should this subheading be Roman numeral II or III in your outline?

10   A **shrieking siren** sends sound waves through the air. The flaps on the sides of your head—your outer ears—catch the sound waves as they pass by. Each outer ear **funnels** the sound waves into a tubelike passage inside your head that leads to the eardrum.

11   Your eardrum stretches across the tube like a skin stretched over a drum. When sound waves hit the eardrum, the eardrum vibrates. These vibrations travel through three connected bones that are smaller than a matchhead.

12   The bones create a new set of waves that enter the **cochlea.** You can see that the cochlea is shaped like a **snail shell.** It's filled with a liquid and lined with tiny, hairlike cells. As the waves pass through the liquid, the hairlike cells begin to wiggle.

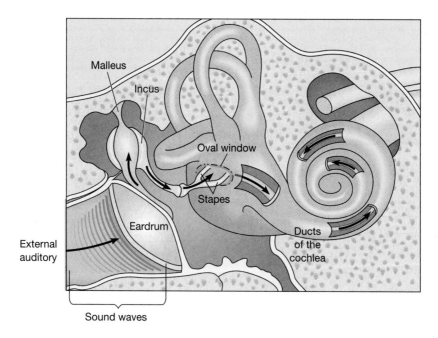

Malleus
Incus
Oval window
Stapes
Eardrum
External auditory
Ducts of the cochlea
Sound waves

---

shrieking   high-pitched and whining
siren   a machine used on ambulances, police cars, and fire trucks to make a loud sound and warn others
funnels   directs from a larger opening to a smaller opening

cochlea   a part of the inner ear shaped like a spiral
snail shell   a spiral-shaped shell of the small soft animal called a snail

whether you're sitting, standing, walking, running, or spinning like the dancer in the picture.

Represent Text Information in an Outline

What important fact from this paragraph should you include in your outline?

13 Notice that the sound of the siren has traveled through air, solid, and liquid. That's quite a trip, and it's a fast one too! In the cochlea, the journey's almost over because the wiggling cells excite tiny nerve cells.

14 In the nerve cells, the sound waves change to electric signals that race along nerve cells to the brain. It's up to your brain to **interpret** the signals and tell you that you hear a siren!

15 Your ears also help you keep your balance. You need your sense of balance to keep from falling. The parts of the inner ear that look like loops help you stay upright—

16 As you move, your inner ears pick up changes in the position of your body and of your head. If you **tilt** or turn your head, these parts of your ear send signals to your brain. Then your brain sends out signals that tell your muscles what to do to keep you from falling.

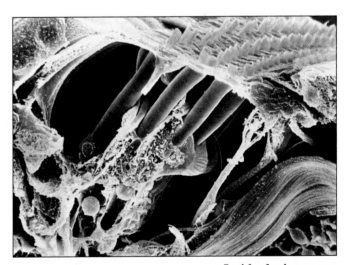

Inside the inner ear.

---

interpret understand

tilt tip to the side

Beyond the Reading

Reading Comprehension

Question-Answer Relationships (QAR)

"Right There" Questions

1. **Recall Facts** What causes sound?
2. **Recall Facts** How does sound travel?
3. **Recall Facts** Where do sound waves change to electric signals?

"Think and Search" Questions

4. **Connect** What two main jobs do your ears perform?
5. **Sequence** What is the first thing to happen when a sound wave reaches your ear?
6. **Analyze Cause and Effect** What makes sounds?

"Author and You" Question

7. **Summarize** What parts of your body help you hear properly?

"On Your Own" Questions

8. **Speculate** How would your life change if you could not hear well?
9. **Raise Questions** What unanswered questions would you research about hearing and the ear? Use your knowledge to think of questions.
10. **Interpret Visual Images** Why do you think page 322 uses an illustration to support the text instead of a photo? How do the different parts of the illustration help you understand the text?

Activity Book
p. 170

Student
CD-ROM

Build Reading Fluency

Read to Scan for Information

You must adjust your reading rate to read fast when you scan. Scanning is looking for the title, headings, subheadings, and key words in a text. With a partner answer these questions.

1. What is the title of the reading?
2. What are the headings?
3. What are the subheadings?
4. What are the key words?

Listen, Speak, Interact

Discuss How Sound Waves Travel

Participate in a shared reading, which will show you how to use clues to get meaning from the reading.

1. With a partner, scan the selection for descriptions of sound waves. To scan the selection, look through the selection quickly.
2. Take turns reading one of the descriptions aloud. First read in your normal voice. Then read in a whisper, or a very quiet voice.
3. Was it more difficult to hear your partner read in a quiet voice? When you read in a quiet voice, do you think the sound waves travel differently than when you read in a louder voice? Use words from the selection to explain your answer.

Elements of Literature

Recognize Descriptive Language

Scientific writing must be very precise (exact). Science writers use descriptive language to help you picture actions. Descriptive language is very precise. It tells you exactly what is happening and helps you form a picture in your mind.

1. Copy the chart in your Reading Log.
2. Use a dictionary to find the meanings of the specific verbs *pluck, vibrate,* and *crunch.* Write the definitions in the chart.
3. How do the specific verbs give you more information than the general verbs?

General Verbs	Specific Verbs
pull	pluck definition: _____ _____ _____
move	vibrate definition: _____ _____ _____
bite	crunch definition: _____ _____ _____

 Reading Log

 The Heinle Newbury House Dictionary

 Activity Book *p. 171*

 Student CD-ROM

Word Study

Identify Words with Greek Origins

Many words in English come from Greek words. Understanding word origins can help you learn new words. For example, the prefix *tele-* means "far" in Greek. How does this help you understand the word *television*?

1. On a piece of paper, make a web like the one shown.
2. Look up words starting with the Greek prefix *tele-* in a dictionary. Write them in your web.
3. What do each of these words mean? Write the words and their definitions in your Personal Dictionary.

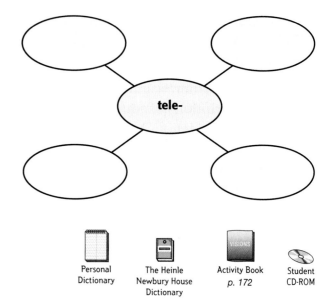

Personal Dictionary   The Heinle Newbury House Dictionary   Activity Book *p. 172*   Student CD-ROM

Grammar Focus

Recognize Subject and Verb Agreement in the Present Tense

A verb in the present tense must *agree* with its subject. If the subject of the sentence is *he, she, it,* or a singular noun, the verb ends in *s.* This is called third-person singular.

1. Look for three examples of third-person singular subjects and verbs. Look in paragraphs 5, 10, and 11 of the selection.
2. Write one sentence with a third-person singular subject and verb.

Activity Book *pp. 173–174*   Student Handbook   Student CD-ROM

Sound	move**S**	in waves.
third-person singular subject	present tense verb	

From Reading to Writing

Write to Inform

Write about how to do something that you know. For example, you might explain how to research something on the Internet.

1. Use a heading and subheadings to organize information. This will help readers identify the parts of the process. Be sure to capitalize the first word and important words.
2. Address the reader directly, using the pronoun *you*.
3. Add specific details and real-life examples to make it easier for readers to understand the process.
4. Illustrate your entry to help explain difficult parts of the process.

> **How to Research Something on the Internet**
>
> ○ **The Internet Service Provider**
>   First, you must have an Internet Service Provider. Some examples are . . .
>
> ○ **Logging On**
>   In order to log on, first . . .
>
> ○ **Key Words**
>   For every topic you research . . .

Activity Book
p. 175

Across Content Areas

THE ARTS

Learn About the Voice

The vocal cords in your **larynx** (voice box) make sound. Men's vocal cords are thicker and vibrate more slowly than women's. Therefore, men have lower voices.

In music, men usually sing the lower notes. Some men can sing higher or lower notes than other men. The same is true for women. There are four main categories of voices, two for men and two for women: **soprano, alto, tenor,** and **bass.**

Copy the chart. Complete it with the four voice categories. Here are some clues.

1. *Alto* is a woman's part, and *tenor* is a man's part.
2. *Soprano* is the highest part, and *bass* is the lowest part.

	Men	Women
Higher		
Lower		

Activity Book
p. 176

CHAPTER 4

The Art of Making Comic Books

an illustrated "how-to" book
by Michael Morgan Pellowski

Reading Make inferences as you read an illustrated "how-to" book.

Listening and Speaking Explain a concept for a character.

Grammar Understand the present conditional.

Writing Write an illustrated "how-to" article.

Content The Arts: Learn about art forms.

Use Prior Knowledge

Discuss Comic Books

What do you know about comic books? Ask and answer these questions with a partner.

1. Do you have any comic books? Which ones?
2. Do you know any comic book heroes? What special powers do they have?
3. What movies have you seen that are based on comic book heroes?
4. Where can you find comic books?
5. How do you think that a comic book is made? Is it made by one person or a team of people?

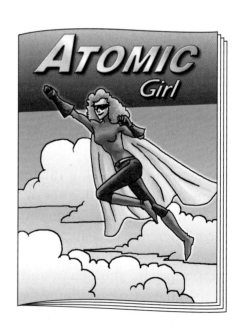

Build Background

The History of Comic Books

A comic book tells a story mostly through pictures and dialogue. The words of the characters are written in balloons above their heads.

Comic books had their origins in newspaper comics. In the 1930s these comics were sometimes reprinted in book form. The comic book characters were often funny (the word *comic* means *funny*).

In the mid 1930s, a new kind of comic book appeared. These books had original stories, not stories reprinted from newspaper comics, and they were about a specific adventure.

In 1938, the comic book world changed when Superman, a superhero, appeared. Since then, superheroes have been the main characters of comic books.

Content Connection

Several popular movies have been based on comic book superheroes.

Build Vocabulary

Learn Words About Art

You can use your own knowledge and context clues to learn words about art.

1. Work with a partner. Read the following sentences. Match the underlined words with their definitions.

Definitions
• person or animal in a story
• special clothing
• an idea

a. You can't begin to write or draw stories until you have a <u>concept</u>.

b. Creating a <u>character</u> is like fitting together the pieces of a puzzle.

c. The rule for <u>costumes</u> is the same as for body type.

2. Check your answers in a dictionary.

3. Write the words and definitions in your Personal Dictionary.

Personal Dictionary

The Heinle Newbury House Dictionary

Activity Book
p. 177

Student CD-ROM

Text Structure

Illustrated "How-to" Book

Illustrations are drawings or other artwork that help you understand a text. "The Art of Making Comic Books" is a **"how-to"** book. It tells how to make comic books. It also uses illustrations to show parts of the process. Here are some special features of an illustrated "how-to" book.

Look for these distinguishing features as you read. Focus on the information in the pictures.

Illustrated "How-to" Book	
Illustrations	drawings and other artwork that explain and add detail
Captions	words next to the pictures that explain what is happening
Step-by-Step Explanation	information that tells you exactly what to do

Student
CD-ROM

Reading Strategy

Make Inferences Using Text Evidence

As you read, you need to **make inferences** to understand. You make inferences by using **text evidence** (words and details) that gives you information.

1. Read the first paragraph of "The Art of Making Comic Books." What evidence tells you that the characters in comic books are made up?
2. In your Reading Log, make a chart like the one shown. Write the inference you can make from the text evidence.

Text Evidence	Inferences
humans fly like birds	characters are made up
teenagers stay young forever	
let your imagination run wild	

Reading Log   Student
CD-ROM

an illustrated "how-to" book
by Michael Morgan Pellowski

Audio

Make Inferences Using Text Evidence

Look at the boldfaced words only. How can you use them to make an inference about the characters in comic books?

1 Biff! Zap! Ka-pow! Welcome to the world of comic books. It's a place where animals walk, talk, and think like people and marvelously well-muscled humans fly like birds. It's a world populated by heroes, villains, and tough **antihero** good guys who act like bad guys.

2 In the timeless universe of comic books, teenagers stay young forever and get in and out of wild **predicaments** in the blink of an eye. The comic book world is filled with **aliens,** monsters, superheroes, detectives, pirates, robots, **mutants,** magicians, **avenging** soldiers, fearless **barbarians,** and anything else overactive imaginations can conjure up.

---

antihero   a hero who does not have the usual qualities of a hero, such as courage or physical strength

predicaments   troubling situations

aliens   beings from outer space

mutants   creatures whose features have changed from normal to strange

avenging   getting revenge

barbarians   characters who are brutal and do not follow any rules

VHOOSH BAM BOOM ZAP POW

3   Imagination! That's the key to unlocking the gateway into the comic book industry. Some comic book stories build on real-life situations of war, crime, history, politics, technology, science, or romance. But most successful comic books use reality only as a **springboard** into a **dimension** beyond belief. When was the last time you bumped into a half-human robot **terminator** or a hairy mutant at the mall? In real life you won't encounter six-foot-tall turtles in the sewers or millionaire ducks who speak with Scottish accents.

4   If you want to be a comic book writer and/or artist, let your imagination run wild. When your imagination shifts into overdrive, you can capture that creative power to produce your own comics . . .

Make Inferences Using Text Evidence

What is the most important quality for a comic book writer to have? Use text clues to help you answer.

---

springboard   a place to start
dimension   (here) another world

terminator   a character who hunts other characters on command

Comic Book Characters

5   To produce a successful comic book, you need a star if the book revolves around a main character, or an interesting **premise** if the book focuses on a theme like horror, UFOs, or crime. If it's a theme book, you may also want to develop a host to introduce stories.

6   Creating a character is your chance to let your imagination run wild. Over the years, comic book stars have ranged from polite **do-gooders** to **off-the-wall** or imperfect folks with acne, **hang-ups,** and even money problems. Experiment with the **absurd.** Go one step beyond. The comic book field knows no boundaries where heroes and stars are concerned.

> **Make Inferences Using Text Evidence**
>
> Draw an inference about the role that imagination plays in creating comic book characters.

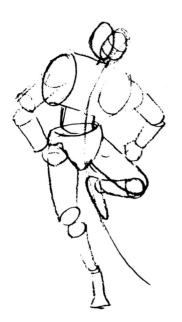  

---

premise   an idea
do-gooders   people who always try to do good things
off-the-wall   somewhat crazy or different

hang-ups   difficulties
absurd   foolish, ridiculous

**Make Inferences
Using Text
Evidence**

The text says to
"take the time to
define and refine
your hero." What
does this phrase
suggest about the
importance of
characters in
comics?

7 You can't begin to write or draw stories until you have a solid concept, so take the time to define and refine your hero. Who knows? The next comic book **best-seller** might be the outrageous character you come up with . . .

Drawing New Characters

8 . . . A number of important issues come into play as a new character takes shape. Some questions to ask yourself are: How realistic do I want this character to look? What kind of body type do I want the hero to have? Slender? **Stocky?** Muscular? Is the character ugly or handsome? Tall or short? Young or old? What **distinctive features** can I create that will set my character apart from others?

---

best-seller a very popular work that many people buy

stocky strongly built

distinctive features characteristics that identify a person

9   Creating a character is like fitting together the pieces of a jigsaw puzzle. You take a bunch of characteristics (hair, build, **facial** features, body type, and so on) and fit them together until you find just the right look for the character.

10   Sometimes it is a good idea to **sketch** a series of heads and faces first and then do a series of various body types. You can even break that process down further into a variety of eyes, noses, chins, and so on. Once you have a wide variety of choices, you can mix and match your sketches until your character has just the correct combination of features.

Make Inferences Using Text Evidence

What can you conclude about how many features you should draw before creating your character?

---

facial of the face

sketch draw quickly without giving many details

Costumes/Clothing

11   The rule for costumes and clothing is the same as for body type. Try several different looks on your characters. What kind of mask should your superhero wear, if any? Should he or she wear boots and a cape? If you're doing an animal character, does the animal dress in human clothes? Experiment with a number of looks before making any final choices.

About the Author

Michael Morgan Pellowski (born 1949)

Michael Pellowski was born in New Jersey. He had many other jobs before writing books for young people. For example, he taught art and physical education. He also played football with the New England Patriots. Pellowski started writing in 1975 and has written numerous books. He writes under his own name and also as Ski Michaels. He created and hosted his own television show for children. Pellowski explained, "I'm interested in three major topics—humor, children, and sports . . . I close my weekly television show with the words 'Don't grow up too fast, because it's great to be a kid.' That sums up my cause in life."

► Do you think Michael Pellowski likes or dislikes comic books? Find evidence in the reading and in his biography above to support your opinion.

Beyond the Reading

Reading Comprehension

Question-Answer Relationships (QAR)

"Right There" Questions

1. **Recall Facts** What is this selection about?
2. **Recall Facts** What is the first step in creating a comic book?
3. **Recall Facts** Name three characters found in comic books.

"Think and Search" Questions

4. **Make Inferences** What can you infer about the characters in comic books? Do they have features based on real people or are the features all made up?
5. **Find the Main Idea** What do you need to make a successful comic book?

6. **Analyze Cause and Effect** How does first sketching different faces and heads help you create a character?

"Author and You" Question

7. **Make Observations** Do you think that creating comic books is hard or easy? Explain.

"On Your Own" Questions

8. **Speculate** Do you think you would be good at creating comic books? Why or why not?
9. **Speculate** If you created a comic book character, what would he or she look like?

Activity Book
p. 178

Student
CD-ROM

Build Reading Fluency

Repeated Reading

"The Art of Making Comic Books" has difficult words. You can learn to read and understand faster if you read one paragraph at a time. Rereading builds confidence.

1. With a partner, read paragraph 1 on page 334 three times.
2. Next, read paragraph 2 three times.
3. Continue rereading each paragraph.
4. Stop after ten minutes.

Listen, Speak, Interact

Explain a Concept for a Character

"The Art of Making Comic Books" provides details about making comic book characters.

1. Reread the selection with a partner. Discuss the different features and types of comic book characters.
2. Brainstorm your own character. As you speak, use evidence and examples to support your ideas. Make a list of characteristics, special powers, and how the character will look.
3. Clarify your ideas. Explain why you want to give your character these qualities.
4. Draw the character with your partner. Make sure each feature is based on your list of ideas.
5. Present your character to the class. Explain each feature. Also explain your reasons for including it.

Elements of Literature

Recognize Writing Style

Remember, **style** is the way writers use language to express themselves.

Michael Pellowski uses an informal writing style in "The Art of Making Comic Books." He does not always use complete sentences.

> What kind of body do I want the hero to have? Slender? Stocky? Muscular?

Now look at the example written in a more formal style:

> What kind of body do I want the hero to have? Should he be slender? Should he be stocky? Should he be muscular?

1. Discuss the informal and formal examples with a partner. How do you feel when you read each one? Which one sounds "friendlier"?
2. Read paragraph 3 and pay attention to the question near the end of the paragraph. What is your reaction to the question? Do you think that this question shows formal or informal style?

Activity Book
p. 179

Student
CD-ROM

Word Study

The Suffix -ian

The suffix **-ian** is often used to tell where a person is from.

   She's a <u>Californian</u>.

The suffix **-ian** can also give you other kinds of information about people.

1. Copy the chart in your Personal Dictionary.
2. Reread paragraph 2 of the reading selection and find two examples of words with the suffix -ian. Write the words in the chart.
3. Look the words up in the dictionary and write them in your chart.

4. Add these words to your chart:

   librarian   technician   comedian

5. If you know their meanings, write them in the chart. If not, look them up and then write them in.

-ian Word	Meaning

Personal Dictionary   The Heinle Newbury House Dictionary   Activity Book p. 180   Student CD-ROM

Grammar Focus

Understand the Present Conditional

A present conditional sentence has a dependent clause beginning with *if*.

In the present conditional sentence, one action depends on another.

   If I study hard, I make good grades.

Making good grades *depends on* studying hard.

Note that when the dependent clause comes first, it is followed by a comma.

1. Read this sentence:

   You need a star if the book revolves around a main character.

2. Decide which of the two phrases above depends on the other.

Activity Book pp. 181–182   Student Handbook   Student CD-ROM

From Reading to Writing

Write an Illustrated "How-to" Article

Write an illustrated "how-to" article. Use the chart to plan.

	Text	Illustrations
Step 1		
Step 2		
Step 3		

1. Tell what you are going to explain.
2. Use a step-by-step approach. Start at the beginning and move to the end of the process. Record the steps from first to last.
3. Use illustrations and captions.
4. Use an informal writing style.

Activity Book
p. 183

Across Content Areas

Learn About Art Forms

People who create art are called artists. There are many different forms of art.

To learn more about these art forms, do an Internet search. Use the key words *painting, sculpture, photography,* or *graphic design.* You can also look for a book on art in your school library. Ask your librarian to help you.

Art Form	Artist	More About the Art Form
painting	painter	The type of paint can make a painting look very different. Some examples are oil paints and watercolors.
sculpture	sculptor	A sculpture is a three-dimensional representation of an object. Sculptors use materials such as clay, wood, wax, stone, or metal.
photography	photographer	A photographer uses a camera. It can be a still camera or a video camera.
graphic design	graphic designer	Graphic designers use technology such as computer programs to create pictures, illustrations, and other visual images.

Activity Book
p. 184

Student
Handbook

Apply and Expand

Listening and Speaking Workshop

Present an Oral Summary of a Reading

Topic

Choose the reading selection that you liked best from this unit. Prepare and present a summary of the reading.

Step 1: Use the Sunshine Organizer to plan your summary.

Answer these questions. Be specific.

1. *What* is the title of the story?
2. *Who* are the characters? Did you like them? Why or why not?
3. *Where* do the main events take place?
4. *When* do the main events take place?
5. *What* was the problem or conflict?
6. *How* did the character resolve the problem?
7. *Why* is it your favorite story?

Step 2: Plan your summary.

1. Use one of these ideas for a strong opening.
   a. Ask a question.
   b. Say something funny.
   c. Make a dramatic statement.
   d. Refer to an authority and use quotes.
2. Make note cards on your key points.
3. Write an ending that states why you liked the story.

Step 3: Practice your presentation with a partner.

1. Stay on the topic.
2. Be confident so that your listeners will believe that you know what you are talking about.
3. Use your note cards.
4. Ask your partner to fill out the Active Listening Checklist.
5. Fill out the Speaking Checklist.
6. Evaluate the feedback from the checklists and revise your summary.

Step 4: Present your summary to the class.

You may want to record your summary on audio or video to share with your family.

Viewing Workshop

View and Think

Evaluate Visual Media

Visual media include signs, posters, television, videos, technology presentations, and movies.

1. Record all the types of visual media you have seen this week in a journal. Tell what important events were shown in each.

2. Evaluate the purpose of each type of media. Is it for entertainment? Does it try to persuade you? Does it give information?

3. Decide the effect of each type of media and how it influences you. If you had to choose only one form of media to view, which one would you choose? Why? Record your ideas.

4. What nonverbal messages do the types of media show? What do nonverbal messages such as gestures and body language tell you?

5. Share your ideas with the class.

Further Viewing

Watch the *Visions* CNN Video for Unit 5. Do the Video Worksheet.

CNN Video

Writer's Workshop

Write a Persuasive Editorial

Writing Prompt

You have been reading about the theme of communication. Your school board is deciding whether to allow students to carry cell phones in school. Write an editorial for your school newspaper. (Newspapers print editorials to give opinions on important topics.)

Your goal is to persuade your audience that your position is correct.

Step 1: Brainstorm.

1. Make a list of all the reasons *for* and *against* cell phones in school.
2. Decide on your opinion. Do you believe students should be allowed to carry cell phones in school? Write your opinion in one or two sentences.
3. List your best reasons for your position.

For	Against
You can stay in touch with your parents.	Phones ringing in class are distracting.

Step 2: Organize your ideas.

1. Put your ideas in order of importance. List the most important idea first.

2. For each idea, list the facts, examples, and evidence that support it.

Step 3: Write a draft.

1. Write an introductory paragraph.
   a. State why you are writing this editorial.
   b. Briefly state your position.
2. Write a paragraph about each of your major ideas. State the idea and give its supporting details.
3. Write a paragraph to conclude your letter. Briefly restate why you are for or against cell phones in school.
4. Make grammar work for you.
   a. Use the present perfect tense to talk about past actions that are important in the present: *I have had a cell phone for six months. It helps me stay in touch with my parents.*
   b. Use the past progressive tense to describe an important action from the past that was in progress: *Last year, many students were using the pay phone down the street. This was dangerous because . . .*
   c. Use present conditional sentences to express results: *If students have cell phones, they stay in better touch with their parents.*
   d. If you use the simple present tense, be sure to add -s to verbs with third-person singular subjects: *My cell phone helps me let people know if I am late.*

> *Our school board is now deciding whether students may use cell phones in school. I am* _____ _____ _____ _____ _____ .
>
>   *First, cell phones are* _____ _____ _____ _____ .
>
> *For example,* _____ _____ _____ .
>
>   *Another important point is that* _____ _____ _____ .
>
> *This is true because* _____ _____ _____ _____ .
>
>   *For these reasons, I firmly believe that* _____ _____ _____ _____ .

Step 4: Revise and edit your editorial.

1. Do you have support for all of your main ideas?
2. Does your editorial make sense?
3. Proofread your editorial to find errors in spelling, capitalization, punctuation, and paragraph indentation.

If you use a computer, use the spelling check or other features to check your work.

4. Collaborate with a partner to organize and revise your editorial. Ask a partner to read your editorial and give you feedback.

5. Revise your draft. Add or delete text as needed. Elaborate on your main ideas (provide more support for them).
6. Review how you have organized your draft. Reorganize or rearrange text so the order makes sense.

Step 5: Publish.

1. Prepare a final draft. If you write your editorial by hand, use your best handwriting. If you use a computer or a typewriter, be sure to check for typing errors.
2. Write a brief cover letter to the editor of your school newspaper. Explain that you would like to have your editorial published. Tell the editor how to get in touch with you.
3. Put your editorial and the cover letter in an envelope and mail or take it to the newspaper. Be sure to keep a copy of the editorial for yourself.
4. Read the newspaper to see if your editorial and your classmates' editorials are published.
5. Read the published editorials. Identify challenges you and your classmates had in writing to persuade.

The Heinle Newbury House Dictionary

Student Handbook

Projects

These projects will help you learn more about communication. Work alone or with a partner.

Project 1: List Types of Foreign-Language Communication

Does your community have forms of communication (media) in other languages?

1. List types of communication in your community that exist in other languages. For example, is there a television station with programs in Korean? Which Web sites can be viewed in Spanish or other languages?
2. List the kinds of communication you could not find in your community. For example, there may be no radio programs in Polish.
3. List your findings in a chart like the one below.
4. Discuss foreign language communication with a partner. Explain how these types of communication connect people across cultures.

Foreign Language Communication in My Community	Foreign Language Communication Not in My Community

5. Of the missing media, which ones do you recommend be started? Write an editorial about your idea and send it to your community newspaper for publication.

Project 2: Design Your Own Media

Have you ever thought about starting a newspaper? Would you like to draw cartoons or make posters? Would you like to host a radio program?

1. Think about the kinds of media you studied in this unit. What types of media do you use each day? Choose a form that you enjoy.
2. Create an example of this media based on one of the selections in the unit. For example, make a newspaper, draw a cartoon, or record a radio program to show something that happens in the selection.
3. Compare and contrast your media to the reading selection.
   a. How is the information the same? How is it different?
   b. What is the purpose of your media? To inform, to entertain, or to persuade? What was the author's purpose in writing the selection?
4. Share your media with the class. Evaluate how your classmates' media influence you. What effect do they have on your feelings and ideas?

Further Reading

Listed below are some books about communication. Read one or more of them. Write your thoughts and feelings about what you read. In your Reading Log, take notes on your answers to these questions:

1. Make connections between different texts. How are all types of communication similar? How are they different?
2. What is the most interesting thing you learned about communication from the books you read?
3. What question would you ask each author?
4. How can you use a book you read as a model for writing? What goals would you set as a writer after reading this book?

How Tía Lola Came to ~~Visit~~ Stay
by Julia Alvarez, Alfred A. Knopf, 2001. Tía Lola comes from the Dominican Republic to visit Miguel's family in Vermont. At first his aunt, who cannot speak English, embarrasses Miguel. Then Tía Lola helps Miguel discover his heritage.

Helen Keller
by George Sullivan, Scholastic Trade, 2001. In this book, the author uses Helen Keller's own writings to tell her life story. We learn about Keller's struggles with being blind and deaf, how she learned to overcome these physical challenges, and how she was able to help others do the same.

Dear Dr. Bell . . . Your Friend, Helen Keller
by Judith St. George, William Morrow & Co., 1993. Alexander Graham Bell, the inventor of the telephone, and Helen Keller were lifelong friends. Bell met Keller when she was six years old and helped her parents find her teacher, Annie Sullivan. This book describes the friendship shared by these people.

Speech and Hearing: Encyclopedia of Health
by Billy Alstetter, Chelsea House Publishers, 1991. This book discusses the connection between speech and hearing and how the brain interprets speech. The book also discusses speech and hearing disorders.

Manga Mania: How to Draw Japanese Comics
by Christopher Hart and Chris Hart, Watson-Gutpill Publications, Inc., 2001. This book shows how to draw in the distinct style of Japanese animation.

Communications and Broadcasting
by Harry Henderson with Lisa Yount, Facts on File, Inc., 1997. This book discusses the history of telecommunications dating back to Samuel Morse's telegraph.

Ancient Communications: From Grunts to Graffiti
by Michael B. Woods and Mary B. Woods, The Lerner Publishing Group, 2000. Ancient civilizations had their own particular ways of communicating. This book discusses the ancient civilizations of India, China, Egypt, the Middle East, Greece, and Rome.

Reading Log

Heinle
Reading Library

Frontiers

The Rocky Mountains: Emigrants Crossing the Plains,
N. Currier and J.M. Ives, lithograph. 1866.

View the Picture

1. A frontier is a place where something new begins. What kind of frontier is shown here?

2. What other kinds of frontiers do you know about?

In this unit, you will read excerpts from a textbook, a novel, two speeches, and a biography. Each selection focuses on people who have explored new frontiers. You will learn about the features of these writing forms and how to write them yourself.

The Lewis and Clark Expedition

an excerpt from
a textbook

Objectives

Reading Use chronology to locate and recall information as you read an informational text.

Listening and Speaking Use inference to act out a story.

Grammar Use appositives.

Writing Write an informational text.

Content Social Studies: Use headings as you read.

Use Prior Knowledge

Explore Ideas About Frontiers

Read the following statements and record your responses on a piece of paper. If you think that a statement is true, write *T.* If you think that a statement is false, write *F.*

1. I would like to be one of the first people to see a new place.
2. I would keep a journal if I explored a new land.
3. When exploring a new place, it is useful to have partners with different skills.
4. It would be easy to explore an unknown land.
5. We can learn many things from people who explore new places.
6. People can have different purposes for exploring a new land.

Discuss your answers with a partner.

Build Background

The Louisiana Purchase

In 1803, the United States bought the Louisiana Territory from France. The Louisiana Purchase added 828,000 square miles of land to the United States. It nearly doubled the size of the United States. At that time, the land only cost about four cents per acre.

Content Connection

Miles and **acres** are measurements in the U.S. system. Here are the amounts in the metric system:

1 mile = 1.61 kilometers
1 acre = 0.4 hectares

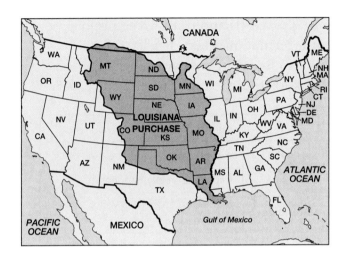

Build Vocabulary

Use a Word Wheel

Brainstorm ideas about a vocabulary word to help you understand it.

1. Brainstorm what you know about the word *expedition*. If necessary, look up the word in a dictionary. You may also use a thesaurus or synonym finder to find words with meanings that relate to *expedition*.
2. Write three words that help you remember the meaning of *expedition*. Write them in a Word Wheel like the one here.

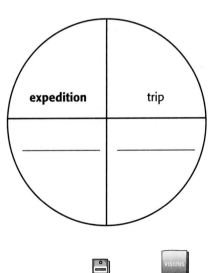

The Heinle Newbury House Dictionary

Activity Book p. 185

Student CD-ROM

Text Structure

Informational Text

"The Lewis and Clark Expedition" is an **informational text.** It tells us facts about something that actually happened. Look for these features when you read:

Informational Text	
Setting	real places
Events	things that really happened
Chronology	told in the order the events happened
Time Sequence	uses time words such as *before, after, finally* to help the reader follow what happened

As you read "The Lewis and Clark Expedition," note important events in your Reading Log.

Reading Log

Student CD-ROM

Reading Strategy

Use Chronology to Locate and Recall Information

As you read, notice that the story is told in the order that the events actually happened. This is called **chronological order.** Remembering the order in which events happened can help you recall information. Time words (such as days, dates, *then, finally*) can help you identify chronology.

1. Read the first page. What is the first important event described on this page? What is the next? Write these events in your Reading Log.
2. Continue listing events in chronological order until you finish the selection.

page 354

1. Jefferson chooses Meriwether Lewis to lead expedition.

2. Lewis chooses William Clark.

Reading Log

Student CD-ROM

The Lewis and Clark Expedition

an excerpt from a textbook

1   Long before the Louisiana Purchase, Thomas Jefferson had been **fascinated** by lands in the West. Who lived there, he wondered? What was the land like? Could the Missouri River possibly lead to a water **route** to the Pacific Ocean? Jefferson wanted to know the answers to these questions.

2   To find the answers, Jefferson sent an expedition to the newly **acquired** land, now called the Louisiana Territory. Jefferson chose Meriwether Lewis, who was an army captain, to lead the expedition. Lewis chose a fellow army captain, his friend William Clark, to share command.

> **Use Chronology to Locate and Recall Information**
>
> What happened before Lewis and Clark were chosen to lead the expedition?

Audio

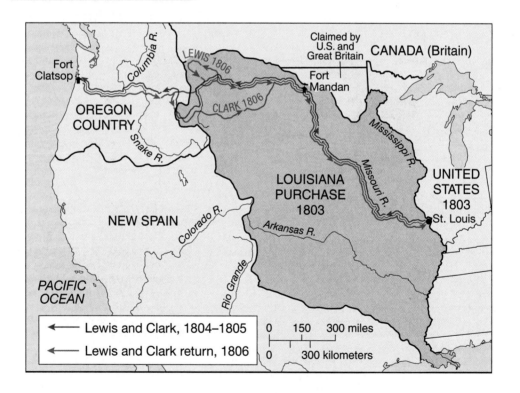

---

fascinated   greatly interested
route   a path along which one travels

acquired   bought or gotten

The Native American Sacagawea guiding the Lewis and Clark expedition. Painting by Alfred Russel.

3   Jefferson told the two captains they had three goals. One was to search for a water route to the Pacific Ocean. The second was to establish **relationships** with the Native Americans they met. Jefferson wanted the Indians to know his "wish was to be neighborly, friendly, and useful to them." The third goal was to pay close attention to "the soil and face of the country," to its plants, animals, minerals, **climate,** and to keep careful, written **records** of their findings. Today, the journals of Lewis and Clark are the main source of information about their expedition.

4   In May 1804, Lewis and Clark and other members of the expedition set out westward from St. Louis, Missouri, along the Missouri River. Follow their route on the map on the **previous** page. The expedition included soldiers, river boatmen, hunters, and York, Clark's slave and childhood friend. During the expedition, York worked at Clark's side much of the time, and had shown he was ready to **sacrifice** his life to save Clark's. Nevertheless, when York later asked to be freed as a reward for his **contributions** to the expedition, Clark refused.

> ### Use Chronology to Locate and Recall Information
>
> If the Louisiana Purchase took place in April 1803, how long did it take Jefferson, Lewis, and Clark to organize the expedition?

---

relationships   connections between people
climate   the type of weather a place has
records   things (usually written) that prove an event happened

previous   coming before something else
sacrifice   give up something valuable
contributions   helpful participation

5   Three boats carried expedition members, equipment, and **supplies.** They did not know it then, but they would not return for another 28 months.

6   During their first winter, they hired a French Canadian fur trapper and his Soshone wife, Sacagawea (sah KAH gah way ah), to act as **interpreters** and guides. Sacagawea helped Lewis and Clark establish good relations with Native Americans along the way. She helped translate Indian languages for the expedition. The baby she carried on her back signaled the peaceful purposes of the expedition.

7   Throughout the expedition, its members faced many **hardships.** They had to paddle their boats against strong river currents. Every now and then, a boat would turn over, sending **equipment** splashing into the water. And there was always the danger of being attacked by dangerous animals, like 900-pound grizzly bears.

> ### Use Chronology to Locate and Recall Information
>
> When did the members of the expedition face hardships?

---

supplies   goods necessary for an operation

interpreters   people who translate one language into another

hardships   difficulties in living conditions

equipment   items needed for a purpose

8   But Lewis and Clark were rewarded with some **fabulous** views. They saw a herd of 20,000 bison stretching across the plain and fast deerlike animals called pronghorns racing by. They crossed the tall, **spectacular** Rocky Mountains. Finally their eyes were filled with the sight of the great Pacific Ocean—"Ocean in view! Oh the joy!" wrote Clark.

9   The explorers finally returned to St. Louis in September 1806. They had not found a water route to the Pacific. But they had recorded and described thousands of varieties of plants and animals, and even brought some back for Jefferson to examine. They had also mapped a **vast** area, opening it to future exploration and new settlers from the United States.

> ### Use Chronology to Locate and Recall Information
>
> If the expedition took 28 months total, in what year would Lewis and Clark likely have arrived at the Pacific Ocean?

---

fabulous   great, wonderful
spectacular   wonderful, exciting

vast   wide

Beyond the Reading

Reading Comprehension

Question-Answer Relationships (QAR)

"Right There" Questions

1. **Recall Facts** What did Lewis and Clark's three boats carry?
2. **Identify** Who was Sacagawea?
3. **Recall Facts** For how long did Lewis and Clark travel?

"Think and Search" Questions

4. **Identify Main Ideas** What did President Jefferson want the two captains to do when they explored the Louisiana Purchase?
5. **Explain** How did Sacagawea help Lewis and Clark?

"Author and You" Question

6. **Analyze Cause and Effect** Why did Clark write "Oh the joy!" when he saw the Pacific Ocean?

"On Your Own" Questions

7. **Compare Events to Your Own Experiences** Have you ever explored a place that was new to you? Describe your experiences.
8. **Ask Questions** What unanswered questions do you have about the selection after reading it? Use what you have learned and your own knowledge to think of these questions.

Activity Book
p. 186

Student
CD-ROM

Build Reading Fluency

Reading Silently

Reading silently is good practice. It helps you learn to read faster.

1. Listen to the audio recording of paragraph 1 of "The Lewis and Clark Expedition."
2. Listen to the chunks of words as you follow along.
3. Reread paragraph 1 silently two times.
4. Your teacher or partner will time your second reading. Raise your hand when you are finished.

Listen, Speak, Interact

Use Inference to Act Out a Story

The reading selection does not include any dialogue, but we can assume that the people talked to each other.

> **Jefferson:** I want to find out what the land to the west is like.
>
> **Lewis:** What do you want to know?
>
> **Jefferson:** Well, who lives there?

1. Read the first two paragraphs of "The Lewis and Clark Expedition." With a partner, write down a conversation between Jefferson and Lewis or between Lewis and Clark.
2. Act out your conversation for the class. Adapt your word choice, diction, and usage to reflect the time when Lewis and Clark lived. They spoke formally.

Elements of Literature

Analyze Characters

Informational texts often discuss **characters** who were historical figures. The two main characters in this account are Lewis and Clark. Other important figures are Sacagawea and York. By reading carefully, you can find out what they were like.

1. Look back in the selection to find information about these people.
   a. What kind of person do you think Lewis was?
   b. What kind of friendship did Lewis and Clark have?
   c. What kind of relationship did Clark and York have?
   d. How would you describe Sacagawea's character?

2. With a small group, explain your answers.
3. Look through "The Lewis and Clark Expedition" to find more traits about the historical figures. Find examples that support your ideas. Also look for evidence in facts and details that tell about the characters.
4. List these people and their traits in your Reading Log.
5. Form three questions about the figures. How would you research answers to your questions?

Reading Log   Activity Book p. 187   Student CD-ROM

Word Study

Use a Thesaurus and a Synonym Finder to Find Synonyms

Synonyms are words that have similar meanings. A **thesaurus** and a **synonym finder** list synonyms for words. These resources are arranged in alphabetical order. Synonyms are listed after the key word that you look up.

> Jefferson chose Meriwether Lewis to <u>lead</u> the expedition.

The entry for the word *lead* in a thesaurus or a synonym finder might be:

> **lead**   guide, show the way, direct, escort, pilot, go in front, head

The chart below lists words in the reading that you could replace with synonyms.

1. Find synonyms for each word in a thesaurus or a synonym finder.
2. Write the words and their synonyms in your Personal Dictionary.

Word in Reading	Synonyms
goal	aim, target
supplies	
attack	

Personal Dictionary

Activity Book p. 188

Student CD-ROM

Grammar Focus

Use Appositives

An **appositive** is a word or phrase that follows a noun in order to give extra information about it.

> Lewis chose a fellow army captain, <u>his friend William Clark</u>, to share command.

> The expedition included York, <u>Clark's childhood friend</u>.

You use a comma before and after an appositive if it is in the middle of a sentence. If an appositive comes at the end of a sentence, use a comma at the beginning of the appositive and a period at the end.

1. Why do you think it is helpful for the author to use appositives?
2. Find another example of an appositive in paragraph 6.

Activity Book pp. 189–190

Student Handbook

Student CD-ROM

From Reading to Writing

Write an Informational Text

Write about a trip you have taken.

1. List the order of events on a piece of paper.
2. Choose the five most important events to include, and write a short paragraph about each.
3. Use chronological order to put the events in the order that they happened. Use time words to help readers understand the chronology.
4. Don't use dialogue. Simply summarize what happened.
5. Exchange your work with a partner after you write a draft. Proofread each other's writing.
6. Discuss how you and your partner can improve your work. Edit and revise your writing as needed.

Activity Book
p. 191

Across Content Areas

SOCIAL STUDIES

Use Headings as You Read

Headings are words in large type. The first word and all important words are capitalized. They are titles for a section of text. You can use headings to locate information as you research.

Read the headings on this page. What do you think the page is about?

On a piece of paper, match the sentences with the heading under which they would go.

1. The earliest European visitors were the Spanish.
2. These people lived in all regions of North America before Europeans arrived.
3. One major French area was called Louisiana.
4. The English established colonies on the east coast of the continent.

People in the Americas

Native Americans
  Xxx xx xxxxxx x xxx xxxxx. Xxxx xxx, xx xxx. X xxxx x xxx xxxxxx, xxx x xx xxxxx.

The Spanish
  Xxx xx xxxxxx x xxx xxxxx. Xxxx xxx, xx xxx. X xxxx x xxx xxxxxx, xxx x xx xxxxx.

The English
  Xxx xx xxxxxx x xxx xxxxx. Xxxx xxx, xx xxx. X xxxx x xxx xxxxxx, xxx x xx xxxxx.

The French
  Xxx xx xxxxxx x xxx xxxxx. Xxxx xxx, xx xxx. X xxxx x xxx xxxxxx, xxx x xx xxxxx.

Activity Book
p. 192

CHAPTER 2

Into the Reading

A Wrinkle in Time

an excerpt from a
science fiction novel
by Madeleine L'Engle

Objectives

Reading Describe mental images as you
read science fiction.

Listening and Speaking Present a story.

Grammar Identify the past perfect tense.

Writing Write a science fiction narrative.

Content Science: Learn about the speed
of light.

Use Prior Knowledge

Record Ideas About Space Travel

In Unit 4, you read about astronaut
Mae Jemison's travels in space aboard the
space shuttle. However, she did not travel
to other planets, as the characters in "A
Wrinkle in Time" do. What do you know
about traveling in space?

1. Copy the Know/Want to
Know/Learned Chart on a piece
of paper.

2. Fill in the chart. In the first column,
list what you know about travel to
other planets. In the second
column, list what you would like to
know. When you learn something
new about space travel, write it in
the third column.

Space Travel		
Know	**Want to Know**	**Learned**
Astronauts have gone to the moon.	Will astronauts ever go to another planet?	Scientists are developing technology to take people to Mars.

Build Background

Travel in Science Fiction

Science fiction stories usually tell about discoveries and inventions that do not exist. For example, people might travel through space in a way that we do not understand today. In this reading, the main character travels through a fifth dimension.

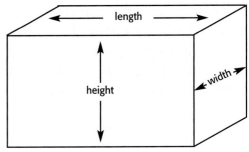

Three dimensions

Content Connection

A **dimension** is a measurement in one direction. In everyday life, we think of three dimensions: length, width, and height. The fourth dimension, studied by the scientist Albert Einstein, is time.

Build Vocabulary

Use Context Clues

You can often guess the meaning of a new word by using **context clues.** Context clues are familiar words in a sentence or nearby sentences that help you understand a new word.

Read the following sentences. There are clues that can help you determine the meaning of the underlined word. In your Personal Dictionary, write the meaning you guess for each underlined word. Check your definitions in a dictionary.

1. Mrs. Who seemed to <u>evaporate</u> until there was nothing but the glasses, and then the glasses, too, disappeared.
2. There was a gust of wind and a great <u>thrust</u> and a sharp shattering as she was shoved through—what?

Personal Dictionary

The Heinle Newbury House Dictionary

Activity Book *p. 193*

Student CD-ROM

Text Structure

Science Fiction

Science fiction is a made-up story based on scientific ideas. Using these ideas, science fiction shows the reader what might happen in the future. As you read "A Wrinkle in Time," look for the features in the chart.

Science Fiction	
Characters	may have special powers
Setting	a time and place in the future or where no one has ever been
Scientific Ideas	imaginary ideas and events based on scientific information

Student
CD-ROM

Reading Strategy

Describe Mental Images

Writers often try to make you "see" what you are reading about. These **mental images** are part of the pleasure of reading. Mental images also help you remember the characters and events in a story.

In "A Wrinkle in Time," Meg and her friend, Calvin, are going to do something that frightens Meg. The author writes:

"Could we hold hands?" Meg asks.

Calvin took her hand and held it tightly in his.

What mental image do you see when you read these lines? As you read the selection, pay attention to the mental images that you see.

Student
CD-ROM

A Wrinkle in Time

an excerpt from a science fiction novel
by Madeleine L'Engle

Audio

Prologue

Meg and her brother Charles Wallace are looking for their father, who is a scientist. He disappeared while doing top secret work on something called a tesseract, which is a way to travel through dimensions. Three mysterious women appear, who call themselves Mrs. Which, Mrs. Who, and Mrs. Whatsit. They take Meg, Charles Wallace, and their friend Calvin across space and time to look for the missing man. Meg is losing hope. Note Mrs. Which's speech: She repeats sounds in words.

1   "My child, do not **despair.** Do you think we would have brought you here if there were no hope? We are asking you to do a difficult thing, but we are **confident** that you can do it. Your father needs help, he needs courage, and for his children he may be able to do what he cannot do for himself."

2   "Nnow," Mrs. Which said. "Aare wee rreaddy?"

3   "Where are we going?" Calvin asked.

4   Again Meg felt an actual physical tingling of fear as Mrs. Which spoke.

5   "Wwee musstt ggo bbehindd thee sshaddow."

6   "But we will not do it all at once," Mrs. Whatsit comforted them. "We will do it in short **stages.**" She looked at Meg. "Now we will **tesser,** we will wrinkle again. Do you understand?"

7   "No," Meg said flatly.

Describe Mental Images

Imagine how Meg looked as she felt her fear.

---

despair   feel hopeless

confident   with strong belief in one's ability or that something will definitely happen

stages   periods of time

tesser   use a tesseract to travel

8   Mrs. Whatsit sighed. "Explanations are not easy when they are about things for which your **civilization** still has no words. Calvin talked about traveling at the speed of light. You understand that, little Meg?"

9   "Yes," Meg nodded.

10   "That, of course, is the **impractical,** long way around. We have learned to take short cuts wherever possible."

11   "Sort of like math?" Meg asked.

12   "Like in math." Mrs. Whatsit looked over at Mrs. Who. "Take your skirt and show them."

13   "*La experiencia es la madre de la ciencia.* Spanish, my dears. Cervantes. *Experience is the mother of knowledge.*" Mrs. Who took a **portion** of her white robe in her hands and held it tight.

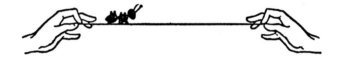

14   "You see," Mrs. Whatsit said, "if a very small insect were to move from the section of skirt in Mrs. Who's right hand to that in her left, it would be quite a long walk for him if he had to walk straight across."

15   Swiftly Mrs. Who brought her hands, still holding the skirt, together.

16   "Now, you see," Mrs. Whatsit said, "he would *be* there, without that long trip. That is how we travel."

Describe Mental Images

What image of Mrs. Who do you have in this paragraph?

---

civilization   a high level of government, laws, written language, art, music, and so on, within a society or culture

impractical   not practical, not sensible
portion   a small piece of a larger thing

17   Charles Wallace accepted the explanation **serenely.** Even Calvin did not seem **perturbed.** "Oh, *dear*," Meg sighed. "I guess I *am* a moron. I just don't get it."

18   "That is because you think of space only in three dimensions," Mrs. Whatsit told her. "We travel in the fifth dimension. This is something you can understand, Meg. Don't be afraid to try. Was your mother able to explain a tesseract to you?"

19   "Well, she never did," Meg said. "She got so upset about it. Why, Mrs. Whatsit? She said it had something to do with her and Father."

20   "It was a **concept** they were playing with," Mrs. Whatsit said, "going beyond the fourth dimension to the fifth. Did your mother explain it to you, Charles?"

Describe Mental Images

Charles is embarrassed. How does he look?

21   "Well, yes," Charles looked a little embarrassed. "Please don't be hurt, Meg. I just kept at her while you were at school till I got it out of her."

22   Meg sighed. "Just explain it to me."

23   "Okay," Charles said. "What is the first dimension?"

24   "Well—a line: —————"

25   "Okay. And the second dimension?"

26   "Well, you'd square the line. A flat square would be in the second dimension."

27   "And the third?"

28   "Well, you'd square the second dimension. Then the square wouldn't be flat any more. It would have a bottom, and sides, and a top."

---

serenely   very calmly, peacefully
perturbed   upset, flustered

concept   a general idea

29   "And the fourth?"

30   "Well, I guess if you want to put it into mathematical terms you'd square the square. But you can't take a pencil and draw it the way you can the first three. I know it's got something to do with Einstein and time. I guess maybe you could call the fourth dimension Time."

31   "That's right," Charles said. "Good girl. Okay, then, for the fifth dimension you'd square the fourth, wouldn't you?"

32   "I guess so."

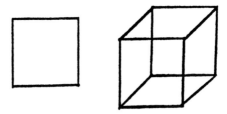

33   "Well, the fifth dimension's a tesseract. You add that to the other four dimensions and you can travel through space without having to go the long way around. In other words, to put it into Euclid, or old-fashioned plane **geometry,** a straight line is *not* the shortest distance between two points."

Describe Mental Images

What image of Meg do you have in this paragraph?

34   For a **brief illuminating** second Meg's face had the listening, probing expression that was so often seen on Charles's. "I see!" she cried. "I got it! For just a moment I got it! I can't possibly explain it now, but there for a second I saw it!" She turned excitedly to Calvin. "Did you get it?"

---

geometry the mathematical study of lines, angles, shapes, and so on

brief short

illuminating giving light to

35 He nodded. "Enough. I don't understand it the way Charles Wallace does, but enough to get the idea."

36 "Sso nnow wee ggo," Mrs. Which said. "Tthere iss nott all thee ttime in the worrlld."

37 "Could we hold hands?" Meg asked.

38 Calvin took her hand and held it tightly in his.

Describe Mental Images

What do you "see" in your mind as Mrs. Whatsit and Mrs. Who disappear?

39 "You can try," Mrs. Whatsit said, "though I'm not sure how it will work. You see, though we travel together, we travel alone. We will go first and take you afterward in the backwash. That may be easier for you." As she spoke the great white body began to **waver,** the wings to **dissolve** into **mist.** Mrs. Who seemed to **evaporate** until there was nothing but the glasses, and then the glasses, too, disappeared. It reminded Meg of the **Cheshire Cat.**

---

waver become unsteady
dissolve disappear slowly
mist a cloudy haze

evaporate change into a gas
Cheshire Cat a character in the story *Alice in Wonderland;* the Cheshire Cat faded slowly until the only thing left was his smile

40   —I've often seen a face without glasses, she thought—but glasses without a face! I wonder if I go that way, too. First me and then my glasses?

41   She looked over at Mrs. Which. Mrs. Which was there and then she wasn't.

Describe Mental Images

What do you "see" happening to Meg in the first sentence of this paragraph?

42   There was a gust of wind and a great thrust and a sharp shattering as she was shoved through—what? Then darkness; silence; nothingness. If Calvin was still holding her hand she could not feel it. But this time she was prepared for the sudden and complete **dissolution** of her body. When she felt the tingling coming back to her fingertips she knew that this journey was almost over and she could feel again the pressure of Calvin's hand about hers.

---

dissolution   slow disappearance

Describe Mental Images

What do you "see" happening to Meg in the first two sentences of this paragraph?

43 Without warning, coming as a complete and unexpected shock, she felt a **pressure** she had never imagined, as though she were being completely flattened out by an enormous steamroller. This was far worse than the nothingness had been; while she was nothing there was no need to breathe, but now her lungs were squeezed together so that although she was dying for want of air there was no way for her lungs to **expand and contract,** to take in the air that she must have to stay alive. This was completely different from the thinning of atmosphere when they flew up the mountain and she had had to put flowers to her face to breathe. She tried to gasp, but a paper doll can't gasp. She thought she was trying to think, but her flattened-out mind was as unable to **function** as her lungs; her thoughts were squashed along with the rest of her. Her heart tried to beat; it gave a knifelike, sidewise movement, but it could not expand.

44 But then she seemed to hear a voice, or if not a voice, at least words, words flattened out like printed words on paper: "Oh no! We can't stop here! This is a *two*-dimensional planet and the children can't manage here!"

---

pressure weight
expand and contract take air in and out

function work

45   She was whizzed into nothingness again, and nothingness was wonderful. She did not mind that she could not feel Calvin's hand, that she could not see or feel or be. The relief from the **intolerable** pressure was all she needed.

46   Then the tingling began to come back to her fingers, her toes; she could feel Calvin holding her tightly. Her heart beat regularly; blood **coursed** through her veins. Whatever had happened, whatever mistake had been made, it was over now. She thought she heard Charles Wallace saying, his words round and full as spoken words ought to be, "*Really*, Mrs. Which, you might have killed us!"

47   This time she was pushed out of the frightening fifth dimension with a sudden, immediate **jerk.** There she was, herself again, standing with Calvin beside her, holding on to her hand for dear life, and Charles Wallace in front of her, looking **indignant.** Mrs. Whatsit, Mrs. Who, and Mrs. Which were not **visible,** but she knew they were there; the fact of their presence was strong about her.

Describe Mental Images

Meg's trip is over. What mental image do you have?

---

intolerable difficult or painful
coursed flowed
jerk a quick, sharp movement

indignant angry because of unfairness
visible able to be seen

Describe Mental Images

What image do you have of Mrs. Whatsit?

48   "Cchilldrenn, I appolloggize," came Mrs. Which's voice.

49   "Now, Charles, calm down," Mrs. Whatsit said, appearing not as the great and beautiful beast she had been when they last saw her, but in her familiar wild garb of shawls and scarves and the old tramp's coat and hat. "You know how difficult it is for her to **materialize.** If you are not substantial yourself, it's *very* difficult to realize how limiting **protoplasm** is."

50   "I *ammm* ssorry," Mrs. Which's voice came again; but there was more than a hint of **amusement** in it.

51   "It is *not* funny." Charles Wallace gave a childish stamp of his foot.

52   Mrs. Who's glasses shone out, and the rest of her appeared more slowly behind them. "*We are such stuff as dreams are made on.*" She smiled broadly. "Prospero in *The Tempest.* I *do* like that play."

---

materialize   appear in solid form
protoplasm   a sticky liquid found in all living things

amusement   entertainment, fun

53   "You didn't do it **on *purpose?***" Charles demanded.

54   "Oh, my darling, of course not," Mrs. Whatsit said quickly. "It was just a very understandable mistake. It's very difficult for Mrs. Which to think in a **corporeal** way. She wouldn't hurt you **deliberately;** you know that. And it's really a pleasant little planet, and rather amusing to be flat. We always enjoy our visits there."

55   "Where are we now, then?" Charles Wallace demanded. "And why?"

56   "In **Orion's Belt.** We have a friend here, and we want you to have a look at your own planet."

---

on purpose intentionally
corporeal with a body

deliberately on purpose
Orion's Belt part of a constellation of stars visible from Earth

About the Author — Madeleine L'Engle (born 1918)

Madeleine L'Engle was born in New York City. Although L'Engle claims not to know exactly how many books she has written, the number is at least 60, including fiction for children, young adults, and adults. L'Engle is best known for combining fantasy and science fiction. "A Wrinkle in Time" was written in 1962. This book was the first book of three about Meg and her family and friends. Madeleine L'Engle has said, "I have written since I could hold a pencil, much less a pen, and writing for me is an essential function, like sleeping and breathing."

▶ If you could ask Madeleine L'Engle a question about this story, what would it be?

Beyond the Reading

Reading Comprehension

Question-Answer Relationships (QAR)

"Right There" Questions

1. **Recall Facts** Does Meg understand how they are going to travel?
2. **Recall Facts** What is the difference between the second and the third dimensions?
3. **Recognize Sequence** Where are the children at the end of the selection?

"Think and Search" Questions

4. **Support with Detail** How does Meg feel when she is in the fifth dimension?
5. **Explore the Main Idea** How is a tesseract helpful to the women and children?
6. **Paraphrase Text** How would you tell someone what the selection is about in your own words?

"Author and You" Question

7. **Draw Conclusions** What do you think is Meg's greatest fear?

"On Your Own" Questions

8. **Speculate** What challenges do you think the author faced in writing this story? What do you think she might have needed to know about to write the story?
9. **Analyze Illustrations** How does the style of the illustrations help you to understand the text? (The style of an illustration is how it looks.)

Activity Book
p. 194

Student
CD-ROM

Build Reading Fluency

Echo Read Aloud

Echo reading helps you learn to read with expression. This is an important characteristic of effective readers. Your teacher will read a line. Then the class reads the same line.

1. Listen to your teacher read a line from "A Wrinkle in Time."
2. Then, read the same line with expression.
3. Continue listening, then reading.

Listen, Speak, Interact

Present a Story

Prepare and present a Reader's Theater performance of a part of the selection.

1. Work in a group of seven students. Six of you will take the role of one of the characters from the reading (Charles, Meg, Calvin, Mrs. Who, Mrs. Which, and Mrs. Whatsit). Group members should read the words that their characters speak. These are the words in quotation marks (" . . . ").
2. The seventh member of the group will be the narrator. The narrator reads the parts between the dialogues.
3. Listen to the audio recording of the part of the selection you will perform. This will help you with pronunciation.
4. Speak loudly enough so that everyone can hear. Use good pitch—not too high or too low. Don't speak too fast. Show feeling.
5. Practice your reading several times.
6. Present your Reader's Theater performance to the class.

Elements of Literature

Understand Mood

An author sometimes sets a **mood** that affects the reader's feelings. The mood may be full of suspense. The reader may not know what is going to happen next. In "A Wrinkle in Time," Madeleine L'Engle sets a mood that makes the reader uneasy (not comfortable) and a little frightened. How does she do this?

1. Read the first two sentences of the selection. What do they tell about Meg's feelings?
2. Notice how different characters talk. Which character in particular seems to make Meg uneasy? Why? How can you tell?
3. Look in the text for other words or phrases that set an uneasy mood in the story. Write them in your Reading Log.
4. Compare your list with your classmates.

Reading Log

Activity Book
p. 195

Student
CD-ROM

Word Study

Understand the Prefixes *un-*, *in-*, and *im-*

A **prefix** is a word part added to the beginning of a word. It changes the word's meaning. The prefixes *un-*, *in-*, and *im-* can be added to a word to give it the opposite meaning.

1. In your Personal Dictionary, make a chart like the one shown.

2. Complete the chart for the words shown from "A Wrinkle in Time."

3. Find another word in the selection with one of the prefixes. Look in paragraph 45.

4. Fill in the new word, its prefix, the root word, and the meaning.

Word in Text	Prefix	Root Word	Meaning
impractical	im-	practical	not practical
unexpected	_____	_____	not expected
_____	in-	tolerable	_____
_____	_____	_____	_____

Personal Dictionary

The Heinle Newbury House Dictionary

Activity Book p. 196

Student CD-ROM

Grammar Focus

Identify the Past Perfect Tense

When authors tell a story that happened in the past, they use different past tenses. The **past perfect tense** is used to talk about actions that have already happened in the story. Here are some examples from the reading selection:

> She felt a pressure she <u>had</u> never <u>imagined</u>.

> This was far worse than the nothingness <u>had been</u>.

The author uses the word *had* with a past participle form of the verb. It describes feelings Meg had before this point in the story.

Find other examples of the past perfect tense in the story. Look at paragraphs 43 and 49.

Activity Book pp. 197–198

Student Handbook

Student CD-ROM

From Reading to Writing

Write a Science Fiction Narrative

Suppose that you are Madeleine L'Engle. What would you make happen next in the story?

1. Reread the end of the reading selection. Make a list of things that might happen next. Select the one that you think will make the best story.

2. Make a sequence timeline like the one shown. Write down what you think will happen next. First, write only the main ideas for each board.

3. Use your storyboard to write your narrative.

4. Set the mood by carefully choosing dialogue and actions.

5. Use the past and past perfect tense when appropriate.

Sequence Timeline

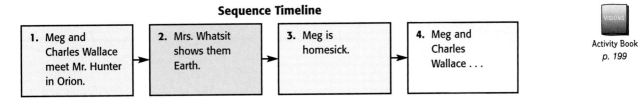

1. Meg and Charles Wallace meet Mr. Hunter in Orion. → 2. Mrs. Whatsit shows them Earth. → 3. Meg is homesick. → 4. Meg and Charles Wallace . . .

Activity Book
p. 199

Across Content Areas

Learn About the Speed of Light

Physicists are scientists who study the nature of the universe. They say that light always travels at the same speed if it is in a **vacuum.** A vacuum is where nothing exists, as in space.

Physicists have measured the speed of light in a vacuum at 299,792,458 meters per second. Most physicists say that nothing can travel at a speed faster than this.

In July of each year, the sun is about 152,500,000,000 meters from Earth. How many seconds does it take light to get from the sun to Earth in July? Use a calculator or a computer program to help you.

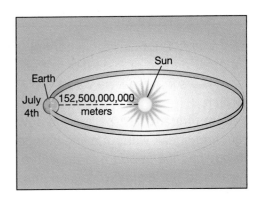

Activity Book
p. 200

CHAPTER 3

I Have a Dream

an excerpt from a speech
by Martin Luther King Jr.

Objectives

Reading Draw conclusions with text evidence as you read a speech.

Listening and Speaking Present a speech.

Grammar Use dependent clauses with *that*.

Writing Write a persuasive speech.

Content Social Studies: Learn about the United States Constitution.

Use Prior Knowledge

Explore Freedom

Read the pronunciations and definitions of **free** and **freedom**.

---

free /fri/ *adj.* **1** not under the control of another person or institution: *After twenty years in prison, he was a free man.*

freedom /ˈfridəm/ *n.* **1** having the power to act and speak without being stopped: *The boy has the freedom to go where he wants to go.* **2** a set of legal rights protected by the government, such as freedom of speech or religion: *Our various freedoms are the bases of our nation.*

---

1. Make a chart like the one shown. Fill in the chart with your ideas. How do you think freedom is expressed at home, at work, and at school?
2. Exchange charts with a partner. Compare your ideas.

Freedom	
at school	can ask lots of questions
at home	
at work	

Build Background

Segregation and Martin Luther King Jr.

In the 1950s, African-Americans did not enjoy the same rights as white Americans. In some places African-Americans were legally segregated from (separated from) whites. For example, African-Americans had to sit in the back of public buses or trains.

In 1955, Martin Luther King Jr. started a political movement in Montgomery, Alabama, to protest against segregated city buses in that city. King's ideas about resisting segregation spread throughout the nation. His nonviolent methods of making change led to new laws and new freedoms for African-Americans.

Content Connection

From the beginning of the history of the United States in the 1600s to the 1860s, many African-Americans were **slaves.** They were owned by other people and they had no rights.

Build Vocabulary

Distinguish Denotative and Connotative Meanings

A **denotative meaning** is what a word usually means. *Home* usually means the place where you live. A word also often has a **connotative meaning,** which is about the images or feelings that the word can give. For example, *home* can also make us think of family, comfort, and safety.

1. Look up the first meaning of the word *dream* in the dictionary. This is the denotative meaning of *dream*. Write it in your Personal Dictionary.

2. In the first paragraph of the reading, Martin Luther King Jr. says, "I have a <u>dream</u> that one day this nation will rise up and . . ." Is he asleep?

3. Describe the connotative meaning of *dream* in this sentence.

4. In paragraph 1, look for these additional examples of using connotative meanings for words. Use your dictionary to find the denotative meanings. Then describe the connotative meanings.
   a. the <u>heat</u> of injustice
   b. an <u>oasis</u> of freedom
   c. the <u>table</u> of brotherhood

Activity Book
p. 201

Student
CD-ROM

Text Structure

Speech

"I Have a Dream" is a speech that was given in 1963 by Martin Luther King Jr. Speeches are written and read aloud by someone who wants to present a strong message.

Before you read the speech, listen to the audio recording. Listen for the features that often appear in speeches.

As you read, write examples of these features in your Reading Log.

Speech	
Personal Style	emotional and exciting; tries to persuade the audience to do something
Direct Address	is presented directly to the audience; uses first person (*I*)
Repetition	repeats key words to help the audience remember
Compares and Contrasts	talks about the past, present, and future

Reading Log

Student CD-ROM

Reading Strategy

Draw Conclusions with Text Evidence

To understand a speech, the listener or reader must **draw conclusions** about what was happening at the time the speech was given. As you listen to or read "I Have a Dream," look for **text evidence** about what life was like for some Americans in 1963. In your Reading Log, record the evidence you find and the conclusions you draw from it.

> *Quotation:*
>
> *I have a dream that one day this nation will rise up and live out the true meaning of its creed, "We hold these truths to be self-evident; that all men are created equal."*
>
> *Conclusion:*
>
> *The United States was not living up to its creed.*

Reading Log

Student CD-ROM

I HAVE A
DREAM

an excerpt from a speech
by Martin Luther King Jr.

Audio

Draw Conclusions with Text Evidence

What quotation helps you draw a conclusion about King's message?

1   I say to you today, my friends, even though we face the difficulties of today and tomorrow, I still have a dream. It is a dream deeply rooted in the American dream. I have a dream that one day this nation will rise up and live out the true meaning of its **creed,** "We hold these truths to be **self-evident;** that all men are created equal." I have a dream that one day on the red hills of Georgia, the sons of former slaves and the sons of former slave owners will be able to sit down together at a table of brotherhood. I have a dream that one day even the state of Mississippi, a state **sweltering** with the heat of **injustice,** sweltering with the heat of **oppression,** will be transformed into an oasis of freedom and justice. I have a dream that my four children will one day live in a nation where they will not be judged by the color of their skin but by the content of their character.

2   I have a dream today!

---

creed beliefs
self-evident speaking for themselves, obvious
sweltering suffering from heat

injustice lack of justice; unfairness
oppression the act of governing or treating harshly

Draw Conclusions with Text Evidence

What does King's description of the governor of Alabama tell you about the tension between people at this time? Give evidence for your conclusion.

3   I have a dream that one day down in Alabama—with its **vicious racists,** with its Governor having his lips dripping with the words of **interposition** and **nullification***—one day right there in Alabama, little black boys and black girls will be able to join hands with little white boys and white girls as sisters and brothers.

4   I have a dream today!

5   I have a dream that one day every valley shall be **exalted,** and every hill and mountain shall be made low. The rough places will be plain, and the **crooked** places will be made straight, and the glory of the Lord shall be revealed, and all **flesh** shall see it together.

* At this time, some southern states threatened to disobey any federal laws that allowed more rights for African-Americans.

vicious   cruel, hostile

racists   people who believe that their race is better than other races

interposition   the idea that a state may not follow a federal order

nullification   the refusal of a state to enforce a federal law

exalted   highly raised

crooked   bent, not straight

flesh   living things

The Liberty Bell

Draw Conclusions with Text Evidence

How can you describe the struggle for freedom at this time? Which of King's words support your conclusion?

6   This is our hope. This is the faith that I go back to the South with. With this faith we will be able to **hew** out of the mountain of **despair** a stone of hope. With this faith we will be able to **transform** the jangling **discords** of our nation into a beautiful symphony of brotherhood. With this faith we will be able to work together, to pray together, to struggle together, to go to jail together, to stand up for freedom together, knowing that we will be free one day. And this will be the day. This will be the day when all of God's children will be able to sing with new meaning, "My country, 'tis of thee, sweet land of liberty, of thee I sing. Land where my fathers died, land of the pilgrims' pride, from every mountainside, let freedom ring."* And if America is to be a great nation, this must become true.

7   So let freedom ring from the **prodigious** hilltops of New Hampshire. Let freedom ring from the **mighty** mountains of New York. Let freedom ring from the

* King quotes from the words to "My Country 'Tis of Thee,"
  a patriotic song.

---

hew   chop or cut   **discords**   disagreements
despair   sadness without hope   **prodigious**   marvelous or amazing
transform   change   **mighty**   having great strength or power

heightening Alleghenies of Pennsylvania! Let freedom ring from the snowcapped Rockies of Colorado! Let freedom ring from the curvaceous slopes of California! But not only that. Let freedom ring from Stone Mountain of Georgia! Let freedom ring from Lookout Mountain of Tennessee! Let freedom ring from every hill and every molehill of Mississippi. From every mountainside, let freedom ring.

8   And when this happens, and when we **allow** freedom to ring, when we let it ring from every village and every hamlet, from every state and every city, we will be able to speed up that day when all of God's children—black men and white men, Jews and Gentiles, Protestants and Catholics—will be able to join hands and sing in the words of the old Negro spiritual, "Free at last. Free at last. Thank God Almighty, we are free at last."

Draw Conclusions with Text Evidence

What conclusion can you make about how King wanted this speech to make people feel?

---

heightening   rising, growing taller

allow   let, permit

About the Author   Martin Luther King Jr. (1929–1968)

Martin Luther King Jr. was born in 1929 in Atlanta, Georgia. As a child, he was angry at the segregation that he saw around him. He helped win equal rights for African-Americans, including the right to vote. In 1964, he was awarded the Nobel Peace Prize. In 1968, King was shot and killed in Memphis, Tennessee.

➤ Why do you think Martin Luther King Jr. wrote this speech? Was it to entertain, to inform, or to persuade? What was the effect on the listener? What was the effect on you as you listened?

Beyond the Reading

Reading Comprehension

Question-Answer Relationships (QAR)

"Right There" Questions

1. **Recall Facts** What does Martin Luther King Jr. say his dream is for his four children?
2. **Find the Main Idea** What does King say will happen when Americans "allow freedom to ring"?
3. **Paraphrase** Paraphrase King's dream.

"Think and Search" Question

4. **Find Details** What does King say can be done if people have faith and hope?

"Author and You" Questions

5. **Identify Symbolism** Why does King include the words of "My Country 'Tis of Thee"?

6. **Understand Author's Purpose** What do you think King wanted people to do after they heard his speech?
7. **Distinguish Opinion** What does "I Have a Dream" tell you about King's opinions?

"On Your Own" Questions

8. **Infer** After hearing this speech, do you think you would have agreed with King? Why or why not?
9. **Draw Conclusions** How do you think the author intended people to respond to this speech? Why?

Activity Book
p. 202

Student
CD-ROM

Build Reading Fluency

Adjust Your Reading Rate

When you read a speech, you can learn to adjust your reading rate. Pause and read like you are giving the speech, "I Have a Dream."

1. Listen to the audio recording of paragraph 7 on pages 386–387.
2. Read paragraph 7 silently two times.

3. Read paragraph 7 aloud to a partner.
4. Read with expression, as if you were giving the speech to an audience.

Listen, Speak, Interact

Present a Speech

It is important for people giving speeches to speak clearly and expressively.

1. Choose one paragraph from the speech to present to the class.
2. Listen to the audio recording of the speech. This will help you distinguish sounds of words. Say words out loud to practice making the correct sounds.
3. Also listen to the audio recording to distinguish intonation (how your voice rises and falls). Say sentences out loud to practice intonation.
4. Make a speech evaluation checklist.
5. Perform the speech for the class. Ask your classmates to fill out the evaluation.

Speech Evaluation Checklist

Did I:	Yes	No
speak clearly?	_____	_____
stand up straight?	_____	_____
use gestures and	_____	_____
body language to	_____	_____
communicate?	_____	_____

Elements of Literature

Identify Audience and Purpose

Every piece of writing should have an audience and a purpose.

To write effectively, you need to know your **audience**—the people you are writing to. Who is the audience for King's speech? How do you know? Record your answers in your Reading Log.

It is also important to have a **purpose**—your reason for writing. Speeches might have one of these purposes:

1. To **inform** (to give new information).

2. To **persuade** (to try to influence the audience's actions or beliefs).
3. To **entertain** (to give people pleasure).

What is the purpose of King's speech? Support your answer by noting evidence from the speech. Record your answers in your Reading Log.

Reading Log

Activity Book
p. 203

Student
CD-ROM

Word Study

Recognize Figurative Language

In **figurative language,** words mean more than their dictionary definitions. When Martin Luther King Jr. writes "a symphony of brotherhood," he is not really talking about music.

Figurative language often uses the connotative meaning of words instead of denotative meanings. Recall that a connotative meaning is about the images or feelings a word gives. A denotative meaning is what a word means most of the time.

1. Choose one of the following examples of figurative speech:
   a. Hew out of the <u>mountain</u> of despair a stone of hope.
   b. Every <u>valley</u> shall be exalted, and every <u>hill</u> and mountain shall be made low.
2. Use a dictionary to find the denotative meaning of the underlined word. Then determine the connotative meaning of the word.
3. On a piece of paper, draw a picture of what the words actually say. Then write a short description of what you think is King's figurative meaning.

Personal Dictionary   The Heinle Newbury House Dictionary   Activity Book *p. 204*   Student CD-ROM

Grammar Focus

Use Dependent Clauses with *That*

Clauses are parts of sentences that have a subject and a verb. Many sentences in "I Have a Dream" by Martin Luther King Jr. begin with, "I have a dream that . . ." The sentence "I have a dream" can stand alone. It is a main clause. However, King adds a **dependent clause** beginning with *that*. It makes what he is dreaming of more specific.

1. Find sentences that begin "I have a dream that . . ." in the reading.
2. Write three sentences about your dreams. Use dependent clauses with *that*. Be sure to use correct punctuation.

Activity Book *pp. 205–206*   Student Handbook   Student CD-ROM

From Reading to Writing

Write a Persuasive Speech

Write a speech about a dream you have to solve a problem in your school or community. You must persuade your audience that the dream is a good one.

1. Make a web like the one shown. Use it to organize your ideas for reaching your dream.
2. Identify your audience and purpose.
3. Use figurative language. Use a dictionary to help you distinguish the denotative and connotative meanings of words.
4. Repeat important words to help your audience remember what you say.

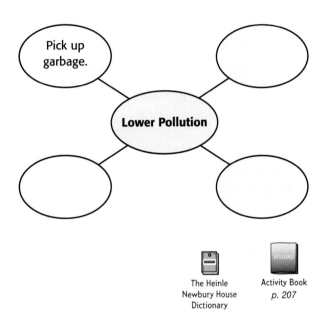

The Heinle Newbury House Dictionary

Activity Book p. 207

Across Content Areas

Learn About the United States Constitution

The **Constitution of the United States** was written in 1787. It tells what the government can do and what kinds of laws the government can pass.

The Constitution has to be **amended** (changed) from time to time. For example, the 13th Amendment made slavery illegal. The 19th Amendment gave women the right to vote.

An important part of the Constitution is the **Bill of Rights.** This lists the first ten amendments to the Constitution. These amendments give Americans basic freedoms such as freedom of speech.

Copy these sentences on a piece of paper. Decide if each one is *true* or *false.*

1. The Constitution cannot be changed.
2. The right to freedom of religion is in the Bill of Rights.
3. The Constitution says how fast you can drive.

Check your answers with your social studies teacher.

Activity Book p. 208

CHAPTER 4

Lyndon Baines Johnson:
Our Thirty-Sixth President

an excerpt from a biography
by Melissa Maupin

Speech to the Nation:
July 2, 1964

an excerpt from a speech
by Lyndon Baines Johnson

Objectives

Reading Distinguish fact from opinion as you read a biography and a speech.

Listening and Speaking Conduct an interview.

Grammar Use the conjunction *yet* to show contrast.

Writing Write a biography.

Content Social Studies: Learn about the branches of government.

Use Prior Knowledge

Talk About What United States Presidents Do

The president of the United States is the leader of the country. He has many important duties (jobs that he has to do).

1. With a partner, make a list of the duties of the president of the United States that you know about.
2. Work with the class to put together a chart with all the duties that everyone has listed.
3. Do you know about leaders in other countries? What duties do they have? Compare and contrast them.

> **President's Duties**
> signs new laws
> command the armed forces

Build Background

Presidential Elections

In the United States, presidential elections are held every four years. First, political parties nominate (choose) candidates to represent them and run for office. Candidates for president and vice president run for office as a team. Then, in the presidential election, citizens vote for the person they want to take office. If the president dies, the vice president becomes president.

See page 401 to learn more about how "Vice President" Johnson also served later as "President" Johnson.

SOCIAL STUDIES

Content Connection

You can vote in a presidential election if you are at least 18 years old and a citizen of the United States. You must **register** (sign up) before voting.

Build Vocabulary

Identify Key Words About Government

Every text has **key words** (important words) you should know in order to understand the text. Identifying these key words is an essential skill.

1. Reread the Build Background section above. As you read, write down any unfamiliar words that you think are important to know.
2. Select one word from your list to define. Try using context clues to find the meaning of the word. Then check your ideas for the definition in a dictionary.
3. Teach your vocabulary word to a partner. Explain why you think the word is important to know and how you found the definition. Then ask your partner to explain a word.
4. As you read the selection, continue to identify key words. Define and record them in your Personal Dictionary.

Personal Dictionary

The Heinle Newbury House Dictionary

Activity Book
p. 209

Student CD-ROM

Text Structure

Biography

Both of the selections in this chapter relate to Lyndon B. Johnson, the thirty-sixth president of the United States. The first selection is a **biography.** Biographies tell the story of a person's life. Look for features of a biography as you read.

As you read "Lyndon Baines Johnson: Our Thirty-Sixth President," notice which events and details the author thinks are important for you to know.

The second selection is a **speech.** Review the features of a speech on page 382.

Biography	
Third-Person Point of View	The story is told by someone other than the biography's subject, using the words *he*, *she*, and *they.*
Chronology	Chronology tells important events in the person's life and when they happened.
Important Details	Details show what the person was like and why the person's life was important.

Reading Strategy

Distinguish Fact from Opinion

A **fact** is something that can be proven. An **opinion** is a belief that may be true, but cannot be proven.

> Our classroom has five windows. This is a fact.

> Our classroom is very comfortable. This is an opinion.

It is important to understand the difference between fact and opinion.

1. Read the titles of the two readings in this chapter. Which do you think is more likely to contain facts? Which do you think may contain opinions? Why?
2. Read and listen to the audio recording of the two selections. Distinguish between the facts and opinions in each. Opinions sometimes begin with "I believe" or "we believe."

Student
CD-ROM

Lyndon Baines Johnson:
Our Thirty-Sixth President

an excerpt from a biography by Melissa Maupin

Speech to the Nation:
July 2, 1964

an excerpt from a speech by Lyndon Baines Johnson

Lyndon Baines Johnson: Our Thirty-Sixth President

an excerpt from a biography by Melissa Maupin

Prologue

In 1960, John F. Kennedy was elected president of the United States, and Lyndon B. Johnson was his vice president. When Kennedy **was assassinated** in 1963, Johnson became president.

> **Distinguish Fact from Opinion**
>
> Is the first sentence a fact or an opinion? How do you know?

1   Just hours after Kennedy's death, Johnson took the **oath of office** as president of the United States. Five days later, he addressed the nation on television. He vowed to carry out all of Kennedy's programs. One important goal was civil rights for all Americans. Kennedy wanted to end **discrimination** against blacks and other minorities in the country. President Johnson **pleaded** with the country to put their differences aside in the memory of the late President Kennedy. "Let us put an end to the teaching and preaching of hate and evil and violence," he said.

---

was assassinated was murdered; usually describes the murder of someone important

oath of office a formal promise to do something

discrimination unfair treatment of someone, especially because of race, gender, religion, and so on

pleaded requested urgently

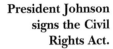

President Johnson
signs the Civil
Rights Act.

Distinguish Fact from Opinion

What are the facts of the Civil Rights Act of 1964? What did this act achieve?

2   Next, Johnson pushed through the Civil Rights Act of 1964. This ended segregation laws that discriminated against African-Americans. Segregation laws kept blacks from entering certain public places that were **reserved** for whites only, such as restrooms, hotels, and restaurants. The Civil Rights Act made such laws illegal. But even with this act, problems with discrimination continued. African-Americans still struggled for equal rights.

---

reserved   set aside for use by someone

About the Author

Melissa Maupin (born 1958)

Melissa Maupin has written many biographies of United States presidents, including Franklin D. Roosevelt, William Howard Taft, Calvin Coolidge, and Lyndon B. Johnson. She has also written a biography of Benjamin Banneker, the famous astronomer and mathematician.

➤ Why do you think the author wrote this biography? Was it to persuade, to inform, or to entertain?

What question would you like to ask Melissa Maupin?

Audio

Speech to the Nation: July 2, 1964

an excerpt from a speech by Lyndon Baines Johnson

Prologue

After a long and difficult **struggle** to get Congress to approve the Civil Rights Act of 1964, President Johnson wanted to tell all Americans about the new law. His speech was heard on television and radio from the White House on the evening of July 2, 1964.

Distinguish Fact from Opinion

Is it a fact or an opinion that the struggle for civil rights "was a turning point in our history"?

1   My fellow Americans:

2   I am about to sign into law the Civil Rights Act of 1964. I want to take this **occasion** to talk to you about what that law means to every American.

3   One hundred and eighty-eight years ago this week a small band of **valiant** men began a long struggle for freedom. They **pledged** their lives, their fortunes, and their sacred honor not only to found a nation, but to **forge** an **ideal** of freedom—not only for political independence, but for personal liberty—not only to **eliminate** foreign rule, but to establish the rule of justice in the affairs of men.

4   That struggle was a turning point in our history. Today in far corners of distant continents, the ideals of those American patriots still shape the struggles of men who hunger for freedom.

---

struggle   a fight
occasion   a special time or event
valiant   brave
pledged   formally promised to do something

forge   make, create
ideal   high standard
eliminate   remove, exclude

5   This is a proud **triumph.** Yet those who founded our country knew that freedom would be secure only if each **generation** fought to renew and enlarge its meaning. From the minutemen at Concord to the soldiers in Viet-Nam, each generation has been equal to that trust.

6   Americans of every race and color have died in battle to protect our freedom. Americans of every race and color have worked to build a nation of widening **opportunities.** Now our generation of Americans has been called on to continue the unending search for justice within our borders.

7   We believe that all men are created equal. Yet many are **denied** equal treatment.

8   We believe that all men have **unalienable** rights. Yet many Americans do not enjoy those rights.

9   We believe that all men are entitled to the blessings of **liberty.** Yet millions are being deprived of those blessings— not because of their own failures, but because of the color of their skin.

---

triumph   a great success, victory

generation   a group of people of approximately the same age

opportunities   good times to do something

denied   refused, rejected

unalienable   not able to be taken away; permanent

liberty   freedom from control

10   The reasons are deeply imbedded in history and tradition and the nature of man. We can understand—without **rancor** or hatred—how this all happened.

11   But it cannot continue. Our Constitution, the foundation of our Republic, **forbids** it. The principles of our freedom forbid it. Morality forbids it. And the law I will sign tonight forbids it.

12   That law is the product of months of the most careful **debate** and discussion. It was **proposed** more than one year ago by our late and beloved President John F. Kennedy. It received the **bipartisan** support of more than two-thirds of the Members of both the House and the Senate. An overwhelming **majority** of **Republicans** as well as **Democrats** voted for it.

13   It has received the thoughtful support of tens of thousands of civic and religious leaders in all parts of this Nation. And it is supported by the great majority of the American people.

President
John F. Kennedy

> **Distinguish Fact from Opinion**
>
> President Johnson says, "That law is the product of months <u>of the most careful debate and discussion.</u>" Does the underlined part of this sentence reflect fact or opinion?

---

rancor   deep, long-lasting, and bitter hatred
forbids   does not permit
debate   consideration and discussion
proposed   suggested, recommended
bipartisan   involving two political parties

majority   more than half, but not all, of something
Republicans   members of the Republican Party, one of the two main political parties in the United States
Democrats   members of the Democratic Party, one of the two main political parties in the United States

14   The purpose of the law is simple.

15   It does not **restrict** the freedom of any American, so long as he respects the rights of others.

16   It does not give special treatment to any citizen.

17   It does say the only limit to a man's hope for happiness, and for the future of his children, shall be his own **ability.**

18   It does say that those who are equal before God shall now also be equal in the **polling booths,** in the classrooms, in the factories, and in hotels, restaurants, movie theaters, and other places that provide service to the public.

Distinguish Fact from Opinion

President Johnson mentions specific places where the law will apply. Is this opinion or fact?

---

restrict limit

ability the skill and power to do something

polling booths places where people vote

About the Author

Lyndon Baines Johnson (1908–1973)

Lyndon Baines Johnson was born near Stonewall, Texas. His father was a state legislator and often took him to see the state government at work. When he was in college, Johnson decided to go into politics, and he worked his way up through Congress. In 1960, John F. Kennedy asked Johnson to run for vice president with him. Kennedy and Johnson won the election, and Johnson began his duties as vice president. In 1963, President Kennedy was assassinated. Johnson became the president of the United States. He is especially remembered for the many civil rights laws that he helped pass.

➤ Sometimes presidents believe very strongly in the laws that they sign. Other times, they are not very enthusiastic about them. Based on your reading of the speech, do you think that President Johnson strongly believed in the Civil Rights Act, or not? Explain.

Beyond the Reading

Reading Comprehension

Question-Answer Relationships (QAR)

"Right There" Questions

1. **Recall Facts** How did Lyndon B. Johnson become president of the United States? When?
2. **Recall Facts** When did President Johnson give his speech about the Civil Rights Act of 1964?
3. **Recall Facts** In what places did the new law make all citizens equal?

"Think and Search" Questions

4. **Find Main Ideas** What did the Civil Rights Act of 1964 promise?
5. **Find Main Ideas** How did President Johnson believe that he could continue the struggle for freedom?
6. **Paraphrase** Explain Johnson's speech in your own words.

"Author and You" Question

7. **Identify Cause and Effect** Why was the Civil Rights Act necessary?

"On Your Own" Questions

8. **Draw Conclusions** Why do you think that President Johnson discussed American history in his speech?
9. **Support Opinions** Do you think that the Civil Rights Act was important? Why or why not?
10. **Compare and Contrast** Compare and contrast Johnson's speech with that of Martin Luther King Jr. in Chapter 3. How are they the same? How are they different?

Activity Book
p. 211

Student
CD-ROM

Build Reading Fluency

Choral Read Aloud

A choral read aloud means the teacher reads aloud together with the class. This helps improve your listening and reading skills.

1. Read aloud paragraphs 7–9, on page 399, with your teacher.
2. Try to keep up with the class.
3. You may point to the text as you read.

Listen, Speak, Interact

Conduct an Interview

In the first selection, Melissa Maupin tells a story from President Johnson's life. The story is told in the third person and tells important facts from his life.

1. You will interview a classmate. Think of five questions you would like to ask him or her. The questions should include facts about his or her life, goals, and so forth.
2. Write your questions on paper or index cards. Interview the person and record the person's answers.
3. Save these questions and answers for the From Reading to Writing section of this chapter.

Where and when were you born?

Interviewer

I was born in Thailand in 1992.

Classmate

Elements of Literature

Recognize Repetition in a Speech

Speechwriters sometimes use **repetition** of a word or a phrase to help the listeners understand. Repetition can also make the speech sound powerful.

1. Reread paragraphs 7–9 on page 399. What phrase is used at the beginning of each paragraph?
2. Find another example of repeated phrases on page 401.

3. Recall Martin Luther King Jr.'s "I Have a Dream" speech. Can you remember the repeated words? If not, go back to page 384 and reread the speech.
4. Choose three of the sentences with repetition that you like best and record them in your Reading Log.

Reading Log

Activity Book
p. 211

Student
CD-ROM

Word Study

Identify Adjectives

People often use **adjectives** to make their sentences more interesting. An adjective is a word that describes a noun.

> One hundred and eighty-eight years ago this week a <u>small</u> band of <u>valiant</u> men began a <u>long</u> struggle for freedom.

The underlined words are all adjectives: *small* describes the size of the band of men, *valiant* describes the men themselves, and *long* describes the struggle. The sentence would not be as interesting if the adjectives were taken out.

1. Look at pages 399–401 and find these nouns.

triumph	search	debate
support	majority	

2. Find the adjective that describes each noun.
3. Look up the adjectives in a dictionary to find their meanings.

Personal Dictionary   The Heinle Newbury House Dictionary   Activity Book p. 212   Student CD-ROM

Grammar Focus

Use the Conjunction *Yet* to Show Contrast

In his speech, President Johnson contrasts people's opinions and facts. To do so, he uses the conjunction *yet*.

1. Find the sentences in President Johnson's speech where he uses *yet* to show differences. Look in paragraphs 5, 7, and 9 on page 399.

2. The conjunction *yet* shows contrast in the following sentences. Copy them on a piece of paper, and fill in the blanks.

   a. I think I am old enough to stay up late. Yet my parents _____ .

   b. I studied all day for my math test. Yet I _____ .

Activity Book pp. 213–214   Student Handbook   Student CD-ROM

From Reading to Writing

Write a Biography

Use the questions and answers you asked a partner in the Listen, Speak, Interact activity to write a short biography. If you prefer, research information about a different person.

1. Evaluate your information. If you are unsure about a fact, ask the person you are writing about or do further research.

2. Use the biography of Lyndon Johnson as a model.
3. Use third-person point of view. Use the pronouns *she, he, it,* and *they.*
4. Use the past perfect tense when appropriate. (See page 378.)

Activity Book
p. 215

Across Content Areas

Learn About the Branches of Government

The government of the United States has three **branches** (main parts).

The **legislative branch** makes the laws. It consists of the House of Representatives and the Senate.

The **executive branch** approves and enforces the laws. The president of the United States heads this branch.

The **judicial branch** interprets the laws (says what they mean). The Supreme Court makes up this branch of government.

Which branch of government does each of these newspaper headlines refer to?

1. **New Transportation Law Passed**

2. **Court Says Schools Must Get More Money**

3. **President Announces New Rules for Workplace Safety**

Activity Book
p. 216

Apply and Expand

Listening and Speaking Workshop

Give a Persuasive Speech

Topic

In this unit, you read about people who helped others. Your school is thinking about requiring students to do community work. Examples of community work are helping the elderly and tutoring children. Is this a good idea? Present your opinion in a speech to the class.

Persuasive Speech

Introduction
State one issue and your position.
Give one argument from the other position and tell why it is not good.
Reason 1 with example and detail
Reason 2 with example and detail
Reason 3 with example and detail
Conclusion
Restate your position. Call for action.

Step 1: Plan your speech.

1. Make a list of reasons for and against the topic.
2. Decide if you are for or against community work.

Step 2: Write your speech.

Introduction

1. State the issue and your position.
2. State a reason on the other side of the issue. Then explain why that reason is not a good one. Give facts and examples to clarify your ideas.
3. Explain that there are many good reasons to support your position.

Reasons and Examples

1. Give three good reasons to support your position. This will help your listeners understand the major ideas of your speech.

2. Use phrases like
   "I am in favor of . . ."
   "I do not agree that . . ."
3. Support each of your reasons with facts and examples. This is your supporting evidence.
4. Be careful not to exaggerate or be disrespectful.

Conclusion

1. Tell what the issue means to you.
2. Urge your listeners to join you in taking action.

Step 3: Practice your speech.

1. Use note cards for each main point.
2. Use the Presentation Checklist.
3. Ask a partner to listen to you and give you feedback.
4. Revise your speech based on your partner's feedback.

Active Listening Checklist

1. I liked _____ because _____ .

2. I want to know more about _____ .

3. I thought the opening was interesting / not interesting.

4. You stayed on the topic. Yes / No

5. I understood the major ideas of your speech. Yes / No

6. I understood the facts you used as supporting evidence. Yes / No

Presentation Checklist

Did you:

1. have a good opening?

2. support your reasons with facts as evidence?

3. support your reasons with examples?

4. tell listeners what the issue means to you?

5. use interesting, specific words?

6. look at the audience?

7. speak so everyone could hear you?

Step 4: Present your speech.

1. Speak clearly and loudly enough for everyone to hear you.

2. Use expression to show that you respect the audience, but you are convinced of your opinion.

Viewing Workshop

View and Think

View Videos of Speeches

Find videos of the two speeches in this unit. Compare and contrast the printed and video versions of the speech.

1. How are the printed and video speeches the same or different?

2. What did you learn from the video that you did not know from the printed speech?

3. Which version most influences how you feel about the speech? What effect does it have on you?

4. How do you interpret the nonverbal messages in the video? For example, what does the speaker's gestures and body language tell you?

5. What do you like and not like about the videos of the speeches?

Further Viewing

Watch the *Visions* CNN Video for Unit 6. Do the Video Worksheet.

CNN Video

Writer's Workshop

Write a Research Report

> **Writing Prompt**
>
> Write a report about a famous person who was the first to do something.

Step 1: Research questions like:

1. *Who* was the first to . . . ? (for example, land on the moon)
2. *Where* did the main event take place?
3. *When* did the main event take place?
4. *How* did the person accomplish his or her goal?

Step 2: Revise questions.

1. Look up sources of information on the Internet, in the library, and in newspapers. You may also look for information in the readings of this unit and other units in your book.
2. Ask new questions as you look up information. Revise your questions and write them down.
3. Use headings and tables of contents to help you locate and organize information. Also use graphic features to locate and organize information. Some graphic features are maps, graphs, time lines, and charts.
4. Ask your teacher to help you interpret the information in the graphic features. What do the graphic features tell you?

5. Review what you learned. Use the information from your research and your own prior knowledge to ask more questions you need answers to.

Step 3: Record information.

1. When you find something useful for your report, summarize it *in your own words*. Then make a note card of the source where you found it. Refer to the Research Process section of the Student Handbook.
2. If you find something that you want to quote in your report (that is, use someone else's exact words), you *must* copy the words exactly and put them in quotation marks (" . . . "). Make a careful note of the source. In your report, you *must* use the quotation marks and show who originally said or wrote the words.
3. Evaluate your research. Review your notes. Make sure your information is useful.

Step 4: Organize your ideas.

1. Choose the parts of the person's story that you want to tell. Organize them in chronological order. Use the headings, tables of contents, and graphic features from your research to help you.
2. For each part of the story, list the facts, examples, and evidence that support it. You will use the outline in the next step to organize this information.

Step 5: Write a draft by hand or on a computer.

1. Write a TITLE for your report.
2. Write an INTRODUCTION.
   a. In one sentence, state what you are going to talk about. (This is your **thesis statement.**)
   b. Explain why this is an important topic to understand.
3. Write the BODY (two or three supporting paragraphs).
   a. In each paragraph, state one of your ideas.
   b. After stating your idea, give supporting details or examples.
   c. Write about your ideas in chronological order.
4. Write a CONCLUSION. Briefly restate your thesis.
5. Write a bibliography, a list of your SOURCES (the places where you got your information).
6. Make grammar work for you.
   a. Use the past perfect tense to talk about past actions that happened before other past actions: *He had already tried to climb the mountain.*
   b. Use *yet* to show contrast: *He was cold and tired. Yet he continued on.*
   c. Use appositives to identify other people in the report: *Diana Chen, his teammate, was a big help.*

Step 6: Revise and edit your report.

1. Proofread your report to find errors in paragraph indentation, spelling, capitalization, and punctuation.
2. If you use a computer, use software such as an online dictionary or thesaurus. Check definitions and spellings.
3. Collaborate with a partner to proofread your report and give you feedback. Also proofread your partner's work and give feedback.
4. Revise your draft. Blend paragraphs together. Use transition words. Combine sentences using conjunctions.

Step 7: Publish.

1. Prepare a final draft. Create a Table of Contents to organize your information.
2. Create a class collection of these reports. Review them for their strengths and weaknesses.
3. Set your goals as a writer based on your writing and the writing of your classmates.

The Heinle Newbury House Dictionary

Student Handbook

Projects

These projects will help you expand what you know about frontiers. Work alone, with a partner, or with a group.

Project 1: Make a Book About a New Place

Everyone goes to new places at some time. Find information and pictures about a new place and make a book about it.

1. Look through magazines and find pictures of several places where you have never been. Cut out these pictures, if you can.
2. Glue each of your pictures onto a piece of paper. On the paper, write the name of the place shown.
3. On a note card, write down some questions you have about these places. Research answers to your questions at your school library or on the Internet. Write the facts you learned at the bottom of the pieces of paper.
4. Use maps that show where this place is located. Use and interpret the maps to answer some of your questions. What do the maps tell you? Write this information next to your pictures.
5. Bind your pages together to make a book. Add to the book as you learn about new places that you might go.

Project 2: Write a Letter to the President

If you could write a letter to the president of the United States, what would you say? Collaborate with a partner to write your letter.

1. Think about something important to you, to your family, or to your community.
2. How can the president help? Make a list of your ideas on a piece of paper or make a draft on the computer.
3. Use correct letter format. Refer to your Student Handbook.
4. In the opening paragraph, state your reason for writing.
5. In the next paragraph, give facts and examples to support your position.
6. In conclusion, tell again what you would like to happen and how the president can help.
7. Revise and edit your letter. Be sure to use the Editing Checklist in your Student Handbook and all the steps you learned in the Writer's Workshops.
8. Sign your letter in your best cursive handwriting when you have finished.

Student
Handbook

Further Reading

The books listed here explore the theme of frontiers. Read one or more of them. Write your thoughts and feelings about what you read. In your Reading Log, take notes on your answers to these questions:

1. In the books you have read, what common characteristics do the characters share?
2. How do the characters deal with the challenges presented by frontiers?
3. How are the experiences you read about similar to your own life experiences?

A Wrinkle in Time
by Madeleine L'Engle, Bantam Doubleday Dell Books for Young Readers, 1973. Meg and Charles, along with their friend Calvin, journey through time and space to find their father, who disappeared while working on a top-secret government project.

Lewis and Clark
by George E. Sullivan, Scholastic, Inc., 2000. Lewis and Clark kept journals of their 1804–1806 expedition to the Pacific Ocean. In this book, read about their journey in their own words.

They Had a Dream: The Civil Rights Struggle from Fredrick Douglass to Marcus Garvey to Martin Luther King Jr. and Malcom X
by Jules Archer, Penguin Putnam Books for Young Readers, 1996. This book chronicles the lives of important African-Americans in United States history.

Taking Charge: The Johnson White House
by Michael R. Beschloss, Simon & Schuster Children's, 2001. President Johnson tape-recorded all phone conversations and Oval Office meetings while he was in the White House. This book allows readers to read his thoughts and conversations about the Civil Rights Act and his meetings with Martin Luther King Jr.

Sarah, Plain and Tall
by Patricia MacLachlan, HarperCollins Children's Books, 1987. This book tells about life on the American prairie. Sarah, a new bride, comes to live with a family on the frontier and must adjust to her new life.

Dragon's Gate
by Laurence Yep, HarperCollins, 1994. This book gives an account of the lives of the Chinese immigrants who built the Transcontinental Railroad in the Sierra Mountains.

Across the Wide and Lonesome Prairie: The Oregon Trail Diary of Hattie Campbell
by Kristina Gregory, Scholastic, Inc., 1997. In her diary, 13-year-old Hattie tells the story of her trip from Missouri to Oregon. She writes about the joys and hardships her family faces as they make the long journey through the frontier.

Reading Log   Heinle
                     Reading Library

Skills Index

274, 312, 405
experience for comprehension, use of, 2, 54, 80, 92, 102, 118, 132, 154, 166, 202, 224, 238, 252, 316, 328
fact and opinion, 192, 388, 394, 396–401, 402
graphic organizers, 2, 40, 51, 201, 215, 240, 279, 304
identify, 24, 36, 51, 61, 98, 99, 114, 131, 186, 248, 253, 312, 358, 393
illustrations
  analyzing, 162
  "how-to" book, 330
images, 88
interpret, 88, 186, 198, 246, 260, 298, 313, 324, 410
judgments, making, 162, 198, 260
knowledge for comprehension, use of, 2, 14, 28, 40, 54, 80, 92, 102, 118, 132, 154, 166, 178, 190, 202, 224, 238, 252, 264, 286, 302, 316, 328, 350, 362, 380, 392
main idea and details, 10, 36, 56, 58–67, 68, 136, 137, 168, 170–173, 266, 268–273, 274, 338, 358, 376, 388, 402
make modifications
  asking questions, 324, 358
  rereading aloud, 11
  searching for clues, 15, 179, 287, 363, 393
  using reference aids, 13, 191
memoir, 204
mental images, 4, 98, 156, 158–161, 364, 366–375
monitor comprehension, 16, 156, 199, 266, 318, 364
narration, 56
outline, 318, 320–323
paraphrase, 24, 212, 376, 388, 402
predict, 24, 30, 31–35, 50, 120, 122–127, 128, 212, 288, 290–297
prior knowledge, 2, 14, 28, 40, 54, 80, 92, 102, 118, 132, 154, 166, 178, 190, 202, 224, 238, 252, 264, 286, 302, 316, 328, 350, 362, 380, 392
purposes for reading, 49, 173, 197, 247
  adjust purpose, 11, 25, 37, 51, 69, 89, 99, 163, 175, 188, 213, 300, 310, 314, 347,

352, 377
  to enjoy, 347, 377
  establish purpose, 77, 151, 221, 304, 314, 347, 352, 377
  to find out, 56, 58–67
  to interpret, 352, 377
  to solve problems, 352, 377
  to understand, 10, 50
questions
  different levels, 10, 24, 36, 50, 68, 88, 98, 114, 128, 142, 162, 174, 186, 198, 212, 234, 248, 260, 274, 298, 312, 324, 338, 358, 376, 388, 402
  different types, 2, 28, 72, 76, 89, 92, 118, 149, 150, 224, 240, 249, 251, 263, 301, 328, 350
  test-like questions, 14, 279, 302
recall facts, 10, 24, 36, 50, 68, 88, 98, 114, 128, 142, 162, 174, 180, 182–185, 186, 198, 212, 234, 248, 260, 274, 298, 302, 312, 324, 338, 352, 354–357, 358, 376, 388, 402
reflect, 198
sequence of events, 37, 99, 104, 105–113, 134, 136–139, 174, 175, 212, 274, 324, 376
setting, analyzing, 50, 98
similarities and differences across texts, 4, 101, 304
speculate, 174, 198, 298, 324, 338, 376
steps in process, 88, 274
study strategies, 234, 265, 324, 352, 382, 403
summarize, 68, 94, 96–97, 142, 245, 324
support inferences, 6, 7, 9, 65, 66, 82, 162, 337, 376, 401
text features
  biography, 168, 304, 394
  diary, 94, 180
  drama, 304
  fable, 4
  fiction, 16, 94, 120, 134, 226, 364
  first-person narrative, 42
  folktale, 254
  historical fiction, 94, 134
  historical narrative, 30, 94
  "how-to" book, 330

informational text, 82, 352, 361
journal, 134
memoir, 204
narrative, 30, 42, 288
nonfiction narrative, 30, 240
play, 104
poem, 4, 156
realistic adventure fiction, 16
realistic fiction, 16, 120
science fiction, 364
scientific informational text, 82
short story, 56, 71
speech, 192, 382
textbook, 318
text's structure/progression, 4
  captions, 330
  fable, 4
  fiction, 226
  first-person narrative, 53, 249
  headings, 318, 361, 408
  inductive organization, 266
  locate information, 180, 182–185, 318, 352, 354–357
  narrative, 53, 249, 288
  recall information, 10, 24, 36, 50, 68, 98, 114, 128, 142, 162, 174, 180, 182–185, 186, 198, 212, 234, 248, 260, 274, 298, 302, 312, 324, 338, 352, 354–357, 376, 388, 402
  subheadings, 318
  textbook, 318
  timeline, 134, 168, 246
  visuals, 36, 59, 88, 162, 317, 330, 343, 354, 376

Content Areas
arts, 3, 263, 327, 329, 341
language arts, 101, 155, 237
math, 145, 177, 351
science, 13, 15, 27, 71, 82, 91, 165, 177, 265, 277, 303, 315, 325, 379
social studies, 29, 39, 41, 55, 81, 93, 103, 117, 119, 131, 133, 167, 179, 189, 191, 201, 203, 215, 225, 239, 251, 253, 287, 301, 317, 361, 363, 381, 391, 393, 405

Culture, 53
common characteristics, 42, 50
compare
  others' experiences, 42, 50, 143
  own experiences, 42, 50, 143, 248

science, 13, 15, 27, 71, 82, 91, 165, 177, 265, 277, 303, 315, 325, 379

social studies, 29, 39, 41, 55, 81, 93, 103, 117, 119, 131, 133, 167, 179, 189, 191, 201, 203, 215, 225, 239, 251, 253, 287, 301, 317, 361, 363, 381, 391, 393, 405

context clues, 15, 179, 287, 363, 393

denotative meaning, 52, 381, 390

derivatives, 52, 81, 236

draw on experiences, 265, 329, 351, 363

figurative language, 25, 200, 234, 390

homonyms, 41

key phrases, 10

key words, 239, 393

listening to selections, 114, 128, 142, 199, 377

multiple-meaning words, 41

personal dictionary, 13, 52, 55, 70, 81, 103, 130, 133, 144, 155, 167, 176, 188, 203, 225, 236, 262, 276, 300, 303, 314, 317, 326, 329, 340, 360, 363, 376, 393

reference aids, 3, 130, 133, 155, 163, 167, 191, 203, 265, 326, 340, 390, 393, 404

related words, 27, 29, 39, 71, 81, 88, 119, 131, 236, 239, 253

repetition, 225

root words, 52, 70, 90, 133, 236, 253, 276, 326, 378

strategies
LINK strategy, 103
word wheel, 81, 351

synonym finder, 3, 13, 167, 303, 360

synonyms, 3, 13, 93, 167, 303, 360

thesaurus, 167, 360

word origins, 52, 81, 90, 236, 262, 276, 326

Word Identification
context, 15, 179, 287, 363

contractions, 164

derivations, 52, 81, 236

dictionary, 53, 55, 81, 90, 130, 155, 203, 236, 253, 340, 390, 393, 404

glossary/glosses, 90, 191, 265, 317

language structure, 12, 38, 70, 164, 176, 188, 214, 308

letter-sound correspondences, 90

meanings, 52, 53, 133, 203, 214, 225, 253, 300, 325, 378, 381, 390, 404, 409

prefixes, 262, 300, 378

pronunciation, 90, 163

root words, 70, 133, 276, 378
Greek, 90, 276, 326
Latin, 52, 236, 276

suffixes, 12, 100, 130, 144, 188, 314, 340

Writing

Connections
authors
challenges, 72, 161, 211, 233, 273, 297
strategies used, 231, 297, 308
collaboration with other writers, 13, 146–147, 175, 213
correspondence
e-mail, 280–281
letter, 148–149
mail, 149, 280

Culture
compare and contrast, 150
others' experiences, 76

Forms
bibliography, 409

biography, 177, 277, 405

book, 410

dialogue, 117, 301

diary, 101, 189

editorial, 344

e-mail, 280–281

folktale, 263

"how-to" article, 341

informational text, 91, 361

instructions, 341

interview
form, 175
questions, 146, 175, 403

journal, 101, 134

letter, 148–149, 410

list, 74, 213, 392, 406

magazine article, 76, 150

memoir, 215

narrative, 74, 301, 379
first-person, 53, 101, 131, 189, 251
historical, 39

persuasive speech, 391, 406–407

play, 117
scene from a play, 315

poem, 11, 13, 145, 165

poster, 76, 150, 282

report, 72–73, 408–409

review, 75

science fiction, 379

speech, 201, 220, 391, 406–407

story, 237
realistic adventure story, 27
realistic story, 131
short story, 71

Web article/page, 76, 220

Inquiry and Research, 218, 282
concept map, 72, 165, 391

evaluation, 405, 408

guest speakers, 76, 148, 150, 220, 277

learning log, 150, 282, 411

on-line searches, 76, 148, 150, 177, 341

organize facts, 148, 216, 282, 408

organize ideas, 235, 344, 391, 408

outline, 235, 408–409

periodicals, 76, 150

presentations, 76, 216, 220

prior knowledge, 148

questions, 89, 146, 218, 220, 282, 397, 403, 408, 410

sources, citation of, 218, 408, 409

summarize facts, 282, 408

summarize ideas, 235

take notes, 235, 408

technology presentations, 72

timelines, 216

Literary Devices
characterization, 51, 53

chronological order, 361, 394, 408, 409

dialogue, 263

figurative language, 25, 391

flashback, 99, 277

incomplete sentences, 129, 131

metaphors, 143

personification, 37, 39

repetition, 391, 403

rhyming words, 11, 163, 165

table of contents, 409

thesis statement, 409

timeline, 39

tone, 187, 189, 199, 201

word choice, varying, 93

Purpose
appropriate form, 361, 412

appropriate literary devices, 11

audience and purpose, 389, 391
appropriate style, 235, 237, 339, 341, 391

Credits

Illustrators

Author Photos

Photos